D1745478

No. 93

Foreign News in the Media: International reporting in 29 Countries

Reports and Papers on Mass Communication

unesco

REPORTS AND PAPERS ON MASS COMMUNICATION

Foreign News in the Media:

International reporting in 29 Countries

Final report of the "Foreign Images" study undertaken for Unesco by the International Association for Mass Communication Research

Editors

Annabelle Sreberny-Mohammadi with Kaarle Nordenstreng,
Robert Stevenson and Frank Ugboajah

Heads of national teams

Grant Noble and Elizabeth Noble - Australia
Kaarle Nordenstreng - Finland
Winfried Schulz - Federal Republic of Germany
J. S. Yadava -India
Annabelle Sreberny-Mohammadi - Iran
Tamas Terestyeni - Hungary
Nabil Dajani - Lebanon
Brajesh Bhatia - Malaysia
A. Kaiser - Netherlands
Frank Ugfboajah - Nigeria
Jersy Oledzki - Poland
Richard Cole - United States
Slavko Splichal - Yugoslavia

1

ISBN 92 - 102265-2
French edition 92 - 202265-6
Spanish edition 92 - 302265-X

Published in 1985 by the
United Nations Educational
Scientific and Cultural Organization
7, place de Fontenoy, 75700 Paris, France

Composed by SAGI, Paris

Preface

The origin of this study may be traced back to Unesco's Approved Programme and Budget for 1977-78 (paragraph 4156) which called for a joint study 'on the image of foreign countries representing different social systems and development stages, as portrayed by mass circulated press in the countries concerned'. On the basis of this mandate, the International Association for Mass Communication Research (IAMCR), readily accepted Unesco's invitation to plan and co-ordinate an international comparative study on how the media present other countries, peoples and related issues to readers, listeners and viewers.

Undoubtedly, the choice of the IAMCR as the co-ordinating institute for such a wide-ranging project reflects the unique position of this association in the international communication research community. The IAMCR was established in Paris at the seat of Unesco, in December 1957. It has the status of a 'non-governmental organization' with Unesco, with whom has a consultative and co-operative working relationship. Over the last thirteen years or so this relationship has grown in strength, starting perhaps with the Unesco Meeting of Experts on Mass Communication and society, held in Montreal in 1969. During this time the Association has participated in several joint research exercises with Unesco.

Amont other things, these have highlighted the major issues and problems in international communications and have questioned some of the basic prevailing assumptions and *modus operandi* all with a view to improving knowledge and awareness about international communications, and with increased international understanding as their ultimate overriding objective.

The present study is a report of a unique international research project that stemmed from the communication debates of the mid-1970s. A co-ordinated comparative research design was agreed on and carried out by thirteen national teams, covering twenty-nine different countries. From modest beginnings, it developed into one of the most ambitious projects ever carried out. The research covered diverse media systems in countries which varied in their level of development, political orientation and pattern of socio-economic organization. The results provide an up-to-date picture of the current situation with regard to international news flows in many parts of the world.

The editors and authors of this volume are responsible for the choice and presentation of the facts and opinions expressed therein, which are not necessarily those of Unesco.

Table of Contents

Acknowledgements

The first acknowledgements must go to Unesco and IAMCR who fathered and then mothered this project. Special thanks are due to James Halloran, President, International Association for Mass Communication Research, who master-minded the study, and whom I should like to thank personally for inviting me to take over the co-ordination and editing of the final report in June 1980. Best wishes and thanks go to Paul Hartmann, the initial co-ordinator and originator of the coding schedule, who was prevented only by ill-health from continuing, and who helped to tidy up the reliability checks and monitored our statistics. Thanks are also due to Richard Cole, Robert Stevenson, David Weaver, Cleveland Wilhoit and Donald Shaw, for the extra materials included in various appendices, particularly the literature review and the analysis of the wire services.

I should also like to thank my three fellow drafters, Kaarle Nordenstreng, Robert Stevenson and Frank Ugboajah, for their hard work and razor-sharp criticism, and invite them to share any praise or blame for the final product. Finally, the main congratulations must go to my fellow participants who responded so amicably to continued hectoring for additional materials to complete the project. Without their tremendous hard work and dedication, often in very difficult circumstances, there would have been no study, and this report truly belongs to all of us.

Annabelle Sreberny-Mohammadi

Introduction

There is little doubt that the decade of the 1980s will see an increase in the struggle between the North and South for a rearrangement of the international order, as it currently exists and operates. The *Brandt Report,* Published in 1980, suggested that the North and the South share "mutual interests" in trying to resolve problems of common concern, but it also accepted most of the South's demands for a New International Economic Order, often repeating these point by point. The *Brandt Report* dealt with the hard facts of hunger and population, the material difficulties of finance, and the dilemmas associated with energy and disarmament.

It was left to another report published in the same year, —*Many Voices, One World*— the result of the lengthy deliberations of the MacBride Commission, to articulate the no less critical issues of communication and information, and to support the demands for a New World Information and Communication Order. One of the major areas of inequality and dependency in the existing information order lies in the processing and dissemination of news. Accusations of bias and distortion in the way the news media portray the developing world, and complaints about the implications of the dominance of the big four Western news agencies have all been raised, suggesting that the Third World is both portrayed as, and indeed is, a handicapped actor on the international stage.

Since the news media are important arbiters of reality, not only at the mass level but also amongst decision-makers, distorted images of the international scene could be a major obstacle for those trying to solve the problems at issue between North and South. It was, in fact, the oft-expressed concern at the way in which the different 'worlds' portray each other through their news presentations, as well as the way in which development issues were covered by the media, that prompted the research effort which is reported in these pages.

Some of the extensive data produced by the research is of specific relevance to national issues and debates, and will be made publicly available in the appropriate form through individual national publications and scholarly articles. What is presented here is a synthesis and broad comparative analysis of the findings based on extrapolations from separate reports produced by each national team. It is, in a sense, the report of reports. If it contributes to our general knowledge and awareness of this important international subject, if it succeeds in clarifying some of the issues in the debate and indicates some new directions for future research, then the report will have amply repaid the efforts of the many national teams who, despite many difficulties, contributed in such a splendid way to this most unusual venture in international research co-operation.

One final point needs to be made before the reader turns to the main report, and this has to do with the very limited nature of this or any other single research project. We are convinced that this research represents an important contribution to one of the major issues of our time, but it is still only a modest exploration of a very complex area. The knowledge we require can only be built up over time, from a co-ordinated and sustained research programme. It is particularly important to make this point with regard to this study because the data from some of the national studies have been used prematurely, in contentious and misleading ways, by outside parties, without the approval, or even prior knowledge, of either IAMCR or Unesco. Here and elsewhere we need to be on our guard against unwarranted generalizations and the dubious application of results in support of ideological positions.

Chapter 1: Background to the Project

... the world consists of individual and national actors, and since it is axiomatic that action is cased on the actor's image of reality, international action will be based on the image of international reality. This image is not shaped by the news media. . . alone; personal relations abroad, diplomatic dispatches, etc., count too —whether less, equally much or more, we do not know. But the regularity, ubiquity and perseverance of news media will in any case make them first-rate competitors for the number one position as international image-former . . .(1)

The context for the projects

During the early 1970s the demand for a New World Information and Communication Order became part of a renewed political action in the anti-colonial struggle by the developing world in general and the non-aligned movement in particular. There was an incrasing recognition of the 'established fact that the activities of imperialism are not confined solely to the political and economic fields, but also, cover the cultural and social fields (2).' With the adoption of the United Nations Declaration on the New International Economic Order, analyses began to show communication and information dependency as both a product and reinforcement of the old order. The demand for a New World Information and Communication Order was first officially introduced at the Non-Aligned Symposium on Information in Tunis in March 1976. It has now become a central part of the struggle for decolonization and freedom from all kinds of dependency; democratization, both internationally and nationally, and demonopolization. The aim is to establish a more authentic and self-propelled form of development.(3)

By the mid 1970s a variety of relevant communication and information issues were being widely discussed. In terms of news flow, the dominance of the Western agencies and the wish to promote alternative forms of information exchange was a vital issue and led to the establishment of the Non-Aligned News Pool in 1975. The constitution of the Pool was formulated at the New Delhi Conference of Ministers of the Non-Aligned Countries in July 1976, and was later ratified at the Fifth Summit of the Non-Aligned Movement in Colombo.

In Unesco-related circles debates on these and similar issues had been taking place for some considerable time. The developing concerns included an examination of international media traffic, of the operation of the major news agencies and of the way in which satellite broadcasting and other kinds of information flows could impinge upon national sovereignty. There was also an attempt at successive Unesco General Conferences to pass a declaration establishing

fundamental principles governing the use of the mass media*; and the vexed issue of the 'free and balanced' flow of information was rarely off the agenda. Increasingly Unesco's research programme reflected these concerns.

The details of, and the various decisions taken in, this continuing international dialogue need not be summarized here. There is already a voluminous and ever-growing literature which covers the important international meetings, the critical debates and their outcomes. For example, a useful and detailed report, written from the North American perspective, is the study edited by Jonathan Gunter.(4) The position of the Non-Aligned Movement can be found neatly summarized by Tran Van Dinh, while more recent meetings are reported in Hamelink's work.(5) There are also the many documents submitted to the MacBride Commission, quite a number of which deal specifically with the concept of a New World Information and Communication Order, as well as the final report itself.(6)

The project

At the nineteenth session of the General Conference of Unesco, held in Nairobi, in the autumn of 1976, there were many heated exchanges about information imbalance and about bias in news reporting, particularly with regard to the portrayal of the developing world.

During the conference a draft resolution, prompted by the Scandinavian countries and later endorsed by India and Yugoslavia, was discussed which invited the Director General to include in the Unesco Programme and Budget for 1977-1978, Section on Free Flow of Information and Communication Policies, 'a study on the image of foreign countries (4)'.* Particular emphasis was to be placed on the 'image given over the past twenty years by mass media in

---

*The Unesco Declaration on Fundamental Principles concerning the Contribution of the Mass Media to Strengthening Peace and International Understanding, to the Promotion of Human Rights and to Countering ·Racialism, Apartheid and Incitement to War was adopted by acclamation on 22 November 1978 in Paris at the twentieth session of the General Conference of Unesco.

---

* This draft resolution was later incorporated into the Approved Programme and Budget for 1977-78, where the following reference to this project was made: "In co-operation with research institutions, a joint study will also be promoted and co-ordinated on the image of foreign countries representing different social systems and development stages, as portrayed by mass circulated press in the countries concerned. " (paragraph 4156).

industrialized countries of the developing countries and of the changing economic and political relations in the international community. The resolution also suggested that the project could be carried out as a 'joint study.' In practice, this would (4) have to meet all their own expenses and provide all necessary materials and human resources while Unesco, together with some such body as the IAMCR, might look after the co-ordination and the publication of results, perhaps providing funds for planning and analysis meetings.

Justification for such a proposal was given in the draft resolution, besides referring to Unesco's relevant research programme, by

> Recalling that by its Constitution Unesco is charged with contributing to peace and security *inter alia* by advancing the mutual knowledge and understanding of peoples through all means of mass communication.

> Recalling also that in the Final Act of the Conference on Security and Co-operation in Europe, the participating States recognize the need for an ever wider knowledge and understanding of the various aspects of life participating States.

> Recalling further the decisions taken by the Fifth Conference of Heads of State or Government of Non-Aligned Countries, endorsing the principle that all countries of the world should have the right to inform and be informed objectively and accurately. . .(7).

The Nairobi Conference thus may be added to the list of important landmarks in the development, at several levels, of an increasingly critical approach to the study of international communications. The particular initiative and what stemmed from it, which is reported here, dealt with only a fraction of the total debate, yet it touched upon two very significant points. First, the resolution was directly concerned that research should be undertaken on the *content* of the mass media, specifically news as distinct, say, from technical infrastructure or professional training. Second, it explicitly placed information issues in the wider context of international relations and changing constellations of global forces. It avoided both the reduction of communication problems to the individual social-psychological level and a remote examination in terms of abstract categories. In short, the media and communication issues generally were to be studied not in isolation, but in the appropriate historical/political/economic contexts.

The problems to be tackled

It is important to note, however, that despite its birth amidst the controversies surrounding a New World Information and Communication Order, this study was never specifically intended as an effort to clarify or analytically justify this particular notion. The main aims of the study were to combat ignorance and prejudice on what was seen as a vitally important issue, to increase awareness, to make it more difficult for conventional rationalizations to be sustained and, to provide a sound base for informed policies and change. In simple terms it sought to do this in those countries which participated in the research, by systematically providing, according to an agreed schedule, information on the quantity and quality of media representations of other countries.

The project was planned as an international inventory of foreign news reporting, having something in common with earlier studies although these covered only a limited number of media systems and collaborating institutions. Amongst the most famous pioneering efforts in this field are the study by Jacques Kayser on *One Week's News,* a comparative study

of seventeen major daily newspapers for a seven-day period, and the study by the International Press Institute (IPI), *The Flow of the News,* both published in 1953. (8) Additionally, a recent study by Gerbner and Marvanyi looked at the 'worlds' presented in selected press systems; Schramm has focussed in depth on Asian media; and several journals have devoted special issues to research on news flows and discussion of news imbalances.(9) Appendix 5 of this report examines a number of recent research studies and compares their findings with those reported here.

It is increasingly recognized that what must be studied is the whole of the communication process, not just one part of it. At the beginning, with this in mind it was hoped that it would be possible to study the 'images of the world' in the minds of ordinary people (in the manner of an early study by Buchanan and Cantril), (10) as well as studying the images presented by the media. However, it became clear at an early stage that this was far too ambitious an aim for this particular project. The necessary time and resources were just not available. It was also recognized that, ideally, the study should have an historical dimension which would enable comparisons to be made, say, over a twenty or thirty year period. Unfortunately, but in the circumstances understandably, quite a number of participants were unable to undertake this task.

International comparative studies of this kind must, of necessity, be limited in nature and scope in order to facilitate realistic execution. Nevertheless, such projects —and this was no exception— have to be designed in such a way as to provide soundly based representative data. The quantitative data presented in this report are drawn from the thirteen media systems studied by thirteen participating teams, plus an additional sixteen media systems covered by one of the teams, namely the United States team. All regions are represented. The results of this part of the study are presented in Chapter 5.

It was also hoped that the study would be intensive as well as extensive in character, not confining itself solely to the use of the formal categories so characteristic of conventional content analysis. Ideally, a delicate interpretative instrument which could penetrate to the real substance of 'image-Guilding', whilst still maintaining the cross-national comparative element, might have been employed. But in practice it proved impossible to develop agreed guidelines for such an ambitious undertaking. In the event, a more limited attempt to analyse selected major stories within each media system was undertaken. The results of this are presented in Chapter 4.

It needs to be emphasized here that the results of this limited study reported here provide an excellent base for follow-up studies which, amongst other things, might attempt what, in this study, was found to be not possible. Let us hope that the opportunity for such studies is not lost.

The plan

In the summer of 1977 Unesco delegated the design, planning and co-ordination of the project to the IAMCR, through its president, James Halloran, at the University of Leicester. Subsequently, in July of 1977 a planning meeting was held in Paris where the outline design was formulated.

After the planning meeting, Halloran wrote (on 26 July 1977) to a number of individual and institutional members of IAMCR, most of whom had previously expressed interest in research collaboration in this area, and who met the international sampling requirements agreed on at the Paris meeting, 'in the hope that you or your institute will be able to take part.'(11) The countries approached at that time included the United States of America, the Union of Soviet Socialist Republics, the Federal Republic of Germany, the

German Democratic Republic, Finland, Sweden, Yugoslavia, and at least one country from each of the developing continents of Africa, Asia and Latin America. In the event, the German Democratic Republic and Sweden did not participate, while the developing world was in a sense more than adequately represented, particularly in the quantitative section of the study.

The study was outlined in the letter as follows:

> The research is essentially concerned with the role played by the media in portraying foreign countries, foreign affairs, etc, to the public —and the consequences of this for social consciousness. It was decided in Paris that the research should not be unduly ambitious and that, in the first instance, we should think in terms of a pilot study which it was to be hoped, would lead to further developments at a later stage. The preliminary design was based amongst other things on the need to have participation from eight to twelve countries in different parts of the world without undue stress on their resources.
>
> . . . In the first instance, the research will be confined to an analysis of agreed samples of press and television content, special attention being given to the mass-circulated press. It is proposed that the work should commence around February/March 1978 and should be completed within twelve months.

In Paris, the basic outline for a 'pilot study' has been agreed upon, including the time periods to be sampled, although the categories for the formal content analysis were yet to be determined. By the end of 1977 the pool of prospective participants as envisaged in the original design was almost complete, and Halloran reported in his Presidential Letter of December 1977:

> Preliminary discussions on this project were held at the July meeting in Paris, when a draft design was prepared. Exchanges have continued both by correspondence and by discussions —the latter with several colleagues who may participate in the study and whom I had the pleasure to meet at the Conference of the Association for Education in Journalism (AEJ) in Madison, Wisconsin in August, at the seminar sponsored by the Instituto Latino americano de Estudios Transnacionales (ILET) in Amsterdam in September, and at the Finnish UNESCO Seminar in Helsinki earlier this month.
>
> I repeat the request made in the June letter. Do let me know if you are interested in this project. For representative sampling reasons it is more important that some countries should paricipate than others, but there is nothing exclusive about this study, so anyone who wishes to take part should get in touch with me immediately. If all those who have signified their willingness to participate play their part by letting me have their comments on the proposed design then we should be able to work out a final agreed design and commence the work by March 1978.

Several more responses were received, and once again the timetable was revised. In February 1978 Paul Hartmann, a Research Fellow at the Centre for Mass Communication Research, University of Leicester, who had been appointed by Halloran as project coordinator, prepared a detailed document operationalizing the design of the study, together with a draft coding schedule and invited the initial working group to pilot test and comment on it. The Warsaw Conference of the IAMCR, in the summer of 1978, provided

an ideal opportunity for further discussion, since it brought many of the potential participants together. Firm decisions on the design and execution of the study were made with the help of the results of a pilot study undertaken by the Finnish team.(12)

By February 1979, final instructions were dispatched, and it was agreed that the first period to be sampled would begin in early April. Eventually, through a hapharrad voluntarism and survival of the most resourceful. The study was carried out by thirteen national teams. Appendix 1 lists the leaders of each team and their institutional affiliation.

The United States team, when they heard the final list of participants, decided to try to expand the sample to include more developing nations. With funds supplied by the U. S. International Communications Agency (ICA), and using the services of foreign students and residents, the United States team coded materials for an additional sixteen countries. A list of these, with descriptions of the national media systems, can be found in Appendix 4. This additional quantitative data is strictly comparable with the rest and thus Chapter 5 is based on a data set of twenty-nine countries. However, the qualitative analysis carried out by the United States team was different from that carried out by the other thirteen participants, whose coders were all present within their respective nations during the period under study, and therefore in a better position to make the appropriate qualitative assessments. Because of these methodological considerations, the qualitative analyses from the additional countries were not included in the qualitative report.

As will be clear from the above, the terms of the original aims were somewhat modified —inevitably so, as the working arrangements were agreed on, the accommodations made and the design amended accordingly. The stages in the development of the project plan have been recalled here in some detail in the hope that the account will provide an illustrative example of the practical and related methodological problems invariably found in comparative international research, particularly with research which entails the participation of several independent persons or institutions in various parts of the world, and from different political systems. In this respect it is not surprising that the demands of the timetable are rarely met, and that many other practical complications stem from the fact that there are so many participants. Still, the fact that so many of the contributors agreed to co-operate in the way they did and that so many lasted the course is an achievement in itself.

It is possible, in such circumstances, that not all the participants will be able —sometimes for very good reasons within their own institutions, which will be funding the research— to keep strictly to the original plan. Consequently, in the end, in some cases the implementation is not always as closely related to the 'agreed design' as one might have hoped at the outset. In a sense, the research exercise in any given country or institution may begin to lead its own life, by no means unrelated to the original problem and its theoretical formulations, but undoubtedly influenced as it develops by a number of pragmatic considerations, sometimes including 'unavoidable' alterations in the measuring instruments. In such cases it is possible that oversimplified, usually quantified pictures may emerge. One of the problems of this form of social scientific research is that in terms of the data obtained 'richness' —even 'validity'— is often at the opposite pole from 'hardness', 'certainty' and 'reliability'.

The research was finally carried out in the spring and summer of 1979. A pre-analysis meeting for all participants was held at Unesco headquarters in Paris in December of that year. There, a deadline of 30 April 1980 was set for completion of national reports. The content of these was strictly defined and limited, each national team being required to produce a thirty-page report consisting of sixteen agreed-upon tables of data and a three-page analysis and interpretation of dominant news stories. These reports form the basis for this synthesis.

A working party of four was selected (Frank Ugboajah, Nigeria; Kaarle Nordenstreng, Finland; Bob Stevenson, United States; and Annabelle Sreberny-Mohammadi, who carried out the research in Iran, but was at that time living in London) and spent a week in Leicester in July 1980 producing a draft report.* The draft report was presented to the 12th Annual Conference of IAMCR in Caracas, Venezuela, in September 1980, and was circulated to all participants for revision and comment. The final version does not differ substantially from the original outline, but embodies a variety of useful comments from participants and other colleagues.

---

* It was at this point that Annabelle Sreberny-Mohammadi was invited by Prof. Hallosan to take over the co-ordination and editing, because of Paul Hartmann's ill health.

Chapter 2: The Design of the Study

After some pilot testing of draft schedules and a great deal of correspondence and debate about the material to be included and how it should be coded, by early 1979 a 'common core' schedule was produced to which all participants had to adhere. This ensured comparability of results, and still allowed participants to code additional materials if they so wished. In practice, few teams did more than the basic requirements, and any historical and other additional analyses will be published in national reports. For the quantitative analysis, our concern here is only with this common core schedule.

Media Sample

The media sample was to include both press and broadcasting, recognizing the vital informational role played by broadcasting, particularly in those parts of the world where literacy is still prevalent. Meaningful comparisons of news presentation between the two kinds of media are notoriously hard to draw since the comparisons are of such unequal and dissimilar forms. Therefore detailed analysis of similiarities and differences between the findings for press and broadcasting presentation of international news is left for national publications to report on. A composite figure for each nation is all that can be presented here.

The press to be sampled were 'three or four daily papers in each country, including wherever possible the largest circulation national daily'. This and the following quotations are taken from the General Guide and Coding Instructions prepared by IAMCR at Leicester. They are reproduced in full in Appendix 3.

For broadcasting, only 'the main news bulletin of the day' was to be selected, both for radio and for television. Analysis was based on a video or sound-only recording.

Beyond such general instructions, selection was left to the discretion of the local investigators as how to best represent their own national media situation: whether to reflect political diversity or a variety of linguistic communities, for example, and what balance of national and regional presses to choose. Chapter 3 presents actual channels selected by each national team with a brief description of the general media context from which these choices were made.

Time sample

The study design called for a sample of two weeks, one of which was to be a chronological week and one a composite week constructed from a three-month period. This provided both an intensive week of news coverage with its specific 'hot'

issues, the established practice in such content analysis studies, and also allowed for extensive coverage over a longer period in which more enduring issues could reveal their significance. The results of this compromise showed little significant difference in the news composition of the two weeks, the 'uniqueness' of specific events merging into the 'typicalness' of the pattern of news reporting. This supports Stempel's contention that any period of four days or more will adequately represent the news pattern in a media system. (1) The actual dates for the study were chosen arbitrarily, far enough in advance to ensure adequate preparation by participants. The chronological week ran from Monday 23 April to Saturday 28 April 1979. The composite week was constructed by selecting the first Monday in April, a Tuesday to weeks later, and so on. This period spanned April to June 1979.

The 'week' was in fact six days, omitting Sundays since many countries publish no Sunday, or equivalent, papers and because these editions tend to break the normal pattern of weekly presentation. Thus the total amount of foreign news as shown in the figures in Table 2 (Appendix 6) under-represents the actual amount of published foreign news. This is perhaps most relevant to the United States and European systems where the 'Sundays' play an important role in reviewing and analysing the past week's events. Clearly too, since only one newcast each for radio and television were included, and vews magazines and periodicals were omitted, our figures do not begin to reflect the complete universe of news reporting available in any country. They do, however, adequately represent that universe for our purposes. The United States was coded both inclusive and exclusive of Sunday editions, and a discussion of the differences in findings plus a warning note about their interpretation can be found in Stevenson's analysis in Appendix 5.

For various reasons there were minor deviations from this sampling schedule. For example, in India three days of the composite week were changed because of strikes or holydays. In Iran, there are no Friday papers, and strikes and New Year celebrations also complicated matters. In Yugoslavia a national holiday and May Day intervened; there are generally no papers or television programmes on Mondays. In such cases, the next available issue broadcast after the missing date was selected for inclusion, and these alterations are not believed to have greatly affected the findings.

Modes of analysis: Qualitative interpretation

From the beginning of the project it was intended that a straight-forward exercise in quantification would be substantiated and balanced by a qualitative analysis of the material. This would flesh out the real news content correct omissions and give more flavour to the kinds of news coverage available within each media system. Such analysis was considered vital if correct interpretation of the statistical data was to be made, since each provided a distinct kind and level of analysis. In the event no detailed, formalized guidelines for participants as to the method for qualitative analysis usable across cultural boundaries were devised. It was suggested that three or four 'dominant news stories which commanded the greatest attention during this period' be identified and summarized with respect to the overall perspective and news angle, the journalistic devices used to draw attention to the selected stories, and the language used to describe the events. Decisions as to what constituted 'dominance' and 'greatest attention' (i. e. length of stories, presence on front page, continual recurrence throughout the period, etc.) were once again left up to the national teams.

This topical analysis was the pragmatic version of the original intention to move away from an inventory of the formal aspects of international news reporting to a deeper analysis of its content. It proved difficult in this kind of multi-national project with severe limitations of resources to devise a more systematic and rigorous method for such interpretative analysis and equally hard to ask for such a laborious and rigorous procedure to be undertaken. The difficulties experienced in this area have however not dispelled the belief that such analysis is a vital scientific counterpart to statistical evidence. The comparisons between the two levels of findings, presented in Chapters 4 and 5 show clearly how erroneous and misleading interpretations made on the basis of only one level may be.

Modes of analysis: Quantification

The formal coding instrument used in this study is a general purpose technique for quantification of news content. Its pedigree stretches to the Golding and Elliott project for the International Broadcast Institute (IBI)* on broadcast news, and to McQuail's analysis of the British press for the Royal Commission.(2)

There are clearly many ways of categorizing news. The method here measures rough volume only and attempts to present the overall structure of international news reporting and the basic foci of attention. The major concern was with the following variables: Where the news occurred; Location; Where the news item originated; Source; Who made the news; Position and nationality of actor; What the news was about; Topic; The news context; Theme. The full coding schedule appears in Appendix 2.

For each international news item a separate coding sheet was completed. This was so designed as to facilitate key-punching of the information on to two eighty-column computer cards. A sample coding sheet is shown in Appendix 3. Key-punching and computation were the responsibilities of each national team, although some loose coordination was provided by the United States. The information was never gathered in one place so additional competition was hard to organize. Each team has agreed to make its data available to interested parties and this does constitute a potentially huge comparative data base ripe for further systematic analysis.

The news item is the basic unit of analysis, most usually distinguished by a headline in the press or by an introductory statement in newscasts. A simple frequency count was made,

and the length of each item in the press was also measured in column centimetres, the total length of the item based on the standard column width for that paper. Broadcast items were timed in seconds. Tests run on the reporting of results by number of items or by length produced very high correlations; see the discussion in Appendix 5. Thus, except for Table 2, all results are reported solely in percentages based on the total number of items. The national reports carry the full data, including lengths, for those interested in further testing. It should also be borne in mind that the standard column width varied from paper to paper, ranging from 3.5 cm. to 8 cm. A more precise method would have been to measure in square centimetres; alternatively, all lengths should have been reduced to a standard width. Neither of these was done, so that the centre column of Table 2 showing the total amount of international news available in one channel on an average day, is not based on one standardized measure. Nor has any account been taken of total page size in newspapers, nor of spatial variations in linguistic scripts.

Only items of international news were coded. The instructions stipulated that items were to be included if they dealt with 'events or situations outside the home country, or events in the home country in which foreign nationals take part or which are presented as having substantive relevance to foreign situations'. This definition is based on the story-type classification originated by Elliot and Golding which allows for the inclusion of 'foreign news at home' and 'home news abroad' as well as the pure type 'foreign news abroad'. (3) Since on this basis all items were neither strictly foreign news nor indeed external news, it was decided to use the appellation 'international news'. There still remains some slight semantic confusion, however, since not all items were truly international either. Each item was coded to indicate whether it was solely a domestic story or concerned 'relations between states as political entities', a rather unwieldy description which was usually interpreted fairly broadly to include items involving more than one nationality of 'actor' (person or party involved).

For newspapers, it was agreed to include only the general news pages for analysis. Any and all specialized sections for example on finance, fashion, travel, etc., or any special reports were omitted. This was intended to maximize the comparability of results, cut coding time, and make the press results more readily comparable to those from broadcasting, where all special programming for sports, documentaries, cultural and current affairs was excluded. As always, the criteria used to select material for inclusion have predetermined the outcome —which in this study has meant the over-representation of international news as dominated by political affairs and political actors. Very little sporting news is included in the press figures, 'soft' news items hardly appear, and even economic and business stories are not well covered. It also complicates the comparison of our findings with those of similar studies. For further discussion of this point see Appendix 5. Specifically, this has also meant an under-representation of the total amount of international news available in the Western press; the teams from the United States, the Netherlands and the Federal Republic of Germany pointed this out in their national reports. It has thus contributed to the tendency evident in the quantitative aspect of this report to over-emphasize the homogeneity of the content of the world's news media systems.

Most of the categories were clearly mutually exclusive and only a single code could be registered. For some, like the source of an item, multiple coding was possible so that totals in tables relating to sources of international news items may exceed the actual total number of news stories. For other

---

* Now known as the International Institute of Communications (IIC).

variables, such as topic and actor, a main category and up to three subsidiary categories could have been registered for each item. It was here that interpretation was most problematic; for example, in judging whether an item on arms sales to the Middle East was presented more as a political or military topic; or, in a piece on the SALT II talks, deciding whether United States President Carter for USSR President Brezhnev was the main actor. In the final analysis presented in the national reports, only main topics and main actors were dealt with.

Locations of events and nationalities of actors were individually recorded and subsequently grouped into eight regions to make the data less cumbersome. The geopolitical grouping adopted was considered to be a 'less than perfect breakdown of the world', but also less contentious than classification into First/Second/Third and more worlds, or other attempts to group nations according to their level of development, or cultural or political outlooks. The boundaries of the eight regions are as follows: North America includes Bermuda; Latin America also includes Mexico, the Caribbean countries and Cuba; Africa does not include Egypt; the Middle East includes Egypt and Iran but not Turkey; Asia extends from Afghanistan to Australasia and Oceania; Eastern Europe includes the USSR and Yugoslavia; Western Europe includes Turkey. 'Other' may include items dealing with the world in general, the United Nations, Unesco, North Atlantic Treaty Organization (NATO), etc., plus, where applicable, space, sea, and so forth.

The twenty-nine media systems included in the quantitative analysis were similarly grouped into eight regions. When reading the results as reported by regional media systems, it is important to remember that, for example, North America is represented by a single media system: that of the United States, while seven media systems were analysed for Africa.

The initial desire to examine international news imagery 'over the past twenty years' by coding the maximum circulation newspaper on the basis of the composite week for the years 1969, 1959, 1949, was finally relegated to an optional extra. A few teams did undertake this additional coding, the results of which will be made available in national reports.

Coding reliability

Each national team leader supervised a group of research assistants and/or students. After initial practice using the centrally-organized coding schedule, during which period general rules were established and a common national approach was cultivated, regular meetings were held by each team to iron out other difficulties and negotiate on problematic items.

Reliability of the coding was checked by having different coders recode about 20 per cent of the material in each national sample. These results were then compared with the original coding. Using Scott's formula for nominal scale data, (4) most teams reported a *pi* coefficient in the region of .7 to .8 for the topic classification (major topic headings only). The Polish team made several such checks and found *pi* ranging from .43 to .96, these being the lowest and highest figures reported by anyone. Apart from this freak low result, the reliability of coding generally was as high as can be reasonably expected with this kind of data. It is certainly high enough for the overall pattern of results to be confidently accepted as meaningful, particularly in view of the large number of items covered by the analysis.

Chapter 3: Participating Nations: Media Systems and Channel Selections

This chapter presents background information about the media systems in each of the participating nations. With thirteen countries to include, only the broad parameters of each system can be outlined with a description of the particular newspapers and radio/television channels that were selected for inclusion in this study. Similar information for the additional sixteen countries coded by the United States team can be found in Appendix 4.

The following information was supplied by the participating teams themselves. The criteria for selection of channels clearly varies from country to country. Some teams questioned the theoretical validity and practical possibilities of examining their complete national media system, and chose to focus on one region only: New South Wales in Australia, and Slovenia in Yugoslavia. In other countries there is no true national paper and the selections draw newspapers from important regional centres, as in the United States and the Federal Republic of Germany. Other teams tried to represent the spectrum of political opinion available through the daily press in their nation, as with many of the West European choices. The Malaysian team chose to represent the variety of ethnic/linguistic communities that comprise their nation, selecting press, radio and television channels in the four main languages (English, Tamil,, Chinese, and Bahasa Malay). The Indian team, on the other hand, for reasons of practicality, only examined the English-language press in India. Many chose privately owned, commercial stations and public service channels in order to compare performance. For obvious reasons comparisons specific to internal conditions are left for national reports to analyse.

At least three daily papers and either or both radio and television were covered in each country, except for Iran where the schedule was received too late to record broadcast news. In many countries even more channels were covered; the maximum was twelve in Malaysia.

NORTH AMERICA

The United States

The United States has about 1,700 daily papers, most of which are relatively small and circulated regionally. They are privately owned. Approximately two-thirds of circulation may be attributed to a small number of newspaper chains, whose revenue is derived from advertising, which generally takes up about half the total space. Broadcast media are also commercial but operate with government license, with three networks supplying most news to locally owned affiliates. The media analysed for this study were the *New York Times,* an influential quality paper, averaging up to 100 pages a day with

a daily circulation of 900,000; the *Washington Post,* a rival to the *New York Times* particularly in the capital, with a circulation of 560,000; the *New York Daily News,* a popular tabloid with a daily circulation of almost 2 million; the *Los Angeles Times,* an influential West-Coast paper with a circulation of 1 million; the *Minneapolis Tribune,* regional, Mid-West daily averaging seventy-five pages and with a circulation of 227,000; the *Charlotte Observer,* a regional, Southern daily with a circulation of 172,000; the *Columbia Broadcasting System (CBS)* evening news programme with Walter Cronkite was also included.

AFRICA

Nigeria

Fifteen newspapers are published in Nigeria, all in English because of the continuing dominance of the colonial heritage; some weeklies are published in local languages, however. All radio-television stations are government-owned and supervised by national corporations which are based in Lagos. The newspapers selected include the *Daily Times,* a tabloid of twenty-four to thirty pages with a circulation of 230,000, published in Lagos. Partly owned by the government, it tends to follow an independent line, is nationalist in outlook and the most popular paper. The *New Nigerian* runs between eighteen and twenty pages, with a circulation of 175,000 from both Kaduna and Lagos. It is wholly owned by government and is an authority on central government policy. *Punch* has ten to twelve pages, a circulation of 200,000 and is published in Lagos. It is privately owned, commercial, with a nationalist orientation and a strong humour angle. Advertising takes 40 per cent of total space in all these papers. Also included in the study were *Fren (Lagos),* the central radio relay station, and *NTA (Lagos)* the television headquarters where national network news originates.

MIDDLE EAST

Iran

This study was conducted in the immediate post-revolutionary period; great changes in organization and orientation were beginning to occur in the media but were not yet fully consolidated. It was an interregnum, and the results should be read within this tumultuous context. The prevailing situation determined selection, since in April 1979 only three major daily papers were functioning; yet had a period even one month later been chosen, the available papers would have been different. *Kayhan* is a national afternoon paper, with estimated circulation during this period of about 400,000. It averaged ten pages, with 33 per cent advertising. *Ayandegan* was a national morning paper (estimated circulation: 300,000), twelve pages long with 20 per cent advertising. It pursued a secular intellectual stance after the revolution until it was closed down by the Revolutionary Council in May 1979. *Etela'at* is a national afternoon paper, ten pages long, with 25 per cent advertising and an estimated circulation of 400,000. It was the leading religious voice during the period of the study but has since been replaced by newer, more radical papers. It was not possible to include broadcasting in the study.

Lebanon

Lebanon's press is privately owned; of the fifty-two daily papers, only two have circulations above 60,000. The press laws are comparatively open when compared with those operating elsewhere in the Middle East, but publishers are prey to the financial inducements of both foreign and local interests to present competing viewpoints. The papers selected for this study were *an-Nahar* (The Day), with the highest circulation; the most prestigious paper, it follows a middle-of-the-road position and is read by Lebanese intellectuals, middle and upper classes and the Greek Orthodox community. Its circulation is highest in the capital, Beirut. *As-Safir* (The Ambassador) is the highest circulation left-of-centre paper, appealing to Arab nationalist intellectuals and the Moslem population; its highest circulation is in the Moslem areas of South and North Lebanon as well as in the Bekaa (east). *Al-Amal* (The Work) is a rightist paper, the organ of the predominantly Maronite Christian Phalangist Party, and is second to *an-Nahar* in the predominantly Christian areas of East Beirut and Mount Lebanon. Both *an-Nahar* and *as-Safir* appear seven days a week, usually with twelve pages on weekdays and sixteen on Sunday, and have 25 per cent and 16 per cent advertising respectively. *Al-Amal* appears in eight pages with no paper on Monday, and has 11 per cent advertising.

The only legal radio station is the *Lebanese Broadcasting Station* which is operated as a government agency, with news prepared by the official news agency of the Ministry or Information, and news bulletins presented every hour. A main newscast at 1.30 p.m. was selected; this lasts half an hour and has no advertising. A number of private radio stations are also operating, a by-product of the civil war. They have been declared illegal by the government. *Tele-Liban* is the only television company, an amalgamation of the two previous companies owned by French interests and the Thompson group. Although the State now owns 50 per cent of the company , it is operated by the commercial staff, while the government maintains control or most domestic news bulletins. The main half-hour evening newscast, with 9 per cent total time given to advertising, was included in this study.

ASIA

Australia

The Australian media are a mixture of national, state and local systems with increasing concentration of ownership. There are two national daily papers, while state dailies have a mainly intra-state circulation. The Australian Broadcasting Commission is non-commercial, modelled on the BBC, while commercial radio and TV stations also operate. The media sampled were *The Australian,* a national daily with a circulation 118,000; two New South Wales regional papers, *Sydney Morning Herald* with a circulation of 263,000, and the *Telegraph* with a circulation of 316,000. The television sample included the ABC evening broadcast and one from a regional station, *9/8 Tamworth, New South Wales*. Radio analysis was based on morning broadcasts from *ABC* and the commercial *2 AD Macquarie* station.

India

India has 929 daily newspapers, with the English press maintaining a slightly higher circulation than the Hindi. Circulation is low, at 1.6 copies per 1,000 population, but readership per copy is higher than in developed countries. The sheer size of the population and the multiplicity of languages mean that no paper has a 'national' circulation although many papers are published out of more than one centre, usually the large metropolitan areas. Generally, about 70 per cent of Generally total cost is covered by advertising, which occupies about 50 per cent of space in the major dailies.

Broadcasting is a monopoly of the central government, as yet both radio and television, the latter, reach only a small fraction of the total population.

The media sample included five English-language dailies, selected for their significant place in the Indian press system, and their coverage of different regions of the country: *The Hindu* (Madras); *Hindustan Times* (New Delhi); *Times of India* (Bombay); *Indian Express* (Cochin); *The Statesman* (Calcutta). The English-language national radio news broadcast at 9 p.m. and the regional English-language television newscast on *Delhi TV* at 9.45 p. m. were also included.

Malaysia

In order to reflect the cultural diversity in Malaysia, media in all four languages were included: English, the language used by the elites and in business; Bahasa Malaysia, the national language; Chinese and Tamil. The highest circulation paper in each language was selected: *The New Straits Times* (English); *Utusan Malaysia* (Bahasa Malaysia); *Sin Chew Jit Poh* (Chinese) and the *Tamil Nesan* (Tamil). The circulation figures for these papers in 1978 were 320,000, 125,000, 170,000 and 25,000 respectively. All are published in the capital, Kuala Lumpur, but are available throughout the country. Radio and television broadcasts were similarly chosen to reflect ethnic diversity.

Eastern Europe

Hungary

All forms of mass communication are state-owned and government controlled. There are six national daily newspapers, and twenty-one regional dailies, as well as one paper each in English and German. The media sampled included *Népszabadsàg* (People's Freedom), the central daily of the Hungarian Socialist Worker's Party, wich has a national circulation of 750,000 and is fourteen pages long, with 15 per cent advertising; *Nepszava* (People's Voice), the Trade Union daily, has a circulation of 280,000, is ten pages long, and carries 10 per cent advertising; *Magyar Nemzet* (Hungarian Nation), the daily of the Patriotic People's Front, has a circulation of 120,000, is twelve pages long and has 20 per cent advertising; *Magyar Hirlap* (Hungarian News), the semi-official government paper, which has a circulation of 50,000, runs twelve pages and has 10 per cent advertising; *Esti Hirlap* (Evening News), mainly distributed in the capital, has a circulation of 290,000, and is eight pages long with 5 per cent advertising. The broadcast news analysed was the *Channel 1* evening news on radio from 6.30 to 7.15 p. m. and the television news on the same channel from 7.30 to 8 p. m.

Poland

⬤ Poland has eighty-one newspapers, which have a total daily circulation of 10.2 million. All the media are public sector property in Poland. The biggest press publisher, the Workers' Publishing Cooperative *(Prasa-Kziazka-Ruch),* publishes and distributes 92 per cent of all daily papers. Radio-television is a single state institution, and registration of the first radio and television set bought is compulsory. There are four radio and two television channels, mostly broadcast from the central Warsaw station, with regional additions. Three papers were chosen for inclusion in this study. *Trybuna Ludu* (Tribune of the People), the largest nationwide daily with a circulation of 900,000, is the organ of the Central Committee of the Polish United Workers' Party and is considered the most politically prestigious daily. Each issue has an average of ten pages. *Zycie Warszawy* (The Life of Warsaw), a morning daily with a circulation of 360,000, contains material relating to city problems in particular; it also averages ten pages. *Express Wieczerny* (Evening Express) is the most popular afternoon daily, with a circulation of 550,000 and an average of eight pages. One evening tele-newscast and two evening radio newscasts on programmes 1 and 3 were also included.

Yugoslavia

The analysis is based only on content analysis of the media in Slovenia, one of the eight republics and autonomous provinces that comprise Yugoslavia. Communications organizations operate under workers' self-management, but ⬤ delegates of users also participate in assemblies to ensure that public influence is exerted on communications policy. The three daily papers published in Slovenia were included in the study. *Delo* has a circulation of 100,000, and *Devnik* 50,000, and both are published in Ljubljana. *Vecer,* with 50,000 copies, is published in Maribor. All three newspapers are published in Slovenian. *Radiote levisija Ljubljana* is the central broadcasting organization, with the bulk of its programmes in Slovenian and occasional Serbo-Croatian; *RTV Koper-Capodistria* transmits in Slovenian and Italian. Except for local radio stations, all broadcast organizations are financially independent, financed by subscription and advertising, and self-managed. Publishing ventures used to be subsidised by the Socialist Alliance Party but now in principle operate in the same manner as the broadcasting organizations. Only the radio newscast of *Radio Ljubljana* was included here.

WESTERN EUROPE

Federal Republic of Germany

There are 120 independent daily newspapers in the Federal Republic, selling 23 million copies each day in a pattern of regional distribution. The only nationally circulated tabloid, *Bild Zeitung,* with a circulation of 5 million, was included in this study. Four quality newspapers were also selected, all of which have a national circulation as well as a strong regional basis and reflect the spectrum of political opinion in the ⬤ Federal Republic. *Die Welt* is published in Bonn, with regional editions for Hamburg and Berlin. With a circulation of 230,000 it averages twenty to thirty-eight pages during the week with one-third advertising. The Saturday edition is 110 pages long, three-quarters of which is devoted to advertising.

The liberal-conservative *Frankfurter Allgemeine Zeitung,* based in Frankfurt, has a circulation of 300,000. It follows the same pattern as *Die Welt:* a twenty-five to forty page weekday edition with 38 per cent advertising, and a 120-page Saturday edition with 80 per cent advertising. The liberal *Süddeutsche Zeitung,* published in München has a circulation of 320,000. Its daily editions vary from thirty-two to sixty pages (40 per cent ads); the Saturday edition has 130 pages (80 per cent ads). *Frankfurter Rundschau,* with a circulation of 185,000, is moderate left trade unionist; its daily editions have between twenty and twenty-six pages with 38 per cent advertising, while the Saturday edition has 100 pages, 82 per cent of which is advertising.

The nationally broadcast news of the two television channels was also included: the *ARD* 8 p.m. programme and the *ZDF* 7 p.m. programme.

Finland

Most of Finland's ninety daily newspapers are provincial; 10 per cent are published in Swedish, the second official language. Of the 2.5 million daily circulation, more than half is accounted for by papers published by politically independent companies which rely heavily on advertising. Another 40 per cent can be attributed to newspapers of political organizations. The papers selected for this study reflect this diversity: *Helsingin Sanomat* is the leading national, politically independent, liberal paper. It is thirty-four to fifty-two pages long, has a circulation of 366,000 and is published in Helsinki. *Aamulehti,* a provincial paper, is an organ of the Conservative Party; it runs between twenty-four and forty pages, has a circulation of 130,000 and is published in Southern industrial Finland (Tampere). *Savon Sanomat* is also provincial and is an organ of the Centre (Agrarian) Party; it has sixteen to twenty-eight pages, a circulation of 76,000 and is published in Eastern Finland (Knopio). *Kansan Uutiset,* a national daily, is the organ of the Democratic Union which includes the Communist Party; it has ten to eighteen pages, a circulation of 55,000 and is published in Helsinki. Broadcasting is mainly operated by a public corporation, although there is some commercially run television. New is operated centrally by the public broadcasting corporation. (5) This study included the main television news report of 20 minutes broadcast at 8.30 p. m., which is regularly viewed by over 50 per cent of the population.

The Netherlands

The Netherlands has fifty independent daily newspapers, seven of which have a national circulation of over 100,000. Newspaper sales total 104 copies for every 1,000 households. Two television channels allocate their time to separate organizations according to the size of their membership amongst the public, while the Netherlands Broadcasting Foundation remains the major broadcaster with particular responsibility for news.

Three newspapers were included in this study. *De Telegraaf* is a national morning paper with a rather 'sensational' format and a right-centre political orientation; it has a circulation of 593,000, and averages forty- seven pages, of which about 50 per cent is advertising. *NRC-Handelsblad,* the main prestige newspaper, is a national evening paper with a liberal intellectual outlook; its circulation is 120,000 and it averages twenty-five pages, with 37 per cent advertising; *Tubantia* is an Eastern-region midday paper with an open and independent line; circulation is 100,000 and it averages forty-five pages with 60 per cent advertising. The *NOS* public-service broadcasting television newscast, which is shown at 8 p. m. and is watched by 23 per cent of the audience was also included.

Chapter 4: International News Events: Their Selection and Interpretation

The first part of this chapter presents a brief summary of the variety of actual events that occurred within the two 'weeks' covered by this study. This is in itself clearly a reconstruction, based on selected sources not eligible for inclusion in the study.

The second part presents the summaries of dominant stories within the media systems of each of the participating nations during this period, and the third and last part tries to synthesize and analyse these interpretative pieces in the light of the findings about news themes.

Part I: THE EVENTS THEMSELVES

Since statistical representation and even media interpretation of events tend to give them less impact as such and make them somewhat 'anonymous', it was felt necessary to reconstruct events occurring within our two 'weeks'. The sources used for this included Keesings Archives, Whitaker's Almanac and British newsparers; the first two, at least, select events on a very different basis from that used by a daily newspaper. (1)

The Chronological Week

The week turned out to be a fairly 'typical' one. It contained no world-shaking events; yet the great diversity of important ones that occurred in every part of the world was typical of the dramatic times in which we live. (2)

Kayser's description of the week he selected over two decades ago could almost pertain to ours, which included a number of stories of great importance to regional and national affairs, particularly in Africa, but none to ensure our week an especially prominent place in world history. It was less dramatic than many, but as critical as most, unique yet typical.

The week began with the continued advance of Tanzanian forces into Uganda and the routing of Amin's troops, the capture of Jinja and Amin's subsequent flight to Libya. Elections held in comparative calm were won by Bishop Abel Muzorewa; the Patriotic Front vowed to continue its struggle, however, and was supported by the heads of the front-line states, particularly Kaunda and Machel. In Asia the destination of boatloads of Vietnamese was a continuing dilemma, while the Kampuchean crisis threatened to spill over into Thailand. Insurgents were struggling against the Taraki government in Afghanistan, while in Pakistan, General Zia announced that military officers would take over key political roles since the civilian cabinet has collapsed. In the Middle East, the Camp David Agreement was ratified amidst Palestinian raids on an Israeli coastal resort and Israeli bombings of Lebanese guerilla bases. Saudi Arabia severed diplomatic relations with Egypt because of the agreement, and talked of introducing sanctions. In post-revolutionary Iran, Prime Minister Bazargan warned of two midwives delivering a baby with a crooked head, and tried to consolidate government power. In Europe, polls predicted that Margaret Thatcher would win the general election and become the United Kingdom's first woman prime minister, while the SALT II talks were held in Vienna. In Eastern Europe, the Government of Poland cancelled the scheduled visit of the Archbishop of Canterbury, while, in the Soviet Union, the Baptist minister of Kiev, George Vins, was released from custody and allowed to emigrate along with Alexander Ginsberg and three others in exchange for the release of two Soviet citizens detained by the United States as espionage agents. North American news dealt with the aftermath of the Three Mile Island accident and the future of nuclear energy policy; central Canada was hit by floods. Further south, there was a volcanic eruption on St. Vincent. Human interest was provided by stories of the first attempt to commit murder with radio-activity in France, and a woman giving birth after undergoing a hysterectomy.

It was a week much like any other.

The Composite Week

A wider selection of stories was caught by our constructed week, which spanned the period from 2 April to 16 June 1979. Domestic political stories included elections in Austria, Canada, Italy, Rhodesia/Zimbabwe, Egypt and the United Kingdom. The Sandinistas were struggling hard in Nicaragua; the Mulder scandal broke in South Africa, and in the Central African Republic Bokassa was accused of violence against children and of violating human rights. Iran was formally declared an Islamic Republic. International items included the Vietnamese routing of the Khmer Rouge and Pol Pot's flight to Thailand, and the dilemmas of South-East Asian refugees. The Presidents Carter and Brezhnev met in Vienna. The Vietnamese and Chinese held border talks, and the Turks and the Greeks negotiated over the future of Cyprus. Israeli Prime Minister Begin visited Egyptian President Sadat in Cairo, Fidel Castro of Cuba made a trip to Mexico, and the deposed Shah of Iran left the Bahamas for Mexico City. The United Kingdom Government protested the cost of its membership in the European Economic Community (EEC). Terrorists were everywhere with Red Brigade bombings in Nuremberg, leftist bombings in Italian cities, Armenians active in Turkey and Corsicans in Paris, while a number of embassies were occupied in El Salvador. Crime was also related to politics, with the hanging of former Prime Minister Bhutto in Pakistan and the introduction of Islamic justice there; the arrest of Sanjay Ghandi in India, and the Thorpe trial in the United Kingdom. Religion tended to centre on Eastern Europe,with the visits of the Archbishop of Canterbury to the German Democratic Republic and Hungary,and the much-publicized visit by the Pope to Poland. Natural disasters included an earthquake in Yugoslavia and flooding in Andhra Pradesh, while a man-made tragedy occurred when a jumbo jet crashed in Chicago. Three Mile Island was nearly a nuclear disaster. 'Soft' stories included the continuing control over the music of Theodorakis in Greece, the Divine Light Mission establishing themselves in Switzerland, and Roman Polanski's expressed readiness to return to the United States for trial. All these, and more, are the intricate human stories from which our data were constructed.

Part II: THE EVENTS THAT DOMINATED INTERNATIONAL NEWS REPORTING

As already described in the chapter on methodology, the desire for a finely grained, interpretative instrument that could penetrate and analyse in depth the actual content of international news was never fulfilled. Instead, each participant was asked to identify and summarize three major news events themes which dominated foreign coverage, examining the overall perspective and viewpoint from which the coverage was presented. The national teams were encouraged to be interpretative and some underlined even the question of selection of these dominant stories. The Australian team wrote, 'In selecting dominant items to discuss here, one is conscious that one's own selection might not be the selection of another person'. (3) They suggested that in talking of the images which news media ascribe to foreign countries we were really talking about the growth of a myth which 'establishes a blissful clarity: things appear to mean something by themselves. (4) From such a viewpoint almost any selection is valid.

While that viewpoint is theoretically defensible, there is less feeling of randomness from the reports themselves. Although not specifically so instructed, most focus on press representation rather than broadcasting, perhaps since it is simpler to determine 'dominance' within the press than within a televised newscast or because the press provides a broader spectrum of stories to choose from. In the main, the reports are notable for their rigour and caution. The last part of chapter summarizes this section of the study, while some comparisons between the findings of the qualitative analysis and those of the quantitative analysis are explored in the concluding chapter. What follows are twelve reports written by the national teams themselves.*

United States

The fall of the Ugandan leader Idi Amin and the troubled Rhodesian election in Africa, uncertainty about the new revolutionary government in Iran, and debate on the SALT agreement signed by Presidents Brezhnev and Carter in Vienna received heavy coverage in the United States media during the period of the study.

The influential *New York Times* reported extensively on the disputed election for Rhodesia's first black premier. The

victor, Bishop Abel Muzorewa, was profiled on the front page as a 'hesitant, sometimes vacillating figure whose capacity for toughness in difficult situations is open to doubt'.

This story also had a domestic focus because of an effort in the United States Senate, opposed by President Carter and most newspapers, to end economic sanctions against Rhodesia. In an 'op-ed' commentary (the page opposite the editorial page in most United States papers, devoted to commentary by people outside the paper's staff) Senator Clairhorne Pell urged a 'go slow' policy on reducing sanctions.

The fall of Idi Amin in Uganda also received heavy coverage. *The Times,* which is circulated throughout the country,described the Amin regime as the 'institutionalized brutality of a state gone insane', and commented, 'yet the world looked on, sometimes horrified but always helpless'. The editorial singled out the United Nations for criticism: 'Its selective concern for the inhumanity of some regimes is shaped only by national or racial values.'

The emergence of Ayatollah Khomeini as the dominant figure in post-revolution Iran was emphasized in several reports in United States chapers. The *Washington Post* questioned the democratic leanings of the regime.

The New York Times offered two commentaries on its op-ed page. Eqbal Ahmad, of the Institute for Policy Studies, argued that Iran could be a landmark and model for other Third World revolutions. And British novelist Frederic Raphael, in a commentary titled 'If the Shah Had Read Aeschylus' suggested that classical literature might be more relevant to modern problems than intelligence reports were.

The United States press focused both on the meeting in Vienna between Presidents Carter and Brezhnev to sign the SALT agreement and on domestic reaction to the treaty, most of which was critical. Of special interest was Mr. Brezhnev's health and how the two leaders would get along with each other.

Other highlights of foreign coverage in the United States press included elections in the United Kingdom and Canada.

The New York Times correspondent in the United Kingdom described both major party candidates in detail, 'A Cluster of New Tory Stars Light Up the Party's Future' and 'Callaghan on the Hustings: Hearty and Reassuring', and marvelled at the simplicity and shortness of a British campaign compared to its counterpart in the United States.

*The New York Times,*on the op-ed page, even ran a tongue-in-cheek commentary by Michael Palin, of the Monty Python comedy group, who predicted a landslide of the 'don't knows'.

The New York Times focused on Canada with a three-part series on the United States' northern neighbour. A feature story on a unique house also described relations between the two countries. The 4,000-mile Canadian-American border, drawn in 1842, 'cuts through the kitchen wall and across the sink (of the Cecille Bechard home), splits the salt and pepper shakers, just misses the stove and passes through the wall to sever the Nadeau family's clothesline and cut off the candy counter in Alfred Sirpis' general store. Ms Bechard, whose home is in New Brunswick and Maine, is a Canadian living in 'almost a narrow third country where nationality matters less than personality, where the currency of each country is acceptable in the other and where bilingual-binational families are so common that a visitor needs a scorecard to keep it all straight.'

The Los Angeles Times, whose circulation and national influence continue to grow, usually devotes the left-hand column on its front page to a long, thoughtful story. During the sample period, stories in this position included 'Oil Brings Limited Joy to Scottish Isles', 'The Somozas: a Tight Grip on Nicaragua','The Yangtze: China's Past Joins Future',

---

'Campaigns in Britain Are Short, Cheap', and 'Amin Career: Anatomy of a Nation's Ruin'.

Other foreign stories given prominent attention in *The Los Angeles Times* included 'Uganda - the Psychology of Survival', 'Soviet dissent Survives, Even in Prison', 'Reporter's Notebook: Heated C. Rations Are Feast in Battered Uganda', 'India Acts to Save Its Sacred Cows', and refugees - a "Fourth World of Misery".'

The regional *Minneapolis Tribune,* which circulates widely in the upper Midwest, ran two lengthy staff-written series. A reporter and photographer spent a month in Mexico and reported daily for a full week. The newspaper's Sunday picture magazine was devoted to 'Mexico/the People/Their Lives'. The *Tribune's* labour reporters spent three weeks in the United Kingdom for a five-part series on 'Britain's Winter of Discontent'. And the *Tribune* was one of several United States newspapers to distribute a quarterly (now monthly) supplement; called 'World Paper', it is now circulated in more than a million copies in three languages in twelve countries. The supplement consists of international news written by leading journalists in different parts of the world.

The Washington Post, particularly influential in the national capital, often runs long stories that tie headline events to broader issues. Some of these stories in the sample period were 'West Bank Vigilantes -Jewish Gunmen Intimidate Arabs', 'US Demand for Adoption Spurs Baby Trade in Guatemala', 'Illegal Entry: a People's Terrifying Survival Tradition', 'Moslems in Europe Test Social Systems, Local Customs', and 'Mislabelled Burgundy Stirs Scandal Among French Growers, Inspectors'. Three lengthy stories focused on Asia: 'Phnom Penh Has New Rules, But Same Deserted Streets, 'Laos Says It Fears Attack by China', and 'Khmer Rouge Seek Sanctuary Through Thailand'. A reporter's 'Letter from Philippines' —a favourite style of Post foreign correspondents— wrote that 'Marcos' Foe Prefers Farce to Force'. The state of women was assessed in 'Emancipation for East German Women' and 'Japanese Women: Pride of Place at Home'. A global problem was examined in 'Tropical Forests —a Threatened Resource'.

Nigeria

African news dominated the topics of international stories across the newspaper media of the period. Most notably, the invasion of Uganda by Tanzanian troops drew varied headlines and comment. The tabloid *Daily Times* (24 April 1979) bannered the headline, 'Uganda Flag Hoisted in UK', with the report that after a two-year break of diplomatic relations between London and Kampala, the Ugandan flag was flying once again in London. It added that the strategic Ugandan city of Jinja had fallen to Tanzanian forces. *Punch* was more interested in the human angle aspects of the crisis. 'Big Daddy's 23 Offspring' was used as a banner to report about Idi Amin's children (28 April 1979). Another report (26 April 1979) alleged that Tanzanian action in Uganda was masterminded by certain western powers. Under a headline, 'Tanzanian Minister Blasts OAU', the paper reported a statement by the Foreign Minister of Tanzania, Mr Benjamin Mkenpa, which criticized the attitude of African governments over the Ugandan crisis.

Both *Punch* and *New Nigerian* (28 April 1979) picked up the report that Amin's fleeing troops were turned back by Kenyan authorities in their attempt to gain entry into Kenya. The latter paper, noted for its Moslem sympathies, added that Idi Amin had been given refuge in Libya. *New Nigerian* made various comments on the crisis under the following headlines: 'Ugandan Minister for Talks in Kenya' (24 April 1979), 'Amin's Last Stronghold Captured' (23 April 1979) 'Uganda Now to Get Petrol Supplies' (25 April 1979).

Also dominant in the news media were reports of the elections which ushered in, in Zimbabwe, the ephemeral government of Bishop Abel Muzorewa. *Daily Times* (27 April 1979) under the leading 'Callaghan Now Pledges', reported the promise of the former British Prime Minister to send an envoy to Zimbabwe to assess the conditions of an all-party conference following riots that greeted the election. The paper also reported that Muzorewa was leading in what it titled 'Sham Elections'. The next day, 28 April 1979, the *New Nigerian* ran an editorial captioned 'A Quisling in Africa' in which it ridiculed the elections that brought Abel Muzorewa to his uneasy and short-lived power. The *Daily Times* of the same date also had an editorial along the same line, with a caption, 'Deadly Hoax in Zimbabwe'. *Punch* was not left out: a headline of 27 April 1979 reported 'OAU Lambasts UK, US on Zimbabwe'.

The peace moves between Israel and Egypt attracted significant media attention. 'Egypt, Israel Exchange Instruments of Ratification', bannered *Punch* of 26 April 1979. All the papers treated the same story under various headlines. They also reported the reactions of Arab and Moslem states. These were mainly about the breaking of diplomatic relations with Egypt and the country's possible isolation from the Arab world.

Equally of interest to the newspaper was the Iranian crisis; the many reports on it were mainly in the style of 'news in brief'. *New Nigerian* was more interested in news of the Ayatollah than other newspapers. It reported in its 'briefs' on various dates about the tightening of security in Iran following the assassination of the chief of the country's armed forces. The movement of troops along the country's borders, riots among Turkish and Kurdish minorities, and some of the Ayatollah's warnings and revolutionary proclamations.

It is rather strange that such a major international news event as SALT, which occurred in this period, received only a passing mention by newspapers. *New Nigerian* with the caption, 'Carter Defends Bids for SALT Agreement', reported President Carter as saying that the only alternative to SALT was nuclear war.

Perhaps the scant treatment of such international news might be due to the fact that during this period Nigeria was preparing for its first popular elections, following the termination of nearly fourteen years of military rule. The editors would naturally be more interested in this exercise than in the reporting of distant international news which had no connections with the immediate expectation of their local constituencies.

Iran

The most significant finding of our study, and one not altogether unexpected in a post-revolutionary situation, was the rather small amount of attention paid to international news as compared to the Pahlavi era, when international news tended to block out domestic reporting, which was severely censored. What international news there was tended to be rather self-centred; over half the total number of news items (453) clearly dealt with Iranian issues, either located in Iran or including Iranian nationals, while many other stories dealt with reactions to and the ramifications of the revolution within the region.

Strictly speaking, there were no dominant stories if that implies stories which were given front-page priority, a large amount of space or appeared frequently throughout the period. The dominant theme that was represented by a number of different stories was the new definition of Iran's foreign policy, especially in regard to Middle Fast issues. Yazdi, the first Foreign Minister appointed after the revolution, announced the newly formulated Iranian foreign policy. This consisted of non-alignment, support for the Palestinians, warnings to certain western powers not to interfere in Iranian internal affairs. The announcement of the severing of diplomatic ties with Egypt, because of its unilateral peace agreement with Israel, received much attention. In a similar vein there were stories about Ayatollah Khomeini demanding the end to all relations with Egypt, because of Egyptian support for the ex-Shah, and reports on Iranian condemnation of the Middle East peace treaty.

These stories alternated as front-page items with a cluster of stories dealing with the Palestinians: Palestinian attacks on Sadat, their appreciation of the Iranian movement, and pictures of Archbishop Capucci visiting Khomeini. The fact that Arafat was the first foreign visitor to celebrate the Islamic victory in Tehran, was also highlighted.

The cumulative effect of these frequently small and diverse items was to present a totally new Iranian stance in and interpretation of events in the Middle East. Emancipating itself from its earlier adherence to the policy of the United States, Iran was moving into the non-aligned camp, developing a Third-World, anti-imperialist stance that was supportive of the Palestinian struggle and opposed to any super-power intentions in the region. Few photos enlivened international news stories, while political cartoons abounded.

The tone of many of the items was an angry and emotional one, prefiguring the demands for the return of the Shah and his wealth. The other crisis already brewing during the period of this study was the Iranian conflict with Iraq. Items noted Iraqi warplanes making incursions over Iranian territory and occasional bombings, the arrest of 'freedom fighters' in Iraq, as well as Iraqi provocation of tribal dissatisfaction in Kurdestan: a foretaste of the teeter into war that seemed imminent in the summer of 1980, and which had become a reality in October.

One of the greatest concerns of the government, picked up often indirectly by the media, was the basic need to protect the revolutionary gains from both domestic and foreign attack. These usually brief news items certainly pointed up clearly the host of problems the new Islamic Republic had to face. The consensual picture presented by these three papers mirrored the general public acceptance of the new foreign policy stance, although disagreements about strategy and tactics were to appear later. Ideological disputes came to the fore over internal social reorganization and planning, while the anti-imperialist stance was widely welcomed.

Lebanon

The Middle Eastern situation, mainly the Palestine problem and its implications for the region, received the most important attention by the Lebanese media under study. Most of the daily front page editorials by an-Nahar and as-Safir were devoted to this subject.

The coverage of Middle East news was devoted to three general areas of Arab news: those events related to the Lebanese civil war; the Palestinian problem and efforts to solve it; and general Arab news. The Syrian forces in Lebanon were seen by al-Amal as occupation forces while the left of centre paper as-Safir saw them as supporting forces. The broadcast media ignored this subject completely.

The most salient issue in the Lebanese media during the period of the study related to the developments in the Camp David agreement. This was presented from two sides. The negotiations between Egypt, Israel and the United States, the problems encountered and the implementation phase comprised the first side. The other side included the reaction of the Arab countries towards the agreement and the breaking of relations between these countries and Egypt.

The general Arab news included inter-Arab items, such as Syrian-Iraqi relations and the Libyan-Egyptian conflict. The internal opposition in Egypt was especially emphasized by as-Safir. Other Middle Eastern topics emphasized by the Lebanese media included Arab-Western relations, particularly the Egyptian-Soviet conflict and the Arab-United States conflict over the Palestine problem, and the issue of oil production and prices.

Next to the Arab news in importance, the situation in Iran played a prominent part in all the Lebanese media. Extensive and detailed news of the new regime and the internal difficulties were reported. Regular pictorial coverage was included in the print media. While the broadcast media and an-Nahar, presented a neutral coverage of Iran, as-Safir was more sympathetic while al-Amal was negative.

Third in the rank of importance came the following news (listed in order of volume of coverage): the SALT II agreement and the Carter-Brezhnev summit, which was extensively but not recurrently presented; the war in Uganda and the Tanzanian intervention; the British elections; the Western Sahara conflict; the nuclear disaster in the United States and the nuclear accident in Europe; the Rhodesian elections; the Chinese-Vietnamese and Chinese-USSR conflicts, and the debate over the United States military bases in Turkey.

The SALT II agreement was especially played up by Lebanese television, which included in its news a special feature prepared by an embassy of one of the parties involved. All the media welcomed the agreement. Left-of-centre as-Safir, however, played up the events in Uganda more extensively, emphasizing the Tanzanian invasion.

Australia

Images of foreign countries, indeed those foreign countries to which images are ascribed, are interpretations and selections, affected by factors which a content study by its very nature can only guess at. It would be naive to suppose that newsworthiness is defined only by intrinsic criteria of information value rather than also by concepts like 'bad news is good news' or 'animals and babies sell papers'.

On the whole, foreign news is not as prominent as home news in the Australian media. Rarely do foreign items figure at the start of broadcast bulletins, or as big front-page headlines in the press. Photographs of visiting entertainers, celebrities or babies born outside maternal wombs do make the front page with headlines. If other types of items make the front page they are placed in side columns and their headings are less black. As a general rule, foreign items are placed on about three inside pages, headed The World, and include some discursive pieces and a column of three or four-sentence snippits.

Thus the nuclear accident at Harrisburg seems to categorize itself as a dominant news item because on the day the news broke it led news broadcasts, and made big front page headlines in the press, which devoted an average of nine items and one editorial to it. These headlines were chilling: 'Nuclear blast threat', 'Explosive signs in reactor'. News stories dealt with workers who were tested for radioactivity, and found to be; be uncontaminated, the fear which hit residents who claimed they had been lied to, the mystery over the cause of the accident and mention of unheeded warnings. There were reported fears in the Federal Republic of Germany and Japan, and a setback to the nuclear industry was predicted. An Australian perspective was introduced with discussion of the Australian nuclear power station at Lucas Heights and calls from Australian politicians for observers to be sent to Harrisburg. In the following weeks Harrisburg disappeared almost entirely from the news. Checks were tightened on other reactors of the same design, and Israeli fears about nuclear power boosted Australian coal exports. Harrisburg was an unexpected event, covered as a crisis, that appeared overnight and disappeared almost as quickly.

The Rhodesian election provided a contrast to Harrisburg in that it was covered fairly consistently as a process, not in front page headlines, but in inside page articles. This item was also included in news broadcasts although it was not a lead story. In the week of the election there was a tendency to present it like any other election: 'election nears', 'counting tomorrow', with profiles of Muzorewa as 'Unlikely leader' or 'Bishop set for PM job'. Even 'Sitole claims irregularities' was couched in a constitutional vein. Rhodesia was not clearly seen as part of an African perspective; rather, the election was 'a dilemma for the West' perhaps because 'Muzorewa looks to West for assistance'. In the weeks before and after polling, more mention of less constitutional issues appeared — 'Guerillas threaten poll' or 'Guerilla war as poll starts'— and a more global perspective was introduced —'UN dismises poll as sham'. Editorials discussed 'the African powder keg'; suggested, give Muzorewa a chance' and introduced an Australian perspective that 'Australia could lead' in recognising the winner. In some sense television news, by presenting moving pictures of actual black Rhodesians travelling in the backs of lorries to bush polling booths, gave a truer image of the realities behind the words 'election', 'polling booth' and 'voting'. Perhaps this conveyed to Australian audiences the elasticity of such concepts, which still pictures did not do nearly so well. And perhaps the image of the elections was one of democracy in action; shadowed but not overshadowed by guerillas in action.

The British general election was also a dominant story, without recourse to big headlines, perhaps because ease of access to material, perhaps because of historical links. It does seem worth noting that African and British elections overshadowed the geographically closer Thai election. In Britain, unlike Rhodesia, the opinion polls could be guides —'Labour outs Tory lead', 'Conservatives cautious about poll'. Unlike Rhodesia too, there were riots, demonstrations, 'clashes with police' involving the National Front, thus 'law and order dominates campaign'. Profiles of contender Thatcher dominated. Callaghan achieved only 'Callaghan versus Thatcher', Thatcher's proposed policies were headlined': 'Thatcher acts on Zimbabwe, EEC and unions'. Editorials also focused on 'the Iron Lady' and commented on 'male chauvinism' as a factor in the election. Non-commercial *ABC television* provided insight with its film items of TV campaign ads, the Northern Ireland campaign; immigrant votes and newspaper allegiances and the Southall and Leicester riots. Australian involvement was minimal.

The Vietnamese refugees came and went frequently in the Australian news media. The issue could be judged as relevant to Australia since its geographical proximity, its small population and high standard of living raise the question of how many immigrants should be taken in. Some immigrants begged the question when they arrived in boats in Northern Australia —'shipwrecked girl allowed Australian entry'. Others had their plight reported from 'Refugee island' or were referred to as 'refugees in Malaysia'. Both regional reactions ('Malaysia says ship them out', 'Japanese papers say refugees a big problem') and world reactions ('UN calls for bigger intake','US to settle 40,000 refugees') were reported. However, Viet Nam itself said little. About a quarter of the stories were concerned with Australian reactions, mainly from present and former politicians. The immigration minister declared 'half who escape perish!' Mr Peacock (the foreign minister) discussed the problem in London, while Mr. Whitlaw (former Prime Minister) did so in the United States. Australia was 'in plan to help refugees' but there were renewed fears of Vietnamese refugees in Australia. Once again, a more vivid image of certain aspects of this news item may have been given by television pictures of refugee camps, in contrast to the prosaic image which views, opinions and pronouncements gave.

India

The political developments in Iran, Uganda, Rhodesia and the signing of the Egypt-Israel peace treaty dominated the foreign news coverage in the Indian media during the period of study. The coverage was a matter-of-fact reporting of the events as they unfolded; the two foreign news agencies, Reuters and AP, were the primary sources of these news events. Often, these major political news items were well displayed on the front page. 'Iran declared an Islamic Republic', was the lead story or was well displayed on the front page in most of the papers studied on 2 April. There were only a few editorials and features on these developments.

The Indian media attempted to give various sides of the picture of events in Iran. On 17 April, news about the execution of five more members of the Shah's armed forces after a summary trial was covered by all the newspapers on the front page; the papers described these army men as 'enemies of Iran's revolution'. The same day, President Sadat's criticism of Khomeini as 'a religious bigot' was also published. Again on 16 June, the ex-Shah's statement that Iran was in a 'bloodbath' was printed and it was noted that he hoped to return as ruler. The Iranian foreign minister's resignation was given front page coverage on 17 April.

On certain days during the period of study, there were many stories about Iran. Many of these were published on inside pages, and were varied in character. On 1 June, there were stories about Arab demands for autonomy and better economic conditions; Iran blaming the CIA for the assassination of Iranian revolutionary leaders; security for top Iranian leaders tightened; and three more SAVAK generals executed. In one feature, the socio-economic implications of the Iranian revolution for India were analysed, the author highlighting the pan-Islamic ramifications of the revolution.

Although it might be stated that the Indian media attempted to give an objective and factural account of the happenings in Iran a slight slant in favour of Ayatollah Khomeini, could nonetheless be discerned.

Considerable coverage was given to the events connected with the Egypt-Israel Treaty. News stories on the isssue published were: Warm welcome to President Sadat on his return home after signing the Treaty; the Baghdad conference decided to impose economic and political sanctions against Egypt; Kuwait and Tunisia recalled their ambassadors from Cairo and stopped all financial assistance; Egypt announced it did not recognize the resolutions of the Arabs and would not allow anyone to influence its attempts to achieve a comprehensive solution to the West Asia conflict; Israel cabinet ratified the Peace Treaty with Egypt; the United Nations Secretary General, Dr Kurt Waldheim, said all interested parties, not so far involved in signing the Peace Treaty should be included in further treaty negotiations; and India stated that the Peace Treaty fell short of a comprehensive solution of the West Asia problem.

India's cautious reaction to the Israeli-Egyptian Treaty was evident from the news reports. Mr Husney Mubarak, Vice-

President of Egypt, visited India to explain to the Indian Leaders the positive aspects of the Treaty. Even so, India's Foreign Minister was of the view that the Treaty did not fulfil the aspirations of the Palestinians and at the same time stated that Arab sanctions against Egypt were too severe.

The reports in the Indian media pertaining to the upheaval in Uganda were overtly sympathetic to the Ugandan revolutionaries fighting Amin's troops. India was the first Asian country to recognize the new Ugandan Government. This story was given front page coverage in the press on 17 April. The other stories on the same day were: Ugandan (Asian) exiles return home; their welcome by the new government; hunt for Idi Amin continues; and three-fourths of Amin's troops surrender to Ugandan-Tanzanian National Liberation Army.

Other stories covered were Chinese recognition of the new Ugandan government 2 May and the United Nations Secretary General's appeal to the world to help Ugandan refugees (1 May).

The news about elections in Rhodesia and the issue of black majority rule were prominently reported by the Indian media. The front-page news story (with photograph) on 25 April had the headline 'Muzorewa is first Black PM of Rhodesia'. Bilateral relations dominated coverage of news from the neighbouring countries (Bangladesh, Pakistan, Sri Lanka, Afghanistan and Nepal) by the Indian media. 'India and Bangladesh agree to stop exodus' was the lead story in *The Hindustan Times* and *The Hindu* on 26 April. Other stories dealt with agreements reached at high level talks to check illegal movement of people across the borders, and to strengthen trade relations and establish joint ventures.

The execution of the former Pakistani leader, Bhutto, was extensively covered and commented upon. 'Clemency pleas by Bhutto's sister' made front page news in most newspapers on 2 April. Readers' reactions to the execution of Bhutto were published in the Letters to the Editors columns.

Political unrest in Nepal and Afghanistan, and the issue of a separate State for Tamilians in Sri Lanka were also given ample attention.

Racial conflicts involving Asian immigrants in England were covered in news stories and commented upon in editorials and features by special correspondents of the newspapers. *Indian Express,* in an editorial titled 'Racism in Britain' on 26 April, commented that the latest outrage in Southall was not an act of a lunatic fringe but of a well organized group of 'rabid believers in unabashed racism'. 'Concern at UK violence against Asians'was a seven-column headline at the bottom of the front page in *Indian Express* on that date. *The Hindu* of the same day also carried a four-column front-page story, 'London Riot: Delhi Demands Probe' in addition to three other stories on the issue and a photograph in the inside pages. There were many letters to the editor as well.

Former United States Ambassador, Daniel Moynihan's story (based on his book, *A Dangerous Place)* about CIA pay-outs to the Congress Party, implicating Mrs. Indira Gandhi, was widely covered and commented upon in the Indian press; on 26 April, *Indian Express* carried a major story on it, with Moynihan's photograph.

Indian papers did not include many editorials, features photos or cartoons in most of their foreign coverage.

There were hardly any news stories about Latin America, Australia, Canada or the USSR. News stories from Africa were restricted to the very troubled zones, namely, Rhodesia, Uganda and South Africa. Viet Nam and Cambodia (in connection with China) were virtually the only South-East Asian countries covered.

To summarize, news from Iran, Uganda, Egypt-Israel and Rhodesia was predominant during the period under study.

News from and about neighbouring countries, though not so startling, was given a fair amount of attention and coverage. The issue of Asian immigrants in the United Kingdom was widely covered and commented upon in editorials and Letter to Editor columns because of historical links between India and the United Kingdom, as well as the emotional involvement and concern of Indian readers.

Malaysia

The marching of Kampuchean refugees into Thailand and the continued influx of the 'boat people' to South-East Asian countries featured prominently in all Malaysian newspapers during the period.

Second in importance were the fall of Idi Amin and the controversial general elections in Rhodesia, the internal squabbles in the northern and southern regions of Iran, and reactions to the Egyptian-Israeli peace pact.

Less prominent were the debate on the SALT Agreement signed by Presidents Carter and Brezhnev, and Mrs. Thatcher's campaign during the British elections, highlighting the probability of having a first woman prime minister in the United Kingdom.

Except for one or two occasions, none of these items made the headlines on the front page of *The New Straits Times,* the largest local English daily; it led off with domestic issues such as the impending hike in petrol prices.

The exceptions occurred during the visit of the United Nations Secretary General Kurt Waldheim to Malaysia, when *The New Straits Times* played up the issue of resolving the refugee problems in the region. The Chinese language newspaper *Sin Chew Jit Poh* was also vocal on this topic and on the follow-up to the border conflict between China and Viet Nam.

Nearly all of the reports in the *The New Straits Times,* based on Reuters or UPI dispatches, highlighted the 'flight of some 80,000 Kampuchean refugees' into the mountain sanctuaries bordering Thailand —provoking fears among South-East Asian countries that the military operations would spill over into their territories. The reports painted a picture of the refugees 'trapped between the advancing Vietnamese-led Khmer forces and Thailand, a country that does not want them'. It was also reported that the Thai troops were put on full border alert with Prime Minister Kriangsak back at the helm after his party won the general elections in Thailand.

Such prominence in *The New Straits Times,* which even carried lengthy feature articles on the refugees' plight, clearly indicated the Malaysian Government's thinking on the Kampuchean crisis. *The New Straits Times,* not only has the largest circulation of any daily in the country, but also fully supports government policies.

During Waldheim's visit to Malaysia, *The New Straits Times*'s second lead on the front page was 'a pledge to provide more UN aid to countries like Malaysia and to solve the refugee problems', but it was reported that he asked for more time so as to take account of delays in making arrangements for the transfer of refugees to other countries.

The news reports concerning Idi Amin and Ayatollah Khomeini found almost equal space in the second and third pages (mainly devoted to world news) of *The New Straits Times,* although *Utusan Malaysia* occasionally played up the problems in Iran on the front page.

The New Straits Times and another independent English newspaper, *The Star* (not included in the analysis), reported on Idi Amin's troops' atrocities in Uganda and his disappearance from his country. A side story from a wire service told of Israeli commandos being engaged to hunt down Idi Amin.

The Malays newspaper *Utusan Malaysia,* together with *The New Straits Times,* gave considerable coverage to Ayatollah Khomeini's proclamation of Iran as an Islamic Republic, and the 'chaotic' conditions prevailing in that country. The downfall of the Shah of Iran and his plight constituted another topic evenly covered through wire service reports.

Several of the Malaysian newspapers, especially *The New Straits Times,* played down the Rhodesian elections. Less prominent still were the Egyptian-Israeli Peace Pact, the Carter-Brezhnev agreement on SALT, and Mrs. Thatcher's election campaign.

The stories on the Egyptian-Israeli pact mainly centred on the reactions of the disgrunted Arab countries that opposed the signing of the agreement.

Reports on SALT featured President Carter's move to gain support from his own people, while the wire reports used featured the human interest angle of Mrs Thatcher's campaign.

Some of the foreign stories deserving attention may have lost out to local news: the newly-elected King took the oath of office during the period of study, providing front-page feature material for two days.

Hungary

The most prominent foreign events given almost daily coverage were the SALT II agreement and the closely-related topic of Soviet-American relations. The meeting between Presidents Carter and Brezhnev in vienna and the signing of the SALT agreement were presented by every Hungarian newspaper under study as the most important geopolitical event of the year.

Next in importance were the political, economic and military relations among the Eastern European socialist countries. Information about meetings and negotiations regarding economic co-operation among them was reported almost every day during the period studied. President Brezhnev's visit to Hungary before the Vienna signing of the SALT agreement, Marshall Tito's visit to Moscow, Warsaw Pact military exercises in Hungary and COMECON sessions received the most intensive coverage. News of the international communist movement and communist party events in foreign countries was closely followed as well.

Much foreign news coverage and commentary concerned East-West relations and détente. Such items generally criticized the United States and the Western European NATO countries. Signs of détente —such as President Giscard d'Estaing's visit to Moscow and the visit of some United States Congressmen to Hungary— received extensive first-page coverage.

Domestic politics in Western European countries, particularly the Federal Republic of Germany and Italy, and Common Market relations were covered nearly every day. The elections in the United Kingdom figured prominently in first-page stories in every newspaper under study.

Arab-Israeli relations and domestic events in Iran were the next most important news stories. The Middle East in general received continuous coverage, as did domestic politics and elections in Rhodesia. Events in Uganda and the fall of Idi Amin were described in some detail but never became front-page leads.

As for Asia and Latin America, only the fighting on the Kampuchea-Thai border and the Nicaraguan events received relatively intensive coverage.

The Hungarian news organs differed little in the ways they covered the most prominent foreign news items; the longest and most important front-page stories were usually the same.

The five papers studied were very similar in their choice of political and other terms, theme emphasis and style. Differences appeared chiefly in the coverage of economic or cultural news, 'less important' items of domestic politics in small countries, diplomatic protocol, catastrophes, entertainment, and so forth.

Poland

During the period studied, the Polish press reported chiefly on a number of major international themes.

Relations between socialist countries and highly developed capitalist states stood at the top of the list, and were reported within the context of détente and the idea of peaceful co-existence. Polish journalists wrote about increasing possibilities of and conditions for development of economic co-operation between East and West, and about the political chances of reconciling differences'; the Carter-Brezhnev meeting, to be followed by the signing of the SALT II treaty, was viewed as one such opportunity.

In the middle of April, i.e. two months before the actual date of this meeting, *Zycie Warszawy* and *Trybuna Ludu* published President Carter's statements on the significance of the SALT II treaty, emphasizing his remark that 'the strategy of peaceful actions is the only rational possibility for both sides.'

Virtually every day the three newspapers studied *(Trybuna Ludu, Zycie Warszawy, Express Wieczerny)* reported on the meetings of the Soviet and United States delegations in Geneva and on progress made in drafting the convention prohibiting the use of nuclear weapons. Some articles noted that not all Americans nor all of the NATO states approved of the existing tendency towards peaceful co-existence of nations; in the United States, for example, certain forces attempted to accelerate the arms race (the Pentagon's armament programmes were discussed). On the whole, however, optimistic conclusions were drawn: the idea of peace would succeed, despite attempts by some pressure groups in capitalist countries, since the societies of these countries were definitely against war. Polish journalists predicted that the United States Congress would ratify SALT II.

The optimism of the polish press was particularly visible during French President Giscard d'Estaing's visit to the USSR and the Carter-Brezhnev meeting in Vienna. French foreign policy was presented by the Polish mass media almost as a model of peaceful co-existence between states of different socio-economic structures and policies. *Trybuna Ludu* referred to the Brezhnev-Carter meeting in the following terms: as 'the Soviet-American dialogue in Vienna'; 'Mutual responsibility for the world's peaceful future'; 'The first meeting of L. Brezhnev and J. Carter'; 'Before the signing —the initialling of the SALT II treaty in Geneva'. Similar big headlines were supplied by *Zycie Warszawy:* 'The agreement, a limitation of the arms race, will consolidate the faith humanity has in obtaining durable peace'; 'Leonid Brezhnev and Jimmy Carter met in Austria's capital'; 'The Vienna summit is the centre of the world's attention'. The following headlines were typical of the coverage of *Express Wieczerny:* 'Before the signing of SALT II'; 'The second day of the summit'; 'The world awaits with hope and optimism the results of the talks in Vienna'. Although the Prime Minister of India, Morarji Desai, visited Poland while the Vienna talks were going on, the Polish press devoted more space to the latter.

The second largest quantity of material published dealt with the situation in the Middle East, including the negative reactions of the Arab states to the Egyptian-Israeli agreement signed at Camp David. *Trybuna Ludu* reported that the Arab world condemned the 'serparatist Egyptian-Israeli treaty' and that those countries disagreed with President Sadat's policy and that of the United States in the Middle East. *Zycie Warszawy* and *Express Wieczerny* drew attention to the economic sanctions applied to Egypt by the Arab countries and to the severing of diplomatic relations with that country. All three newspapers also published negative appraisals of Israeli policy towards the occupied Arab territory, pointing out that the right of the Palestinian nation to have its own land was not respected. Israeli's attack on Lebanon was described as 'a dangerous tactic increasing tension'. Referring to Israeli sources Israel's policy was described as 'a tendency to strengthen the position of rightist forces and towards a creation of an atmosphere of perpetual threat to all Lebanese who do not support conservative groups'.

The third most important theme was the China-Viet Nam conflict. The Chinese Government was accused of carrying out a hegemonistic policy towards Asian countries and of provoking borderline conflicts with Viet Nam. All coverage of that theme (signed by the Polish Press Agency PAP) referred to the Vietnamese information agency, VNA.

Other items frequently covered included the fighting in Uganda against Amin, and the civil war in Nicaragua between 'the regime troups of the National Guards and the National Liberation Front "Sandinista" army'. The domestic situation in Iran following proclamation of the Moslem Republic and armed civil fighting taking place in some parts of the country were also reported. The majority of this material was prepared by PAP on the basis of agency news from London, New York and Paris.

Federal Republic of Germany

Foreign news reporting by the media during the period under study was dominated by three topics: the crisis in Iran, the SALT II negotiations, and the elections in Rhodesia.

News about political developments in Iran seldom appeared prominently in the daily newspapers; the one exception was the left-liberal *Frankfurter Rundschau,* which usually gave Iran page-one treatment. Like the daily press, the two television networks reported relatively consistently about the Iranian crisis, although rarely at the beginning of the news programme, i.e. as the lead story.

The Revolutionary Tribunal's death sentences and the subsequent executions dominated the news; an atmosphere of extreme uncertainty and menace in Iran was projected in such headlines as: 'The Ayatollah wants to see more blood;' 'Over 20 executions in Teheran, including three former ministers of state'; 'Horror over blood justice'. The revolutionary situation was often compared with conditions under the Shah's regime; reports frequently concluded that Khomeini even outdid the Shah in his persecution of critics and enemies. The Ayatollah's measures were said to be determined by a mania for revenge and retaliation, rather than by justice. The political atmosphere was characterized as 'chaotic' or 'anarchistic'; the revolutionary Council and the government were said to work frequently against each other. Censorship of the Iranian media was especially criticized.

The second most important topic was the SALT II negotiations. As a rule, however, only short items appeared in the daily newspapers about the actual progress of the talks. Longer front-page stories were carried in mid-May, when agreement was reached on the wording of the pact, and in mid-June, when the Carter-Brezhnev meeting took place in Vienna. Television networks also placed reports on SALT II at the beginning of their news programmes in mid-May and again in mid-June.

In general, news of SALT II was reported with a mixture of sobriety and scepticism. The positions of Moscow and Washington were said to be irreconcilable; some reports doubted the treaty could be enforced. Still, the importance of the treaty was emphasized, and hope was expressed that President Carter would be able to push the SALT II resolutions through the United States Senate.

The election campaign in Rhodesia appeared in the foreign news sections on the inside pages of most papers; only the election results were published on the front page. Few of the stories were accompanied by photos or drawings illustrating background information. In the television reports studies, news of Rhodesia usually came in the middle or at the end of broadcasts.

The elections were presented only in a very limited sense as 'free and fair'. It was pointed out that they were conducted under martial law. Nonetheless, a positive evaluation was usually made: it was noted that in spite of everything, the electorate had declared its aversion to terrorism and disorder. It was emphasized that Zimbabwe-Rhodesia could develop freely only if sanctions were less severe. Participation by the guerilla organizations in solving the Rhodesia problem was viewed as absolutely necessary, since they were already excluded from the elections. The implication was that the United States and Europe should exercise caution and discretion in their political policies towards Rhodesia, and should refrain for the time being from recognizing the government.

In addition to the three most prominent topics in the foreign news reporting, three other foreign events were given substantial coverage: the nuclear accident at the Harrisburg atomic energy plant, the peace treaty between Israel and Egypt, and the fall of Idi Amin in Uganda.

Special attention as paid to the Three-Mile Island (Harrisburg) incident. It was mentioned time and again in domestic political discussions as a threatening sign on the horizon, especially when the debate centred on nuclear politics in the Federal Republic of Germany.

Finland

Fifteen news items were covered extensively in all four daily newspapers studied during the specified period. (If we disregarded the provincial agrarian newspaper *Savon Sanomat* the list of such items would be considerably longer.) In rough chronological order they were: Arab-Israeli relations, Rhodesian elections, the Harrisburg nuclear plant catastrophe, British elections, racial riots in the United Kingdom, the oil tanker catastrophe in the Baltic, Iranian events, the earthquake in Yugoslavia, Tanzanian intervention in Uganda, the UNCTAD conference in Manila, fighting on the Kampuchea-Thailand border, visits of Giscard d'Estaing and Tito to Moscow, Nicaraguan events, the SALT II agreement, and the Carter-Brezhnev summit in Vienna.

It is quite obvious that very few of these events had such a pervasive presence in the pages of the Finnish newspapers that they could be singled out as dominant news stories. The three major events (receiving almost daily coverage) were the question of Arab-Israeli relations, the upheaval in Uganda and the situation in Iran. Next in importance were the elections in Rhodesia and Great Britain, as well as the SALT proceedings, including the Carter-Brezhnev summit. The catastrophes in Harrisburg and in the Baltic (off the southern coast of Finland) dominated all the foreign news on certain days, but did not prevail consistently in the headlines. The SALT negotiations constituted a typical frame of reference for news of this period, although seldom with big headlines.

The complex of Arab-Israeli relations was a standing theme on the 'hard news' pages, particularly in the leading paper *Helsingin Sanomat*. The latter derived its information (directly and through the national news agency) chiefly from the big Western agencies; the information usually, however, underwent considerable editing. *Helsingin Sanomat* typically used both Arab and Israeli sources and thus attempted to strike a balance. Similarly, the leftist *Kansan Uutiset* tried to achieve balanced treatment of this topic in general. Furthermore, unlike the other papers included in the Finnish study, except for the Soviet papers, the *Kansan Uutiset* used the TASS news agency for about one-fifth of its foreign coverage.

The coverage of Arab-Israeli relations clearly illustrates how even the latent orientation of a medium affects its way of presenting a day's news. For example, on Thursday 17 May, *Helsingin Sanomat* carried the following items on Arab-Israeli relations:(1) the Moslem delegations 'walk-out during the Israeli speech at the UNCTAD conference;(2) resignation of the Lebanese government;(3) goal in Lebanon: national unity government;(4) profile of former prime minister of Lebanon. *Kansan Uutiset* reported on (2) and (3) but added that (5) the Lebanese President Sarkis had had negotiations with the Syrian President before the government resigned, and that (6) the right-wing parties of Lebanon were unified. The two provincial papers gave the topic more limited coverage: the conservative *Aamulehti* carried only items (1), (2) and (3), and the centrist *Savon Sanomat* only items (2), (3) and (4).

During the entire period under study it may be stated that, in general, all four papers informed their readers of the main events each day, with such headlines as: 'Arab diplomats leave Cairo while Israeli government accepts Begin's plan to visit Cairo', 'Attack by Arab guerillas against El Al plane in Brussels', 'Palestinians attack settlement on the West Bank', 'Israelis attack in South Lebanon', 'Exchange of peace treaty documents in Sinai', 'Security Council demands UN troops to all parts of Southern Lebanon', 'Cease fire on the front', 'Begin claims that Israel will never give up Golan', 'Walk out at UNCTAD', 'Lebanese Government resigns', 'US and Soviet Union could not agree on prolonging of UN troops presence'. But the particular items —indeed the whole framework— with which each paper surrounded this 'common core' were striking different. In the conservative *Aamulehti,* headlines on 27 April ran as follows: 'Palestinians explode bomb in Israeli train', 'Syrian planes fly over Beirut', and 'Begin proposes Nobel prize to Carter', while the other three papers focused on Israeli attacks on Palestinians, wih *Kansan Uutiset* adding that Israeli planes were seen over Beirut.

As far as the other two dominant news stories (events in Uganda and Iran) were concerned differences between the four newspapers were less apparent. Regardless of their political standpoints the papers relied on exclusively Western sources, chiefly Reuters and AFP (transmitted by the home agency); *Helsingin Sanomat* and *Aamulehti* also used AP and UPI.

In the sample, news items on Uganda appeared in *Helsingin Sanomat* ten times, in *Aamulehti* five times; and in both *Kansan Uutiset* and *Savon Sanomat* four times. A comparison of *Helsingin Sanomat,* the leading independent newspaper, and the communist-oriented *Kansan Uutiset* reveals the following differences: On 2 April *Helsingin Sanomat* reported that Tanzanian planes had bombed Entebbe; *Kansan Uutiset* did not carry any news of this. On 17 April, both papers reported on the verified stories of horror in Uganda and the killing of four western journalists by Amin troops. On 23 April both papers reported the liberation of Jinja. On 24 April *Helsingin Sanomat* informed its readers of an alleged visit by Amin to Libya and Iraq; *Kansan Uutiset* did not report on those suspicions and instead added more material on the

cruelties of the Amin regime. Next day, only *Helsingin Sanomat* reported that British companies were claiming restitution from the new Ugandan Government for the losses they suffered due to nationalization during the Amin period. On 26 April *Helsingin Sanomat* ran lengthy feature stories about the situation in Uganda, one by *The Los Angeles Times* and the second by *The Washington Post. Kansan Uutiset* using Reuters material, reported on the negotiations by Yusf Lule with the Kenyan Government officials and on their decision to refuse former Amin soldiers entry to Kenyan territory. *Helsingin Sanomat* furthermore reported on a massacre by Amin troops in Tororo (28 April), the invasion of Lira by Tanzanian troops (17 May) and the Arab countries' refusal to extend further assistance to Amin (1 June).

Significantly there were no discrepancies between the two papers which could be attributed to their different political standpoints. The leading independent paper simply is better able to devote attention to smaller news stories and invest in services of big foreign dailies than a smaller (party) paper. It is worth mentioning, however, that during the whole sample period *Kansan Uutiset* informed its readers more extensively about the events in Nicaragua than any other Finnish paper - thanks to a heavy coverage of Nicaragua by TASS.

The four Finnish papers covered the developments in Iran much the same way they had covered Uganda. Iran was mentioned in the headlines of *Helsingin Sanomat* ten times, in *Aamulehti* seven times, in *Kansan Uutiset* six times and in *Savon Sanomat* three times during the sample period. In addition, *Helsingin Sanomat* printed a lengthy editorial background article about the Kurdistan problems. No significant differences in the way of editing the news materials could be identified. A comparison of the four newspapers shows only that liberal *Helsingin Sanomat,* conservative *Aamulehti* and leftist *Kansan Uutiset* did not differ very much regarding the volume and variety of their coverage, whereas the agrarian *Savon Sanomat* carried considerably fewer storie on Iran —and on foreign affairs in general.

Netherlands

The major items featured in the Netherlands during this period (in approximate chronological order) were: Arab-Israeli relations, with an emphasis on South Lebanon because of the presence there of a detachment of Netherlands troops under United Nations command; the Rhodesian elections; the Harrisburg nuclear plant disaster; the Tanzanian intervention in Uganda; events in Iran; the earthquake in Yugoslavia; the British elections; racial riot in Britain; the visits of Giscard d'Estaing and Tito to Moscow; the SALT II Agreement and the Carter-Brezhnev summit in Vienna. The Netherlands press also covered several meetings of NATO officials, the increases in oil prices, the Vietnamese boat refugees, the May Day demonstrations and a proposition by a South African commission to abolish apartheid in the country's business firms. In addition, a good deal of attention was paid to a specifically Netherlands problem —the illegal residence of Turkish immigrant workers.

Naturally, only a few of these items can be considered as dominant news stories. Four of the events received almost daily coverage; Israeli-Arab relations; the Rhodesian elections; the events in Uganda, and the situation in Iran. The Harrisburg catastrophe, although not reported on every sample day, also claimed much attention. On the first day of the composed week, and also on the fisrt day of the whole period under study, 2 April, all three papers ran front-page articles with large headlines. The inside pages gave more details and comparisons were made between the Harrisburg nuclear plant and nuclear plants in the Netherlands and elsewhere.

The quality newspaper, *NRC-Handelsblad,* and the provincial paper, *Tubantia,* in subsequent weeks, carried more news about the disaster, or referred to it in connection with several other news events. *Tubantia* brought Harrisburg into its discussion of a storage centre for nuclear waste in Ahaus, a town in the Federal Republic of Germany but close to Enschede, the border town in the Netherlands where *Tubantia* is published.

Similarly, all three papers studied referred to the SALT negotiations and NATO meetings in several different connections, as they did with oder articles on nuclear power and arms which appeared during the study period. Thus it seems that the Harrisburg disaster provided a typical frame of reference for news.

Arab-Israeli relations, in one form or another, consistently formed a lead article on the 'foreign' pages of all three newspapers. Netherlands participation in the United Nations military command made the fighting in South Lebanon a 'hot' news topic; stories covered both the fighting itself and the issue of extra payments for 'our boys in Lebanon'.

Both *De Telegraaf,* the largest circulation newspaper in the Netherlands and, by that country's standards, the most 'sensational' as well as the provincial *Tubantia* derived most of their information from the big Western news agencies, especially for news items. More descriptive articles —for instance about the Egypt-Israeli peace treaty— and also big stories (such as the Arab guerilla attack on the El Al plane in Brussels and its aftermath) were provided by the papers' own correspondents, whose stories tended to relay facts without much comment. Nevertheless, the *Telegraaf* paid more attention to the Israeli than to the Arab side of the conflict. For example, it reported that the Israeli army had had enough and had decided to attack the Palestine terrorists and their bases systematically and not just incidentally, without saying what the Palestine reaction to this might be. The quality newspaper, *NRC-Handelsblad,* carried abundant news about Arab-Israel relations; most of it came from its own correspondents in Tel Aviv, Cairo and Beirut, and tended to cover all sides of the question in detail.

All three papers devoted a good deal of attention to the Rhodesian elections and the new black Prime Minister Muzorewa. The *NRC-Handelsblad* in particular provided detailed accounts from its correspondent in Africa of what was considered the dishonest running of those elections and their impact on the attitude of the other African states, black as well as white. The wavering attitude of the United States and the United Kingdom towards recognition of the government, and the reasons for it, filled many columns. The *Telegraph* and *Tubantia* relied chiefly on Western press bureaux for their information, although the *Telegraph* used one article from its correspondent in Johannesburg. African sources were hardly ever used in any of these three papers.

The Tanzanian intervention in Uganda and the fall of Amin were reported by all newspapers, with the same kinds of variations. The *NRC-Handelsblad* gave the widest coverage, mostly from its own correspondents. The other two newspapers gave shorter reports from the news agencies.

The events in Iran were covered almost daily by the *NRC-Handelsblad.* In particular, the struggle between the ethnic minorities and the executions of the pro- and anti— Khomeini sympathisers were given extended treatment. The *Telegraph* carried no news of the executions but devoted a few brief items to the struggle of ethnic minorities. Apart from short factual reports, *Tubantia* provided a half-page commentary on the Iranian question, strongly criticizing Khomeini's policy.

The three papers differed in their approach to and amount of foreign news. The *NRC-Handelsblad* gave abundant news on all questions, viewed from all sides, and drew mostly on its own correspondents; for the shorter articles it used Western press bureaux. *Tubantia* and the *Telegraph* relied almost exclusively on Western press agencies but confined their treatment to the factual. None of the three ever used IPS* or TASS.

The *Telegraph* especially made more room on its front page or its main foreign page for such stories as a hotel strike in Spain (troublesome for Netherlands tourists) or the fatal fall of a Netherlands citizen in an escape attempt from a Viennese prison, than for the activities of the Ayatollah or the problems of Muzorewa.

Part III: HOW INTERNATIONAL NEWS IMAGERY IS CREATED

Although some of these reports are more interpretative than others, together they give some idea of the differences in focus and perspective which do exist, both within a single media system and between systems, but which tend to get blurred by the forced oversimplification of statistical information.

The basic 'menu' of 'hot' topics was quite limited and fairly universally covered. The stories included two African items (Uganda and Rhodesia) and a Middle East focus (the Camp David Agreement and the Palestinian issue, and the Islamic Republic in Iran). From Europe came news of the SALT II agreement and the issue of détente. Some variety of this basic 'menu' can be found in all systems bar the Iranian, Australian and Hungarian.

A list of items of secondary importance would include the China-Viet Nam fighting, a major concern in the Polish press presumably because it involved intra-socialist conflict; the Kampuchean refugees and Vietnamese boat people in the Australian and Malaysian media, where these issues aroused regional concern and at the same time represented a potential demand on national resources; and the Harrisburg (Three Mile Island) incident in the Australian and Netherlands press but not in the American. A general concern with regional affairs was evident in the Malaysian and Hungarian systems. Iran conformed least to the 'standard' approach to international news; its orientation was the most introspective and regional.

A number of standard journalistic devices can be distinguished in the presentation of international news stories. One was the frequently visible effort to maintain impartiality and balance in reporting a particular international item. In dealing with the events in Iran, the record of the infant Islamic Republic was compared with the time when the Shah was in power; as these were arguably quite incomparable periods, the fledgling Republic was put at a disadvantage. At the same time, reporting of highly partial statements by others, such as Sadat's comment on Khomeini, did not seem to make the impartiality of the news channel itself less credible. In another typical media procedure, complex international processes were reduced to the psychological profiling of central political actors — Muzorewa was labelled 'vacillating', Khomeini was 'revengeful'— and situations were stereotyped as 'chaotic'

---

* IPS (Inter Press Service Third World News Agency), which is based in Rome, is a non-profit journalists co-operative. It focuses on Third World issues and events and emphasizes the reporting of 'processes' in the developing world.

or 'unstable'. The similarity of language used by different media in reporting the same event suggests that such epithets originated in the international wire service reports, but that remains to be thoroughly investigated.*

Although the two major African stories were repeatedly amongst the dominant topics they were rarely, if ever, reported with any 'African' perspective or using African sources; the Nigerian press was an exception. Thus, the Rhodesian election was examined from the standpoint of the end of colonial rule and the need for Western discretion in dealings with the new government.

How the Muzorewa government might be received by other African states, or how the balance of forces in the continent would be reshaped, were aspects scarcely discussed. Concern about the election procedure itself can be found in a number of the reports studied; the only African media system included in this section of the study, the Nigerian, in fact called the process a racist 'sham'.

Coverage of the Middle East situation, with its more obvious political stances, showed perhaps the widest spectrum of treatments from the generally pro-peace stories put out by AP and UPI (see Appendix 6) to the more nuanced reporting in, for example, the Finnish papers, which told of renewed attacks by both sides and restated the unfinished problem of the Palestinians. The Polish press emphasized the Arab condemnation of Egypt's 'separatist' actions, criticized the United States interference in the area, and generally presented Israel in a negative light. These two country examples show that whereas statistics simply tally up the number of stories on the Camp David Agreement, qualitative analysis brings out the differences in perspective hidden by the figures. The reactions to SALT II are another example: whereas the Hungarian and Polish papers were almost jubilant about the rationality of striving for peace and the progress of détente, many of the Western newspapers studied took a far more sceptical, even cynical, attitude.

In short, the twelve brief country reports presented in Part 2 of this chapter are rich in material for revealing divergencies in orientation, perspective and journalistic approch. They warrant a rigorous qualitative analysis.

We will now attempt a brief comparison of dominant topics with the themes contained in news items. (This information was collected in the formal content analysis but was considered to fit better into this section of the report.)

Each news item was coded for the presence or absence of any of thirty-three 'themes and references' which had to be 'quite clearly present in the news item in a way that would be recognized by almost anyone'. In practice, it was difficult to determine clearly the presence or absence of many of the themes and the list itself was rather arbitrarily constructed, including 'Fascism' but not 'Zionism', 'détente' but not 'non-alignment', 'population explosion' but not 'refugees'. Some themes seemed to overlap with and be no more than extensions

of topics, while others tapped conceptual frameworks and ideological positions not explored elsewhere. One limitation of the analysis resulted from the fact that since value-direction was not analysed, the mere presence of such a theme as 'imperialism' still gave little clue as to the angle of presentation, while 'nuclear arms' could include both proliferation and limitation. Although multiple coding was possible, the findings show that usually less than half the items actually contained any theme at all, while others contained several, somewhat confusing the statistics. Given these difficulties, only the three most frequently coded themes within each national media system are presented in Table 1.

Using the above criteria, Table 1 shows that only twenty of a possible thirty-three themes appear, and the degree of repetition is quite striking. The most frequently mentioned themes are as follows:

Terrorism appearing	13	times
Human Rights	12	,,
Independence		
Religious/Ethnic Antagonism	7	,,
Nuclear Arms	6	,,
Imperialism		
Ecology	5	,,
Energy		
Racialism	4	,,
Communism		
Détente		
Development of Third World	3	,,
Eight other themes	10	,,

The amount of overlap and concentration on a limited number of themes, and their ready association with dominant news stories, suggests that themes signal the general context of debate and discussion, providing limited explanatory background for immediate news events. Thus, 'nuclear arms' and 'détente' are the wider referents for stories stemming from the SALT II Agreements, and reflect the East European concern already mentioned. 'Ecology' is perhaps prompted by the Three Mile Island incident. The more political themes could be related to a variety of news stories, depending on one's predelictions. Hence 'terrorism', 'independence' and 'racism' could all be used in the Rhodesian context, while 'religious antagonism', 'imperialism' and 'human rights' would pertain to reports on Iran, and so on. Clearly, a detailed analysis of themes by topic and location would clarify this point. In general, the listing of themes echoes the dominance of 'hard' news items, specifically political stories, and especially within the Third World. The prominence of the terrorism theme may be accounted for by a universal interest in violence as a major news-value. Moreover, this phrase provides a catch-all category for all kinds of exceptional political activity.

Themes are better indications than topics of the actual content of international news; perhaps they are merely handy linguistic pegs on which to hang stories. If so, they indicate to what extent the international language used in such reporting is taken for granted.

---

* Appendix 6 provides some comparative materials on wire-agency content during this period.

Table 1 : The three most frequently mentioned themes

	Terrorism	Human rights	Religions - ethnic antagonism	Independence	Communism	Energy	Rich/poor division	Imperialism	Racism	Home nation benefactor	Individual freedom	Subversion	Nuclear arms	Aid to developing countries	Development of Third World	Political independence	Ecology	Home country benefactor	Population growth	East-West detente	Democracy	Racialism	Economic self-sufficiency
Latin America																							
Argentina	X	X		X																			
Brazil	X	X			X																		
Mexico	X	X				X	X																
North America																							
United States	X	X	X																				
Africa																							
Algeria				X				X	X														
Ivory Coast				X						X	X												
Kenya	X	X	X							X													
Nigeria						X		X				X											
Tunisia			X	X									X										
Zaire				X									X	X									
Zambia	X			X					X														
Middle East																							
Egypt	X	X		X										X									
Iran	X		X					X															
Lebanon		X						X								X							
Asia																							
Australia	X					X										X							
India				X									X						X				
Indonesia	X	X													X								
Malaysia		X										X			X								
Thailand		X	X															X					
Eastern Europe																							
Hungary				X									X							X	X		
Poland													X			X				X			
USSR							X						X							X			
Yugoslavia		X		X													X						
Western Europe																							
Federal Republic of Germany	X				X								X										
Finland	X												X						X	X			
Greece	X		X										X										
Iceland	X		X	X																			
Netherlands		X		X		X																X	
Turkey				X														X					X

31

Chapter 5: The Structure of International News Reporting: a Survey of Twenty-Nine Countries

This chapter analyses the statistical findings obtained from the content analysis conducted according to the common core schedule described in Chapter 2. The thirteen national teams described so far were not the only ones involved: The United States team managed to muster both material and human resources to code materials for another fourteen countries.(1) It further diversified the sample of countries, including more developing nations, and with the help of foreign students or foreign residents of the respective countries, covered the following additional media systems:

Latin America: Argentina, Brazil, Mexico
Africa: Algeria, Ivory Coast, Kenya, Tunisia, Zaire, Zambia
Middle East: Egypt
Asia: Indonesia, Thailand
Western Europe: Iceland
Eastern Europe: USSR

Colleagues at other United States institutions also added Greece and Turkey. Descriptions of these sixteen additional media systems, in addition to information on the actual channels selected for inclusion in this study, are to be found in Appendix 4. The following discussion is thus based on a comparative analysis of twenty-nine national media systems, covering all geopolitical regions.

Description of the results

The amount of international coverage

It was felt that the diversity of media channels represented in this study, both within and between nations, would best be shown by constructing a fictional 'average news day'. The aim of this approach was to provide some indication of the amount of international news reporting an audience could expect to find daily within each of the channels selected. The figures in Table 2 must be handled with some caution since they are the products of our design and definitions, and are based on non-standardized entities.

Yet they do reveal, for instance the varying patterns of international news content in élite/quality versus popular/mass papers; the differences between the *New York Times* and *New York Daily News* figures, or between *La Opinión* and *Crónica* in Argentina, or between the *Nigerian Daily Times* and the *New Nigerian* are examples. Some press systems have a large amount of international news reporting, i.e. at least one newspaper devotes over 50 per cent of its general pages* to such coverage. These include Argentina *(La Opinión)*, the Ivory Coast *(Fraternité Matin),* Tunisia *(La Presse* and *L'Action),* Zambia *(Zambia Daily Mail)* Poland *(Trybuna Ludu* and *Zycie Warszawy)*; Yugoslavia *(Delo)*; the USSR *(Pravda* and *Izvestia)*; and the Federal Republic of Germany *(Die Welt* and *Sueddeutsche Zeitung).* At the opposite end of the spectrum, there are press systems in which not one paper under study devoted over 25 per cent of its overall news output to international reporting. These were Egypt, Iran, Thailand, Greece and Iceland.

For the electronic media, eight television channels (in Algeria, Ivory Coast, Tunisia, Zambia, Lebanon, Malaysia, Thailand and the Netherlands) devoted 50 per cent or more of broadcast time to international news, as did seven radio channels (in Kenya, Zaire, Egypt with an incredible 92 per cent Lebanon, Australia, Malaysia, and Poland).

Although a broad spectrum of types of channel is represented for both press and radio-television, broadcast or telecast news tends to focus on a smaller number of international news items, which constitute a greater total percentage of available newscast time than that constituted by international press items as a percentage of the overall news output. This difference may be accounted for by the production and availablity of international news film and interview material. It is also perhaps related to public ownership of broad casting media since providing international news is very costly and not generally in high demand.

It is not clear what would constitute the most desirable balance between strictly domestic and international news reporting within a media system. It is clear, however, that more external news is not necessarily always desirable: it has been suggested that a large amount of foreign news can be the direct corollary of repression and censorship over domestic news-reporting. As we did not begin to examine domestic coverage we cannot take this issue further, although it remains an important topic for further investigation.(2)

Comparisons of item length show that the newspapers differed considerably in their format and structure. There is a dramatic difference in length by column centimetres of press text. Large amounts (a daily average of over 1,300 columns centimetres) of international news can be found in some of the newspapers in the United States, Argentina, Brazil, Mexico, the Ivory Coast, Tunisia, Lebanon, Malaysia, Yugoslavia, the USSR, Finland, and the Netherlands. The Latin American countries stand out in the developing world, as they Rave mass circulation/high advertising press systems.

---

* This is clearly not the same thing as amount of Total editorial space which we did not calculate.

Table 2 : Amount of international news on an average day

	Average Number of stories	Average* length		Average per cent of overall news output constituted by ** international news
		col. cms	secs.	
North America				
United States				
New York Times	33	1297		39
Washington Post	26	1429		42
Los Angeles Times	21	1029		25
New York Daily News	14	518		19
Minneapolis Tribune	14	495		30
Charlotte Observer	11	542		
Television - CBS	4		266	19
Latin America				
Argentina				
Clarín	20	1372		43
La Opinión	27	1111		53
Crónica	21	551		25
Radio - Rivadavia	11		255	na***
Television - 11	3		226	na***
Television - Tele Noche	4		349	na***
Brazil				
O Estado de Sao Paulo	29	2041		33
Jornal do Brasil	24	1365		28
Mexico				
El Universal	40	1764		33
Excelsior	39	1742		43
Africa				
Algeria				
El Moudjahid	35	1219		44
Television	13		1140	68
Ivory Coast				
Fraternité Matin	22	1459		51
Television	33		1320	82
Kenya				
Nairobi Standard	13	626		45
Daily Nation	14	569		36
Radio	15		540	64
Nigeria				
Daily Times	9	350		5
New Nigerian	3	248		16
Punch	2	60		13

	Average Number of stories	Average* length		Average per cent of overall news output constituted by ** international news
		col. cms	secs.	
Radio	3		203	17
Television	1		59	3
Tunisia				
La Presse	36	1494		76
L'Action	25	1100		51
Television	14		85	77
Zaire				
Elima	9	532		29
Salonga	7	264		25
Radio	18		1140	61
Zambia				
Zambia Times	13	607		43
Zambia Daily Mail	13	643		81
Radio	10		420	47
Television	7		480	80
Middle East				
Egypt				
Al-Ahram	30	1014		25
Al-Akhbar	38	635		17
Al-Gomhuria	30	619		12
Radio	14		660	92
Iran				
Kayhan	15	138		16
Etela'at	12	145		18
Ayandegan	11	109		17
Lebanon				
an-Nahar	48	1789		35
as-Safir	57	1892		41
al-Amal	31	1072		30
Radio Lebanon	22		1117	62
Tele-Liban	13		1062	65
Asia				
Australia				
Australian	23	826		29
Herald	30	802		28
Telegraph	16	514		46
Radio - ABC	7		309	52
Radio - 2ad	2		53	18
Television - ABC	6		550	30
Television - 9/8	2		802	16
India				
Hindu	24	514		24
Times of India	33	543		21

	Average Number of stories		Average* length		Average per cent of overall news output constituted by ** international news	
			col. cms	secs.		
Indian Express	22		474		24	
Hindustan Times	27		476		23	
Statesman	32		473		29	
Radio		5		165		18
Television		6		302		34
Indonesia						
Kompas	11		503		18	
Sinar Harapan	14		732		34	
Merdeka	27		1219		44	
Radio		6		391		na***
Television		9		1175		na***
Malaysia						
New Straits Times	39		1237		39	
Utusan Malaysia	18		621		16	
Sin Chew Jut Poh	37		1632		26	
Tamil Nesan	18		579		23	
Radio English		7		323		54
Radio (Bahasa Malaysia)		13		630		35
Radio (Chinese)		5		258		43
Radio (Tamil)		5		228		38
Television (E)		10		485		54
Television (B)		10		465		39
Television (C)		9		402		45
Television (T)		7		270		30
Thailand						
Siam-Rath	9		451		17	
Thai-Rath	18		573		20	
Dao-Sham	4		292		11	
Radio		2		360		19
Television 3TV		14		1140		58
Eastern Europe						
Hungary						
Nepszabadsag	55		660		32	
Nepszava	43		570		25	
Magyar Nemzet	60		660		31	
Magyar Hirlap	61		730		37	
Esti Hirlap	25		460		30	
Radio		16		960		33
Television		11		720		40
Poland						
Tribuna Ludu	42		1087		73	
Zycie Warzawy	26		677		58	
Express Wieczerny	30		419		45	
Radio 1		9		465		41
Radio 111		6		158		55
TV News		8		717		26

	Average Number of stories	Average* length		Average per cent of overall news output constituted by ** international news
		col. cms	secs.	
Yugoslavia				
Delo	50	4354		60
Dnevnik	24	1694		39
Vecer	12	766		19
Radio	11		540	36
USSR				
Pravda	35	1444		55
Isvestiya	25	1434		55
Komsomoskaya Pravda	15	797		46
Television	8		504	32
Western Europe				
Federal Republic of Germany				
Bild-zeitung	31	351		41
Die Welt	59	1196		52
Frankfurter Allegmeine	50	1110		48
Sueddeutsche Zeitung	65	1004		60
Frankfurter Rundschau	37	802		41
Television - ARD	14		515	17
Television - ZDF	15		530	24
Finland				
Helsingin Sanomat	26	1315		39
Aamulehti	18	673		23
Kansan Uutiset	14	624		22
Savon Sanomat	11	411		10
Television	5		441	36
Greece				
Ta Nea	16	970		18
Iceland				
Morgonbladid	25	897		23
Thjodviljinn	11	609		24
Dagbladid	11	349		16
Radio	6		234	20
Television	4		267	18
Netherlands				
Telegraaf	16	755		26
NRC/Handelsblad	38	1647		42
Tubantia	23	783		17
Television-Nos	6		584	53
Turkey				
Milliyet	27	1126		33

* Standard column width varies from paper to paper radio and ; television broadcasts vary in total length from five minutes to one hour. No adjustment has been made for these variations.

** Not the same as total editorial space because of our omission of certain sections of newspapers.

*** n.a. = not available.

Nigeria and Iran were the only countries in which no paper provided more than 400 column centimetres on average. The small amount of international news in Iran's case can be partially explained by its post-revolutionary introspection; while in Nigeria, the return to civilian rule after a period of military government also meant unusually high attention to purely domestic issues.

Differences in the total amount of international news coverage are attributable not only to the actual length of the paper (total number of pages per issue) but also to editorial policy. The *New York Times*, averaging seventy-five to one hundred pages, and *Pravda*, averaging six pages, have comparable amounts of international news while the percentage of international news in relation to the overall news output is higher in *Pravda*. Similarly, within Australia, for example, the *Telegraph* has a smaller amount but larger percentage of international coverage than the *Australian*.

Variations between radio and television seem to present no clear picture. In Zambia, roughly the same number of items constitute 47 per cent of the radio newscast but 80 per cent of the television broadcast. In Poland the reverse is true, with international news constituting a higher percentage of radio news than of television. In Malaysia, it is language which is determinant: all English-language channels carry greater amounts of international news than the Chinese, and far more than the other two language channels. Table 2 thus serves to highlight the descriptive analyses of the national media systems and underlines the diversity in organization and production of the world's press and newscasting systems.

It must be remembered that when a single composite figure for each nation is presented subsequently in this report this figure is based on a range extending from one channel only (a single newspaper coded in Greece and Turkey) to seven channels in the United States, Australia, India, Hungary, and the Federal Republic of Germany, and twelve channels in Malaysia. From now on, also, only number of items is reported, not length, since tests have shown that over large quantities of content there is little difference between the two figures. This issue is elaborated on in Appendix 5. Those interested in more detailed breakdowns of numbers of items compared to amount of space covered, as well as many other nuances and idiosyncracies that have of necessity been left out of this general report, may refer to the individual national reports.

The format of presentation

Each news item was coded according to its manner of journalistic presentation, i.e. whether presented as a straight news story, as an editorial, or as a feature. In general, these categories pertain mostly to the classification of items in the press, for in broadcasting, general opinion and analysis are usually separated from the newscasts themselves. These figures are not presented here, since in every country studied over 80 per cent of all items were presented simply as news, except for the USSR and the Federal Republic of Germany, where a significant amount of editorializing was noted. This result is to be expected due to the fact that we coded only the general news pages, so that by definition most feature articles were excluded.

The limited amount of editorial space devoted to international news is important, however, and we would suggest a future project that would examine editorials alone for their focus and perspective on international news.

In this study no evaluations of prominence were used, as, for example, the positioning of a news item on the front page or as the first item in a newscast. Thus, all items are dealt

with in the analysis as though they were of equal value although clearly in both press and broadcast news, a hierarchy of importance is presented to the audience.

For the printed press only we analysed the number of items dealt with solely by a picture with caption (no other text) and those for which a picture was used to support the text. Findings ranged from no pictures at all used to illustrate international news (Nigeria) to pictures constituting 40 per cent of the total items (Iceland). Most countries fell within the 10-30 per cent range of all items. (See News Format in Table 3). The use of pictures reflects both infrastructural difficulties (mainly the expense of obtaining photo-wire services) and different traditions and habits of journalism, not to mention the sheer 'picturability' of certain news stories, there is a discernible difference between privately and publicly controlled presses: the former tend to use greater numbers of pictures dealing with a variety of topics, while inclusion in the latter is based on different kinds of journalistic and political considerations. The differences between Western and Eastern Europe show this pattern clearly. However, a far more detailed study of the use of pictures in press coverage of international news is called for. The manner in which different areas and issues are 'imaged' in the press could be compared to film/direct reportage as used in radio-television newcasts.

'International News' and the question of Story Type:

This project focused on all news items that were not merely domestic news stories. However the question of subject-matter is not entirely clear. Not all items dealt with *external* news since some, using the 'story-type' classification, were designated as 'foreign news at home'; similarly, not all items were completely foreign, since many involved domestic actors in 'home news abroad'. It was decided to use the appellation *'international'* news throughout this study since it echoes the demands for a New World Information and Communication Order, which provided the impetus for this project. Yet subsequent classification which distinguishes between news items dealing with one state alone and those involving two or more clearly shows that not all items were strictly *'international'* either. (See Table 3).

Dealing with data from twenty-nine media systems all over the globe, one would have expected quite divergent maps of the world to be presented in international news reporting. What rapidly became apparent was the great similarity of reporting in all the systems we covered. For all countries except the USSR, the bulk of items fell into the simple category 'foreign news abroad', comprising between 50-85 per cent of all items (See story type in Table 3). The only other anomaly is Nigeria, which has a very high recorded number of unclassifiable items. The USSR is the only country where the top two categories, both relating in some manner to domestic concerns, out-numbered 'foreign news abroad', the proportions being 54 to 40 per cents. In addition to the USSR, there are another ten countries (United States, Algeria, Tunisia, Zaire, Egypt, Iran, India, Thailand, Hungary, and the Federal Republic of Germany) where 30 per cent or more of international news items bore some ethnocentric relation. In the main, in twenty-two countries out of twenty-nine, 'foreign news at home' included a larger number of items than did the category 'home news abroad', reflecting the general news media tendency to report on certain kinds of actors in a culturally familiar context.(3)

In the six countries where the reverse pattern was found (that is, there was more 'home news abroad') the explanation lies in the media's tendency to focus on particular individuals of national stature. The Polish media, for instance, focused on the background to the Pope's tour and the Iranian on attempts to secure the return of the Shah; media in the USSR focused on the SALT talks and the summit meeting. Clearly the story type classification may reflect the real relations and global involvements of the world powers, which could explain the high level for the USSR and the moderately high level for the United States. It also reflects specific journalistic attempts to create national relevance (often at the expense of other perhaps more important news values), and to make international news palatable, i.e. more meaningful and assimilable for home audiences, by building in frequently weak and sometimes irrelevant connections to domestic issues. However, 'own country' concern may indeed be seen as a useful learning and even politicizing device. For example, in the case of Iran the high percentage of international items presented a critique of existing foreign relations of dependency and reflected the post-revolutionary reassessment of foreign policy and its shift toward non-alignment.

It also means, however, that the amount of international news items was inflated by domestic stories with a foreign flavour. A subsequent distinction was made between truly international items (those that dealt with relations between states*) and those items dealing with foreign domestic news occurring in a single country. Many of these international items may thus include some of the above described stories with a home focus. This is most easily seen in the USSR figures, where the very high home focus was reflected in the high ratio (82 per cent) of strictly international items. Six of the ten other countries mentioned above (Algeria, Tunisia, Zaire, Egypt, Iran and India) also recorded high levels of international items: 65 percent or more. Latin America generally manifested the least international concern.

It is somewhat difficult to interpret these findings. On the one hand, it could be argued that the attempt to make connections between events and establish pattern in world affairs is in line with the explanatory and educational tasks of the news media. The more politically self-conscious the media system, the more will opportunities be seized to select items and write-in angles that relate international events to one's own situation. This might, on the other hand, reflect big-power chauvinism and a spurious internationalizing of basically local events.

Our data does not allow us to discover how the news media structure the pattern of international affairs through the web of geographical linkages that is presented. Nor is the actual content of these international relations clear: did they, for example, involve top-level political discussion or a happenstance cultural exchange? Nor do we know if the countries involved were portrayed as equal actors in the relationship, or if instead a systematic hierarchy of dominant and subordinate actors was shown. National data might be processed further so that some of these issues could be clarified.

The 'news world' of the world's media system

The geography of international news deserves close scrutiny. Table 4 shows the figures for 'location of events'. Perhaps

the single most important finding was the degree to which the reporting of international news by this large number of media systems was similar in structure, although not in actual content.

Every country, except Yugoslavia and Poland, reported more news from within its own geopolitical sphere than from any other region: between 30 and 63 per cent of all international news items. Thus the main focus was on regional events; only secondarily was attention given to news breaking in other parts of the world and to the various metropolitan centres that command the attention of the peripheral areas.

In the following discussion, it should be remembered that when we refer to the 'regional media system', we are referring only to those national systems that were included in this section of the study; for example, three systems (Argentina, Brazil and Mexico) constitute the sample for Latin America. However, when reference is made to 'own region as an object of focus' and potential source of international news, then clearly the entire geographic region (as we have defined its parameters) is the pool for news items: in this example, the whole of Latin America.

A region-by-region geographical breakdown shows that the United States —the only North American media system included in the study— has a comparatively low rate of concentration on its own region's news: 26 per cent. Yet, since that region as an object of attention is comprised of only three countries —the United States, Canada and Bermuda— this figure once again reflects the high level of domestic concerns which are subsumed under our definition of international news. After 'own region', the United States media paid equal attention to western Europe and the Middle East, and quite a high level of attention to Asia.

In the Latin American media systems, 'own region' accounted for approximately 30 per cent of all news items. Next in order of attention, Mexico looked toward the United States, for obvious geopolitical reasons, while Argentina and Brazil turned more towards Western Europe, where their erstwhile mother countries are located. Argentina also paid substantial attention to events in the Middle East.

In Africa, regional concern ran high, accounting for approximately 50 per cent of all items; the elections in Rhodesia Zimbabwe and the collapse of Amin in Uganda were the main stories. Six of the seven African media systems gave second priority to the Middle East, their territorial gateway to Europe and Asia. A particularly significant focus was evident in the two Maghreb nations, Algeria and Tunis, undoubtedly because of cultural concerns about the Islamic Republic in Iran, and the Arab reaction to the Camp David settlement. Western Europe was the third area of attention, perhaps because of former colonial ties to the United Kingdom and France.

For the Middle Eastern countries, 'own region' again comprised about 50 per cent of the total. Lebanon then looked primarily towards Western Europe; Egypt paid equal attention to Western Europe, North America and Africa, while Iran focused somewhat more on Asia.

In Asia itself, 'own region' drew a range from the comparative low in Australia to 65 per cent in Malaysia, the highest rate anywhere. Like some of the Eastern European countries, Australia seemed to fit least into its geopolitical region; its strong concern with Western Europe and North America reflected both its Anglophone heritage and its tendency to identify primarily with Western industrial nations. For asian news media outside Australia, Western Europe and the Middle East were the next most newsworthy regions.

---

* This was usually very broadly interpreted to include a variety of visits, cultural exchanges, sports matches, as well as high-level diplomatic contacts. The full definition is included in the Coding Schedule, Appendix 2.

Table 3 : Data Relating to News Format and Story Type

	News format		Story Type			
	Percentage concerning relations between states	Percentage with pictures (press only)			Home news abroad	Other or uncertain
	%	%	%	%	%	%
Latin america						
Argentina n-1017	40	15	3	6	74	17
Brazil n-630	34	16	1	3	78	19
Mexico n-1188	30	21	6	10	71	12
North america						
United States n-1487	42	22	11	21	59	9
Africa						
Algeria n-935	80	7	8	29	63	1
Ivory Coast n-390	66	13	3	22	70	5
Kenya n-501	57	33	4	15	74	7
Nigeria n-205	39	0	3	8	36	54
Tunisia n-1303	74	9	9	21	70	1
Zaire n-919	74	12	13	22	64	1
Zambia n-516	58	17	5	13	77	6
Middle East						
Egypt n-1322	74	14	14	24	61	1
Iran n-453	70	1	23	18	51	8
Lebanon n-2049	61	17	8	15	76	2
Asia						
Australia n-1032	25	18	4	13	83	0
India n-1649	65	3	10	20	67	3
Indonesia n-811	44	18	11	16	71	2
Malaysia n-2070	57	16	5	21	71	4
Thailand n-580	35	25	20	32	63	2
Eastern europe						
Hungary n-2931	48	3	19	25	55	0
Poland n-713	40	10	12	9	72	8
USSR n-997	82	10	29	25	40	6
Yugoslavia n-1144	56	10	14	12	68	6
Western europe						
Federal Republic of Germany n-3068	32	12	15	15	69	1
Finland n-881	49	25	5	9	79	7
Greece n-205	28	37	6	3	85	5
Iceland n-689	31	44	8	9	75	8
Netherlands n-991	39	30	10	15	72	4
Turkey n-327	59	16	14	13	58	15

Table 4 : The Location of International News (in percentages)*

	North America	Latin America	Africa	Middle East	Asia	Eastern Europe	Western Europe	General
	%	%	%	%	%	%	%	%
North america								
United States n-1487	**26**	7	10	16	14	6	16	5
Latin america								
Argentina n-1017	13	**32**	5	20	3	3	18	6
Brazil n-630	12	**29**	5	14	7	6	23	4
Mexico n-1188	23	**30**	5	10	7	3	16	6
Africa								
Algeria n-935	3	3	**50**	21	3	5	13	3
Ivory Coast n-390	3	2	**56**	11	5	5	11	7
Kenya n-501	8	1	**46**	13	7	4	11	11
Nigeria n-205	8	5	**50**	11	13	0	8	4
Tunisia n-1303	7	2	**36**	24	6	4	16	5
Zaire n-419	5	2	**53**	16	4	3	12	6
Zambia n-516	8	1	**46**	17	6	3	14	6
Middle East								
Egypt n-1322	13	2	12	**48**	8	2	13	3
Iran n-453	10	6	8	**49**	10	5	12	1
Lebanon n-2049	7	2	9	**54**	4	5	15	4
Asia								
Australia n-1032	20	2	10	9	**32**	4	22	2
India n-1649	15	2	8	12	**40**	4	17	4
Indonesia n-811	9	3	7	15	**46**	3	13	4
Malaysia n-2070	7	1	4	11	**63**	2	11	2
Thailand n-500	8	2	7	11	**51**	4	13	4
Eastern europe								
Hungary n-2931	6	4	5	7	9	**47**	19	4
Poland n-713	8	6	8	6	10	**27**	27	7
USSR n-997	7	3	4	6	15	**34**	14	18
Yugoslavia n-1144	9	4	5	16	9	**22**	26	7
Western europe								
Federal Republic of Germany n-3068	14	4	8	10	9	11	**43**	3
Finland n-881	10	2	9	14	10	14	**36**	4
Greece n-205	22	2	3	8	4	9	**50**	3
Iceland n-689	18	3	9	10	6	4	**41**	9
Netherlands n-991	9	4	10	16	7	6	**44**	5
Turkey n-327	13	3	3	16	6	5	**52**	3

* The figures underlined show the highest percentages for each region.

Eastern Europe reported the least 'own region' news. In both the Polish and Yugoslav news media, Western Europe received as much news attention as did Eastern Europe itself, if not more. This may have been precipitated by concern for détente and the outcome of SALT talks, yet it also reveals an interesting cross-cutting of cultural-historic ties with the contemporary divisions in Europe. No other region stood out prominently as a focus of news attention. Yugoslavia's focus on the Middle East was inflated by inclusion of the Mahgreb in this region during coding. The USSR showed a strong focus on Asian news, 'own region' under a different classification, and also reported 'general news' (i. e. with unspecified location) more frequently than any other country. This catch-all category includes activities at the United Nations and other intergovernmental agencies, as well as events originating in space or at sea. Probably it was the Soviet tendency already mentioned to internationalize news events which was reaffirmed here.

Western European systems focused to the extent of 40 to 50 per cent on 'own region' followed by attention to the Middle East and North America. The Federal Republic of Germany and Finland were the only two countries in the study whose news media paid significant attention to Eastern Europe, an orientation relating to both history and geographic proximity.

Table 5, constructed from this information, ranks the location of international news by region. The regional concentration shows up clearly in the diagonal line of ones running from the upper-left-hand corner to the lower-right across the table. This seems to be as close to a universal pattern as we can find, namely that for all media systems geographical proximity is a dominant orientation for determining newsworthiness. This observation validates similar findings in other studies conducted in the past decade (see the evidence in Appendix 5) and may reflect a true sense of regional identity, the product of shared historical fortunes, cultural similarities and economic interrelationships. On the other hand, it may well be a media-imposed identification that masks rivalries and tensions, and sub-groupings within regions.

Details on the actual break-down of focus of attention within 'own region' and comparisons of balance and reciprocity of attention must be left to the national reports; once again, we have to sacrifice depth for the broad mappings of general findings.

Beyond this there seem to be two main determinants of coverage. One is semi-permanent attention paid to the metropolitan centres. Other studies of international news dating from the mid-1960s up to the present have continually identified the Western metropolitan areas, covered by our two regions of Western Europe and North America, as occupying the top rank in international news geography , these areas have indeed been called the 'consistent news-makers'(4). Except for to the SALT II discussions and some fascination with the possibility of a woman prime minister in Britain, Western Europe did not show up as the backdrop for particularly important events during this period, at least as described by the qualitative reports, yet the region ranked first. North America, which seemed to appear only through discussion of the Harrisburg (Three Mile Island) incident, ranks third, while Africa, despite all of the dominant news stories occurring during this period, ranked only fifth. This finding seems to support the notion that news geography is primarily a matter of news history, and that the news capitals which are best covered in terms of the production and distribution of news stories thus systematically occupy central positions in the world news geography.(5) This also reflects the continuing orientations of the peripheral nations toward the metropolitan centres in the post-colonial world, a prime determinant of news focus suggested by Galtung many years ago.(6)

Geographical proximity and former colonial orientations have thus been established as the two leading criteria. It is perhaps only at the third level that critical events in other parts of the world are selected for inclusion: news values of sensation, drama, world significance allow parts of the Third World to wax and wane in news attention depending on the particular period of time and the specific events occurring. The peripheral areas tend to provide the 'hot' news; once the heat has subsided, these areas rapidly disappear from the news spotlight. The intense Middle East focus included the

Table 5 : Rank Ordering of Regions in International News

Regions in the news	Participating media systems in regions						
	North America	Latin America	Africa	Middle East	Asia	Eastern Europe	Western Europe
North america	1	3	5	3	3	6	2
Latin america	6	1	8	6	8	8	8
Africa	5	6	1	4	5	7	5
Middle East	2	4	2	1	4	4	3
Asia	4	5	5	5	1	3	5
Eastern europe	7	6	7	7	6	1	4
Western europe	2	2	3	2	2	2	1
General	8	8	5	8	7	4	7

ratification of the Camp David Agreement and the aftermath of the Iranian Revolution, both 'hot' topics. In Latin America, however, the world's news media determined that 'nothing much was happening'; it was the region to which least attention was paid, since no coups or natural catastrophes 'demanded' attention. The other region that was generally ignored was Eastern Europe.

International news geography across all twenty-nine nations thus produces a structure remarkably similar to the mapping of events. It conspires to render certain areas of the world almost invisible, particularly developing regions outside 'own immediate region', and Eastern Europe everywhere but in Western Europe. Obviously, since the areas that comprise the Third World constitute four of our seven geographic regions (the eighth category being the 'general, non-specific' location) and a huge assortment of nations and peoples, news items about the Third World are numerically preponderant. But this states the case too baldly; it obscures what remains one of the central problems of international news geography, namely that much of the developing world is invisible in the news focus of the other part, and the flow of news between the different regions of the 'Third World' is extremely poor. Regions which might be presumed to share certain kinds of dilemmas and occupy structurally similar positions within the established international political and economic order in fact know or seem to care little about each other.

Frequently, concern about the balance of news coverage has been voiced. Looking at the ranking of regions in Table 5, one can distinguish between 1) a balanced reciprocity of focus, where, for example, Western Europe and North America give each other most attention after 'own region'; and 2) a mutual reciprocity of ignorance, where Latin America ranks eighth in the African media and Africa ranks sixth in the Latin American. Imbalance can be seen in the manner in which Latin America and Western Europe represent each other, and in the general neglect of Eastern Europe by media systems of other regions. Clearly, these relationships change over time, depending on the established news-worthiness of real events. It seems clear, however, that the pattern distinguished here is not simply a casual 'snapshot' but in fact reflects the deep and systematically reiterated structure of international news geography which has been described in many studies.

The issue of the representation of the developing world is not significantly clarified by our clustering of nations into geopolitical groupings. Our regions contain both highly industrialized nations with a high standard of living and nations struggling to provide enough for their populations: for example, our 'Asia' includes both Australasia and Japan. Because it also includes China and Indo-China, it allows no separate analysis of the manner of representation of socialist societies. 'Africa' includes South Africa, and the 'Middle East' includes Israel and various nations belonging to the Organization of Oil Exporting Countries (OPEC). Our intention here is not to defend any particular way of dividing up the nations of the world, but rather to emphasize the theoretical difficulties involved and to caution against any confusion that may be prompted by our simple geographic clusterings. Clearly, if further studies are really to penetrate the reciprocal imagery of developed and developing nations, more sophisticated groupings are indispensable.

'News Geography' through nationality of actors

An important secondary dimension in the construction of international news geography is the nationality of actors represented in international news reporting. Analysis of the nationality factor provides a marginally yet intriguingly

different picture from that derived from a ranking of the regions. As with all subsequent discussion about actors, the figures here deal with 'main actor' only. Each news item was coded for 'main actor' and up to three subsidiary actors. Because this proved in practice to be a difficult distinction to make, only the figures for main actor have been drawn upon here.

The regional focus is also present, but not quite as prominent as for location of event. For example, in 48 per cent of all items there is an African focus on 'own region'. This figure drops to 42 per cent for Africans as actors. The Western European focus averaged 41 per cent for the region as location of event but 40 per cent for West Europeans as actors in the international news scene. Eastern Europe showed the opposite tendency, with 'own region' averaging 32 per cent but 'own actors' averaging 35 per cent. Undoubtedly this reflects the focus on 'home news abroad', discussed earlier. The fact that all Middle East countries showed a high level of interest in all stories with a regional focus, may have helped inflate their position as top-ranking region overall. In comparing figures from Table 4 and Table 6 we find that North America maintained an almost identical pattern for focus on own region and on own nationals.

Overall, only the Middle East and Eastern Europe showed greater interest in 'nationality of actor' than in 'location of event'. For the former, this involved a number of stories on the exiled Shah, as well as Middle Eastern actors at the United Nations and other international forums; for the latter, the important issues were the SALT II talks and the Carter-Brezhnev summit. Eastern European 'visibility' improved considerably in terms of the nationality of actors in international news, signifying the mobile presence of East European actors on the world political scene compared with what the media considered a lack of news-worthy information emanating from Eastern Europe (the 1980 events in Poland were an outstanding exception).

The position was reversed for Western Europe during this period since it was the scene of significant news events such as the SALT talks, although the major actors in these events were not the focus of attention.

There seems to be no systematic priority accorded to either 'location of event' or 'nationality of actors'; their degree of prominence depended on the particular events taking place. The shifts in rank by order of prominence do not necessitate any alteration in the previous arguments about the determinants of news attention; they do suggest that to look at one indicator alone may be slightly misleading with regard to the news profile of particular areas such as Eastern Europe. It thus clouds further the issue of 'balance' in news attention, and how it is to be determined; apparently there is no single universally applicable yardstick to be advocated. In overall ranking, Africa, despite all of its 'dominant' stories, as discussed in Chapter 4, ranked only sixth; North America, seemingly invisible apart from the Three Mile Island incident, nonetheless ranked third. The general issue of the desirable balance between the 'consistent news-makers', and 'hot spots' and the current 'pockets of invisibility' remains to be tackled.

The focus of the news

The subject-matter of international news was initially coded with a set of forty-eight topic and sub-topic headings. For each news item, the main topic and up to three subsidiary ones could be coded.* The results presented here are based on the

---

* The full coding instructions appear in Appendix 2.

Table 6 : Nationality of Actors in International News (figures shown are percentages)

	North America	Latin America	Africa	Middle East	Asia	Eastern Europe	Western Europe	General
North america								
United States	**26**	6	10	16	14	7	15	5
Latin america								
Argentina	14	**32**	6	21	2	5	15	6
Brazil	13	**23**	5	16	8	8	23	4
Mexico	24	**28**	5	11	7	4	15	7
Africa*								
Algeria	3	4	**39**	25	3	6	11	9
Ivory Coast	7	2	**46**	11	4	2	19	8
Kenya	11	1	**45**	16	6	4	10	8
Tunisia	8	2	**30**	30	5	4	14	8
Zaire	6	1	**49**	17	4	3	14	7
Zambia	8	1	**43**	17	6	4	13	8
Middle East								
Egypt	14	2	12	**45**	6	5	9	6
Iran	10	4	9	**48**	12	5	8	3
Lebanon	9	3	8	**53**	4	3	13	4
Asia								
Australia	22	2	9	11	**27**	4	22	3
India	12	2	8	14	**45**	4	11	5
Indonesia	12	2	6	18	**38**	3	11	11
Malaysia	9	1	4	12	**53**	3	8	9
Thailand	9	2	7	13	**44**	5	11	8
Eastern europe								
Hungary	6	4	4	6	8	**44**	17	12
Poland	6	4	5	7	7	**30**	16	25
USSR	8	4	4	7	15	**43**	13	7
Yugoslavia	9	4	6	16	9	**22**	26	10
Western europe								
Federal Republic of Germany	14	3	7	9	8	12	**32**	7
Finland	12	3	8	14	9	13	**34**	6
Greece	24	2	3	9	5	8	**45**	3
Iceland	19	3	8	11	6	7	**36**	11
Netherlands	11	3	9	16	7	6	**39**	9
Turkey	12	2	4	16	7	5	**47**	8

* Except Nigeria

Notes : — The underlined figures pertain to 'own region'
— As the figures have been rounded off to the heavest whole digit, in certain cases they do not always add up to 100 %.

totals for the eighteen topic headings only, leaving analysis of sub-topics for the national reports.

In general, politics dominates international news reporting. For all but three countries, the top two categories — international politics and domestic politics— comprised between 32 and 66 per cent of all items. The exceptions were Nigeria and Australia, with lower percentages and Iran, with an astonishing 73 per cent. Since military stories and those dealing with economics often also contained a political angle and could sometimes be coded either way, even more political material lies buried in these categories. The four 'hard' news topics (international politics, domestic politics, military and defence and economics) accounted for the bulk of stories in almost all the national systems. This finding is largely a consequence of our initial decision to code only the 'general news' pages of the press, which by definition deal mostly with 'hard' news, since 'soft' items are assigned to their own special pages or sections in a paper. It is thus impossible to look for balance in terms of topics covered in data.

However, the pattern of concentration on the four hard news topics seems to fall into two distinct ranges, for the industrialized and developing worlds (to the extent that our regions indicate that distinction). For the industrialized regions (North America and both Western and Eastern Europe), concentrations fall within the range of 45 to 65 per cent of all international news; only the Soviet Union diverged significantly from this with more hard news items: 73 per cent of the total. In the developing regions (Latin America, Africa, Middle East) the degree of concentration was higher ranging from 65 to 85 per cent. The main exceptions were Mexico, with 58 per cent, and Nigeria, with a very low 37 per cent. The anomalous region was Asia, which followed the advanced world pattern, perhaps more understandably in Australia than in Thailand or Indonesia. Economics as a single category did not show great prominence although the Third World's structural position in the current international economic order has most to do with its 'underdevelopment'.

A far more important issue, beyond the general presentation of the frequency of topics in international news reporting, is how those topics broke down by region and whether there were systematic patterns in the topics through which different regions were represented. A recurrent complaint in the debate on the structure of international news coverage is that the Third World is most usually represented by 'negative' stories. The project was not designed to confront this issue directly, since we did not deal with substantive content in depth, never analysed 'bias' and can merely assume, for purposes of discussion, that certain topics may reflect a negative 'crime and crisis' syndrome.

A cross-tabulation of topic by location of event was run to reveal the 'news profile' of each region*. These rich data allow for a two-fold analysis. One concerned the manner in which the news media of each region presented the world to their audiences; the second concerned the way in which each region was objectivized in international news.*

---

* Since this generates a full page table for each country, it was decided to omit presentation of the actual figures which can be obtained from the Centre for Mass Communication Research, University of Leicester.

* It must be remembered that, as for other tables, no statistical analyses of Table 8 have been run nor chi squares produced. Thus, the following discussion is a relative rather than rigorous assessment of the performance of each system compared to some national average. The actual number of items in each column varied greatly, with certain percentages based on very small n's indeed.

Table 7 : How the regions ranked in terms of nationality of actor

	Actor from							
	North America	Latin America	Africa	Middle East	Asia	Eastern Europe	Western Europe	General
North america	1	7	5	2	4	3	6	8
Latin america	3	1	6	4	6	6	2	6
Africa*	5	8	1	2	6	7	3	4
Middle East	2	8	4	1	5	3	6	7
Asia	3	8	6	2	1	7	3	5
Eastern europe	6	8	7	6	4	1	2	3
Western europe	2	8	7	3	6	4	1	5
Overall rank by actor	2	8	6	1	5	4	3	7
Overall rank by location of event	3	7	5	2	4	6	1	8
Overall rank	3	7	6	1	4	5	2	8

The United States media showed international politics concentrated in Eastern Europe and the Middle East, with a strong 'foreign news at home' focus as well. Africa was covered in terms of domestic political stories, while reporting on the Middle East was dominated by military issues. Crime reporting dealt with both Europes, while natural disasters were picked up in Latin America and Eastern Europe. News of economics was confined to Latin American locations; the conclusion seems to be that ties between the Americas are less political or cultural than they are economic.

The Latin American media presented a pattern similar to the North American with regard to political and military reporting. Economic questions were viewed with a primarily regional focus, while crime stories centred on Western Europe and the United States. There was a pronounced emphasis on religious news in Eastern Europe, especially Pope John Paul II's trip to Poland, while from the United States came items on science and on natural disasters, as well as human interest stories.

For the Eastern European media, international politics had a strong home basis, while domestic politics were featured in reporting on Latin America, Africa and the Middle East. Markedly greater attention was paid to economic topics than in other media systems. Hungary and the USSR highlighted culture in Latin America and Africa, respectively, while crime was shown in Western Europe. The United States was presented through sports items and science with some attention to ecology and natural disasters. 'Own region' was presented in terms of economic issues, culture and sports. In general, there was a discernible focus on more 'positive' reporting (science, culture, etc.), than on 'negative' stories such as crime, with a broader span of topics represented than in other media systems.

In Western European media, Eastern Europe was most prominent in international politics; Africa, followed by Latin America, led in the 'domestic politics' category. There was a generally high level of interest in crime stories, which were located in Latin America and Western Europe itself. There was a comparatively high focus on human interest stories, especially from the United States and ecology/natural disaster topics in the United States also received some attention. The Western European media systems showed a far greater-range interest in these kinds of 'softer' news items than was apparent in either the socialist or developing worlds.

In the African media, Eastern Europe and Africa itself dominated international political reporting. Items from Latin America concerned domestic politics and those from the Middle East dealt with military topics. Crime received considerable attention among news items from Western Europe and Latin America, natural disasters appeared in reporting from Eastern Europe and Latin America, and there was a meagre sprinkling of other 'soft' news.

In Middle Eastern media systems the political focus in general was on Africa and Latin America. Iran showed a greater concern with international political items than any other national system, a fact that may have stemmed from the new revolutionary orientation towards independence and non-alignment. Iran also exemplified most dramatically the trend in the developing world to concentrate on 'hard' news, with minimal amounts of other soft news items. Egypt reported far more stories on international aid than did other systems and displayed a surprising interest in stories from Latin America on social services, personalities and human interest; the latter seem, however, to have been part of the Middle East focus on the exile of the Shah of Iran, first in the Bahamas and later in Mexico.

The Asian media by comparison, paid attention to a far wider range of topics. They did concentrate on the top 'four'

hard news topics but not as markedly as the media in other developing regions. News of international politics came chiefly from Eastern Europe and also from the United Nations, Unesco, etc., as grouped in the non-specific location category we labelled 'other'. News from Africa and Western Europe, concerned domestic politics, while the Middle East dominated reporting of military news. Own region was presented through economics and crime, with a sprinkling of items on culture, religion, sports and ecology. Crime reporting in general was quite abundant with perhaps the greatest diversity in soft news focus to be found in any region.

Moving away from the manner in which each region reports the other regions, a clearer perspective on the image of regions as presented in the world's media can be had by looking at each region as the object of attention in the media throughout the world.

In terms of overall coverage, North America was relatively under-represented in both international and domestic politics. However, it received a greater than average amount of attention when it came to crime, entertainment and personalities, natural disaster and ecology (the latter because of the Harrisburg nuclear accident).

Latin America tended to receive above-average attention with regard to domestic politics —chiefly as a reflection of the Nicaraguan revolution— but had a lower-than-average showing in international politics; this situation mirrored the region's current disengagement from the world political arena and its engrossment in internal affairs. The region tended to generate more than an average amount of crime reporting, and either far more or less than average reporting on military affairs and economic questions.

The Middle East received above-average attention with regard to international politics, and even more with regard to domestic politics; universally, and not surprisingly, it generated a higher than average number of military and defence stories. There was a certain amount of attention to crime in the area, but aside from this, the region was invisible.

The amount of reporting on political affairs in Asia ranked low to average, with military issues over-represented. Crime, international aid and a certain number of natural disasters, usually floods in India, were also associated with the region.

Eastern Europe, as a focus of attention in the world's international news reporting, was under-represented in terms of domestic politics, economics and military topics, but rather over-represented by stories on international politics, which is primarily a reflection of the USSR's global rote (1) in softer news category (2) natural disasters figure prominently, because of an earthquake in Yugoslavia, while because of the Polish visit by the Pope and the Archbishop of Canterbury's trip to the German Democratic Republic and Hungary, there was a substantial focus on religious items.

Western Europe was generally under-represented in terms of international politics, despite the Vienna SALT talks — and military news. Domestic political items received above-average attention, as did crime and human interest stories.

An overwhelming proportion of stories on Africa had to do with political items, and there was an average proportion of military and defense items. Crime stories figured prominently, and there was a discernible focus on culture and human interest items. It is interesting to note that in the African media themselves, African items were reported predominantly as international politics; revealing a tendency to draw political connections in 'own region' reporting which did not spill over to reporting by other regions.

Generalizing from this data set, we may conclude that in the present study the West was more represented by crime and human interest stories than the developing world, while natural disasters and other tragedies were 'hot' news items wherever

Table 8 : Topics in International News (figures shown are percentages)

	International politics	Domestic politics	Military	Economics	International aid	Social services	Crime	Culture	Religion	Science	Sports	Entertainment	Personalities	Human interest	Student matters	Ecology	Natural disasters	Other
North america																		
United States n-1487	18	21	16	9	2	2	12	2	2	2	2	1	1	3	0	2	4	2
Latin america																		
Argentina n-1017	24	27	10	9	1	0	9	1	1	3	3	0	1	3	0	0	6	2
Brazil n-630	18	37	10	10	1	1	11	1	3	2	0	0	0	3	0	0	2	1
Mexico n-1188	18	20	6	14	1	1	9	4	3	4	5	1	3	6	0	0	4	1
Africa																		
Algeria n-935	48	18	15	5	1	2	3	1	0	1	0	0	0	1	1	1	2	2
Ivory Coast n-390	28	21	10	12	1	4	6	1	1	3	2	1	1	1	1	0	2	7
Kenya n-501	25	21	11	8	5	1	14	1	1	2	1	1	1	3	1	1	1	3
Nigeria n-205	12	11	7	7	2	3	9	10	0	6	6	0	13	0	0	3	4	7
Tunisia n-1303	39	20	14	8	1	0	4	2	1	2	2	0	1	1	0	1	2	2
Zaire n-419	46	18	9	7	3	2	4	1	1	0	2	0	1	2	1	0	1	4
Zambia n-516	28	24	11	7	3	1	14	1	1	1	2	0	0	2	1	0	3	3
Middle East																		
Egypt n-1322	30	22	21	7	3	1	5	1	2	2	1	1	1	2	0	2	3	0
Iran n-453	58	15	5	5	1	0	2	1	2	0	0	0	0	0	0	0	0	10
Lebanon n-2049	37	13	15	6	1	0	5	5	1	2	8	0	1	1	0	1	1	5
Asia																		
Australia n-1032	7	19	12	10	2	0	13	1	3	5	0	2	5	4	0	2	4	12
India n-1649	22	19	12	13	2	1	12	3	2	6	0	0	1	3	1	0	2	2
Indonesia n-811	17	16	12	16	7	1	6	4	1	3	3	1	1	6	0	1	5	2
Malaysia n-2040	19	16	12	16	6	7	7	2	1	3	0	1	1	4	0	1	2	4
Thailand n-500	17	15	13	8	3	5	9	1	1	2	1	1	1	3	1	4	4	12
Eastern europe																		
Hungary n-2931	19	17	12	16	2	1	4	10	1	6	1	0	2	1	1	1	2	3
Poland n-713	19	19	11	10	3	3	5	6	1	4	1	0	0	4	0	2	3	9
USSR n-997	41	18	8	6	1	2	1	5	0	5	7	0	0	3	1	0	1	1
Yugoslavia n-1144	25	18	8	14	3	1	4	3	0	5	3	0	2	3	0	2	2	6
Western europe																		
Federal Republic of Germany n-3068	17	21	10	8	2	1	14	1	1	2	0	2	2	7	0	0	4	5
Finland n-881	16	19	18	13	1	2	7	1	1	2	2	1	0	3	0	8	2	7
Greece n-205	15	19	8	3	2	4	8	1	2	8	8	1	1	6	1	2	3	7
Iceland n-689	17	20	5	10	1	1	5	7	1	2	2	5	5	10	0	3	6	3
Netherlands n-991	12	20	14	12	2	5	13	1	2	2	1	0	2	5	0	6	1	3
Turkey n-327	31	9	3	13	9	1	5	1	1	1	5	1	2	2	0	5	3	0

Table 9 : Actors in International News (figures shown are percentages)

	Head of State/Government	Other leading Govt./ruling party offcl	Non-leg. opposition	Non-Govt. leg. pol. circles	Local govt. official	Diplomat/ambassador	Regular military	Irregular military	Industry	Workers union	Pressure groups	Religions	Sports	Media	Academic scientific education	Police	Judiciary/lawyer	Criminals/prison	Celebrities/show business	Aristocracy	Nation(s)	United Nations	Inter. Govt. bodies	Other intel. bodies	People, citizens	Other	Non-human
North america																											
United States n-1487	14	26	0	5	2	2	7	4	3	1	1	3	1	2	2	1	1	3	—	1	3	—	1	1	9	2	4
Latin america																											
Argentina n-1017	16	23	1	5	2	4	7	4	4	2	—	2	3	2	4	1	1	2	1	—	4	—	1	—	6	3	2
Brazil n-630	17	28	2	8	2	2	5	3	5	2	—	3	1	6	4	4	2	1	1	—	4	—	—	—	5	2	1
Mexico n-1188	14	19	1	5	2	4	4	3	6	2	—	3	6	2	5	1	1	2	3	1	4	—	1	—	8	1	2
Africa																											
Algeria n-935	23	37	3	2	1	4	6	3	2	2	1	—	—	2	2	1	—	—	—	—	3	—	1	1	1	4	1
Ivory Coast n-390	21	31	1	4	1	2	5	1	5	1	1	2	1	1	3	—	—	1	2	—	2	—	3	3	2	3	4
Kenya n-501	36	4	1	5	1	3	6	4	2	1	2	3	1	2	2	2	2	3	1	—	4	1	3	—	4	4	3
Nigeria n-205	14	11	—	3	—	1	2	1	—	—	1	—	1	1	1	1	1	—	—	1	3	1	1	—	1	57	—
Tunisia n-1303	19	34	1	3	1	5	5	3	4	—	—	2	1	2	3	1	—	1	1	—	3	—	2	1	2	2	3
Zaire n-419	25	28	1	5	3	6	3	1	2	1	1	1	2	1	3	—	—	1	1	—	6	—	3	—	1	3	3
Zambia n-816	17	27	2	7	1	2	5	4	2	1	1	1	2	2	2	3	1	3	1	—	3	—	1	1	4	3	3
Middle East																											
Egypt n-1322	22	32	—	4	5	4	6	3	5	1	—	2	1	2	2	1	—	1	1	—	2	—	1	—	1	3	4
Iran n-453	17	29	5	4	1	6	6	7	2	2	1	4	1	2	2	—	—	—	2	—	1	—	1	—	4	3	1
Lebanon n-2049	18	22	—	5	2	5	5	4	1	1	—	2	9	4	1	—	1	2	—	—	5	1	1	1	4	1	4
Asia																											
Australia n-1032	11	16	—	6	1	2	5	3	3	1	1	4	—	3	3	3	1	3	5	2	4	2	1	—	10	1	9
India n-1649	16	28	1	6	1	3	4	2	2	1	1	2	1	3	6	1	1	1	1	—	8	2	2	1	8	—	2
Indonesia n-811	14	28	—	2	1	3	4	2	5	2	1	1	3	1	3	1	1	2	1	1	2	1	2	—	4	6	10
Malaysia n-2040	6	40	1	1	1	3	5	4	2	3	3	0	1	2	1	2	1	1	2	1	1	3	3	2	1	10	2
Thailand n-500	18	22	1	4	4	3	8	3	3	1	1	1	1	1	2	1	—	1	2	1	2	—	—	—	9	6	5
Eastern europe																											
Hungary n-2931	14	18	1	5	1	3	4	3	7	3	—	1	1	3	6	1	1	1	6	—	1	2	3	3	4	4	3
Poland n-713	21	15	1	4	—	3	4	3	3	2	—	2	1	—	2	3	—	—	2	3	—	1	2	1	1	26	2
USSR n-997	21	18	—	6	1	8	2	1	3	2	1	—	7	4	7	—	—	—	—	—	7	—	1	1	10	—	2
Yugoslavia n-1144	14	23	1	4	3	2	4	3	4	1	1	—	4	3	5	1	1	1	1	—	2	3	2	1	6	4	7
Western europe																											
Federal Republic of Germany n-3068	16	19	1	6	1	1	4	4	2	1	2	2	—	3	3	2	2	3	3	1	6	1	1	—	13	3	2
Finland n-881	16	21	1	4	1	3	6	4	4	2	1	2	2	3	4	1	1	1	1	—	7	2	2	1	7	1	3
Greece n-205	23	10	—	5	1	1	5	3	2	1	3	1	9	3	11	1	1	1	1	—	7	2	2	1	16	3	2
Iceland n-689	8	17	—	5	3	3	3	5	2	1	1	6	3	4	1	—	2	9	1	—	1	1	1	1	12	3	6
Netherlands n-991	11	17	1	6	2	1	4	5	4	2	3	2	1	2	1	1	1	3	1	—	4	2	1	4	10	4	7
Turkey n-327	14	36	—	5	1	3	1	2	3	2	3	2	5	2	2	2	—	—	1	—	1	1	4	2	5	1	2

Table 10 : Sources of International News (for press only)* (figures shown are percentages)

	Home country agency	Reuters	UPI	AP	AFP	TASS	Other agency	Own staff	Other medium home	Other medium foreign	Other source	Unidentifiable
North america												
United States n-1430	4	6	9	22	—	—	—	36	1	1	6	11
Latin america												
Argentina n-814	—	—	11	8	14	—	20	1	—	1	11	40
Brazil n-630	—	—	1	—	—	—	—	13	—	4	12	70
Mexico n-947	—	—	19	13	22	—	30	12	—	1	13	8
Africa												
Algeria n-775	32	4	—	—	8	—	—	4	—	2	—	54
Ivory Coast n-262	—	2	—	—	2	—	1	13	—	1	—	84
Kenya n-501	2	3	6	6	3	—	—	11	—	1	18	44
Nigeria n-165	2	3	1	2	13	—	—	9	2	12	5	52
Tunisia n-1132	2	—	—	—	3	—	—	3	—	—	—	92
Zaire n-197	2	—	—	—	—	—	1	10	—	—	1	87
Zambia n-516	40	24	—	—	9	—	1	11	—	2	10	40
Middle East												
Egypt n-1157	5	4	4	5	9	—	3	12	—	1	23	35
Iran n-453	4	12	5	19	17	1	15	2	1	3	4	20
Lebanon n-1663	1	21	12	4	33	1	18	10	1	13	3	29
Asia												
Australia n-1059	19	11	7	1	—	1	41	—	—	5	16	
India n-1793	21	15	—	15	9	1	3	21	—	11	5	8
Indonesia n-629	26	5	2	13	31	—	4	27	—	—	6	16
Malaysia n-1387	4	30	11	8	6	—	4	23	—	2	1	
Thailand n-377	1	—	—	28	5	—	—	18	—	1	15	34
Eastern europe												
Hungary n-3209	16	3	2	2	4	6	3	12	1	6	1	54
Poland n-557	49	—	—	—	—	—	2	39	5	—	1	5
USSR n-898	—	—	—	—	—	55	—	23	—	1	15	10
Yugoslavia n-1016	24	4	5	3	5	1	4	14	—	4	2	37
Western europe												
Federal Republic of Germany n-2897	27	11	1	12	5	—	—	30	5	5	17	17
Finland n-817	9	23	11	3	7	5	6	27	—	3	2	28
Greece n-	3	7	7	27	5	—	3	11	—	6	15	22
Iceland n-	—	26	—	18	—	—	1	26	—	4	2	29
Netherlands n-	6	12	6	9	8	—	3	34	—	1	5	23
Turkey n-	42	3	—	14	13	—	3	36	—	6	1	4

* Multiples coding; totals may exceed 100 percent.

they occurred. On the other hand, it seems that the Western press in general was keener on human interest 'soft' news items than were the media systems of developing nations; perhaps this reflects their dissimilar political systems and types of economic organization. An African tabloid, for example, is probably less sensational and carries a greater proportion of 'hard' news items than its equivalent in the West. The developing world was not an important source of 'soft' news items, and was not greatly interested in reporting such items in regions beyond its own. As we have already noted, the amount of reporting from other developing regions tended to be low anyway, supporting McQuail's finding that 'in general, the lower the coverage the more it seems to concentrate on a few topics, reflecting the specific events of the time sampled'.(7)

The people who make international news

As politics dominates the topics of international news, it is only natural that political figures dominate in a classification of actors. The first two categories, including heads of state, chief executives, legislatures and parliaments and ruling party activity, embraced 25 to 60 per cent of all actors coded (see Table 9). However, even when this figure was at the lower end of the range, few other categories of actors commanded much attention. That international news is dominated by political news with political actors is another universal finding of our study.

Few other individual categories ever accounted for over 10 per cent in any of our national data sets. The only exception was 'people, citizens' category in the reporting of Australia, the USSR, the Federal Republic of Germany, Greece, Iceland, the Netherlands (and in the United States and Thailand at 9 per cent). It is perhaps a coding quirk that reduced this category to a catch-all residual category embracing all of the otherwise unclassifiable actors, including Harrisburg inhabitants, Kampuchean refugees and Iranian demonstrators. The only other two kinds of actors ever to receive over 10 per cent attention were academics and scientists in Greece, and non-human actors' in Indonesia. The otherwise low level of 'non-human actors' substantiates the finding that disasters and accidents received relatively little attention during the period of our study.

Reporting on crime accounted for a higher percentage of all topics than criminals, lawyers and police combined, reinforcing the idea that many of the actors in crime reporting are political actors. A cross-tabulation of position of actor by topic would answer this and similar questions, and remains to be undertaken in some secondary analysis.

The sources of international news

Perhaps the most contentious aspect of the entire debate on international news reporting has been the role of the Western news agencies as the dominant creators and 'gatekeepers' of such news.

It proved very difficult to identify sources of international news. Identification was attempted for the printed press only, since most electronic newscasts give practically no such information. Yet even for newspapers, practice varied in the extreme: was a given item attributed to any source at all? how was that attribution made? Thus the findings presented here need to be handled with particular care, and complemented by other studies made on the same issue.

The first observation relates to the large number of items whose source was simply unidentifiable from the newspaper itself: as high as 90 per cent in Tunisia, 84 per cent in the Ivory Coast, 70 per cent in Brazil (see Table 10). In only a handful of countries were fewer than 20 per cent of all items not identifiable (Turkey, India, Mexico, the USSR, Indonesia, Australia, Iran; the Federal Republic of Germany also, but

this figure includes 'other' sources). In principle, it is of course possible to go beyond the printed columns and trace the whole process of international news gathering and editing; this would be along the lines of the work undertaken by Phil Harris and Oliver Boyd-Barrett but clearly beyond the scope of the current project.(8) Thus, from our data alone, it is unclear whether, for example, Ivory Coast news was filtered through a national news agency, taken directly from agency wires in the press room or independently gathered.

Given this methodological limitation, it is not surprising that at first glance the 'big four' agencies (AP, AFP, UPI and Reuters) do not seem to dominate the situation. In only four countries did newspapers explicitly derive over 50 per cent of their international news items from the 'big four' (Mexico, Iran, Egypt, and Indonesia) while papers in most other countries attributed beetween 20 and 50 per cent of them. This leaves only Eastern Europe (although 17 per cent of reporting in Yugoslavia came from the 'big four'), certain African countries and Brazil, where the level of unknown sources is high. The next major source of international news for most systems was either the home news agency or the staff of the national media institutions themselves. 'Home country' was an important source (over 20 per cent of all news items) for Africa, Zambia, Australia, India, Indonesia, Hungary, Yugoslavia, the Federal Republic of Germany and Turkey. 'own staff' accounted for over 20 per cent in the United States, Australia, India, Indonesia, Poland, the USSR and all of Western Europe except Greece. Other countries tended to derive percentages in double figures from 'own staff', excepting Argentina, Algeria, Tunisia and Iran. The difficulty here is that claims that items actually originate from home sources may simply mask their true origination elsewhere and represent the secondary gatekeeping role being played by national agencies in translating, editing and generally controlling the news off the wires.

Yet again, perhaps what is most significant in Table 10 is what does not appear. The amount of news credited to TASS, which provides inexpensive services, is minimal (at most 1 per cent) in all nations except Eastern Europe, Finland and the Federal Republic of Germany. Even within Eastern Europe, while the USSR derived 55 per cent of its news from TASS, Hungary took only 6 per cent and Yugoslavia a minimal 1 per cent.

'Other agencies' also played a spotty role as news originators. Although they are important in Argentina and Mexico (mostly the Latin American agencies), and in Iran, Lebanon, Indonesia, Yugoslavia and Finland, in general they do not yet constitute impressive sources. It was unfortunately not part of the study to note which agencies were mentioned by name. One may also question what it is about certain large news agencies that is not yet fully accepted and utilized by other nations, especially by those who speak out vociferously about Western dominance in news gathering. Given the huge expense and large infrastructure a newspaper needs to keep its own correspondents abroad, geographical and political pools for news would seem to be a good solution; yet the practice is still not well-established or well-utilized. Neither the Non-Aligned News pool nor Inter-Press Service (IPS) occupies any significant place among accredited sources. The continued dominance of the 'big four' agencies as agenda-setters for international news is best revealed by the remarkable correspondence between the overall balance of content from the wires themselves (see Appendix 6) and that found in our twenty-nine media systems. This corroborates Schramm's findings for Asia, although he also pointed out that for specific stories selected, tone and orientation may differ.(9) In fact, the suggestion from our qualitative analysis is that much of wire language is also adopted and there is far less real secondary gate-keeping than there might be room for. As Boyd-Barrett concludes in his recent book, 'there is no strong evidence to suggest that over time the quantitative importance of the 'big four' agencies has diminished.(10)

Chapter 6: Summary and conclusions

Problems and limitations of the study

As indicated earlier in this report, international comparative research on the scale of this study is limited by its very nature. It invariably entails some form of compromise and is not always uniformly put into practice.

In the early stages of the preparatory work in this research it was agreed, in the interests of simplicity and comparability, to code only the general news pages in the press. We were aware that this approach has its limitations. Commenting on this point, the German team wrote as follows:

> This is because the serious newspapers contain special sections in every issue dealing with the economy, arts and leisure, sports, and local news, etc; the tabloid publishes an extensive sports section, and television broadcasts, in addition to general news programmes, special programmes on the economy, culture, and of course sport events. All of these contents are, however, excluded by definition from this study. Only the general news portions (and the main television news programmes), which are almost completely filled with pure political reports, are analysed. Subject areas and themes like the economy, arts and leisure, and sports, are thus underrepresented in the findings, as are the actors in these areas.(1)

The narrowing of the scope of our work meant that comparisons with earlier work were not easy to make. Moreover, and this is of particular importance when considering 'development news', one might find that it is the non-hard news sections —for example, special reports or features and irregular accounts— which provide the main substance of 'development journalism'.

It is wise to remember, however, that regardless of whether we had decided to cover the total contents of the media, including advertising, or only editorial copy excluding advertising, neither of these methods could have been guaranteed to generate data of a higher quality that the data which was actually obtained. Furthermore, had we adopted the wider approach, we might not have obtained such a clear picture of the markedly different functions and compositions of newspaper in various regions of the world.

With regard to one or two other debatable or controversial points, the non-inclusion of Sunday papers is dealt with in Appendix 5, while the specific criticisms of, and idiosyncracies in, particular coding categories have been dealt with in earlier sections, as has classification of countries into 'developmental' zones.

Still, whatever the limitations and imperfections may be, there can be no doubt that a rich and extensive body of data has been generated by this study-far too much, in fact, to be fully explored here. For example, the differences in the ways, in which print and electronic media structure international news and the manner in which different constraints with regard to time, space and limited resources impinge on the selection of news items are not adequately covered. Differences in perspective, between various linguistic communities, between papers of different political affiliations, or between public and private broadcasting systems must also await further analysis. Generally speaking, the need to present a common denominator, permitting comparability, in a relatively concise report, taken together with the individuality of the national reports, led us to impose deliberate limitations on the way in which we used the data. But further analysis, at least in some countries, is a distinct possibility.

In passing, it is also worth commenting on the reasons underlying some of these problems. Some of them stem from the fact that centrally organized and co-ordinated computational facilities were not available, and it was not possible to gather all the data into one bank for speedy checking and analysis. Individuals and/or institutions, all of them responsible for their own funding, had to proceed as best they could and with the facilities available in their own institutions. There is no doubt that budget constraints, limited manpower and ohter commitments prevented some teams from keeping to agreed deadlines, and severely limited the possibility of asking for additional data and computational analysis. It cannot be overemphasized that lack of adequate funding presents a serious problem for projects of this kind, with regard to both the conception and the execution of the design. Lack of funds prevented some interested nations from participating, and prevented others from participating as fully as they would have wished.

Nevertheless, the fact of participating in this type of international research is in itself a useful exercise in co-operation and communication. It needs to be emphasized that the results apart, there is much to be learned at a variety of levels, particularly with regard to methodology, from these collaborative ventures.

Finally, before attempting to summarize the findings, a word of warning is in order about the frequently detected tendency in works such as this to make unwarranted generalizations, and dubious applications in support of ideological positions. It is important to make this point here in view of the fact that the data from some of the national studies have been used prematurely, in contentious and misleading ways, by outside parties without the approval, or even prior knowledge, of either IAMCR. Essentially, what is provided by this research is a systematic account of the parameters and structures of international news reporting, with the main focus on the manifest content of news, categorized in commonly accepted categories. An attempt was also made to analyse the material systematically in a more subtle and qualitative manner, but it is important to see this as a tentative first step along a very difficult path.

Summary of findings

On the whole the results of this work tend to substantiate the findings of other studies of news coverage, although these other studies were based on different coding principles, samples and times. That the findings presented here bear out the general results of similar studies reinforces the notion that a news week is indeed 'unique' in terms of the particular events occurring, but 'typical' of the general structure of news habits and formats through which events are filtered and into which all stores are slotted. As Harris has pointed out, 'Events occur everywhere —the stratification is in their coverage'.(2)

One of the most striking things to emerge from the analysis of this mass of data is the identification of a particular pattern of attention to different types of news which seems to be present in virtually all the media systems studied, no matter what their differences in other respects. The study covered a wide range of media systems which were characterized by a variety of political standpoints and developmental orientations. These differences are not reflected, however, in the figures in the tables which outline the parameters of international news presentation. This is not to suggest that the actual content of international news reporting is the same, for example, in the *New York Times, Pravda* and *El Moudjahid,* but what does appear to have become almost universal is the selection of the same foci in international news reporting.

This is particularly noticeable in the attention given to political news, both in terms of topics and actors. This emphasis was present in all the media systems studied. Admittedly, to some extent this must be a function of our methodology —the decision to code 'general news' pages only— yet the same emphasis is also present in broadcast news, where the severe constraints of time might be expected to produce an even narrower thematic focus. Other research supports this general finding.

Looking at geographic representation, the other universal finding is the prime importance of regionalism. In all the national media systems studied much attention and emphasis were given to events occurring within, and actors belonging to, the geographical region in which the country was situated. For example, Nigeria featured African news most prominently, while Argentina featured Latin American stories, and so on. The only exceptions to this general pattern were the Polish and Yugoslav media systems, where Western Europe attracted as much attention as did Eastern Europe. These were the only instances where the geo-political regional groupings were cut across by other criteria, which could be cultural, historical or related to major events of the time. In designing the research no other kinds of cultural, ideological or developmental blocs were constructed to examine international identifications, nor did any such constructs emerge from the analysis.

After the regional stress, a second level of attention was identified, namely the 'consistent news-makers': the United States and Western Europe. The nature of the news coverage depended on the nature and extent of the old colonial and the newer neo-colonial economic and political ties between the centres and the peripheral nations. It is important to note that although neither region was a prime location for 'dominant news stories' as described in the interpretative, qualitative

analyses, they both figure prominently in the quantitative accounts of news coverage of different areas.

Only at the third step is the focus levelled at what may be referred to as the 'hot spots' of the period covered in the study, in this case primarily the Middle East. Obviously, these 'spots' vary from time to time, but on the whole the developing world seems to appear under this heading more than the other 'worlds'.

In this case, too, comparisons between the qualitative analysis and the results generated by the quantitative method are instructive. Africa as a region was repeatedly described as providing 'dominant stories', mostly in relation to Idi Amin and Uganda, and the elections in the then Rhodesia. Despite these important stories, however, the region as a whole, in quantitative terms of overall coverage, achieved only a middle ranking.

Finally, we must draw attention to the areas of invisibility: those parts of the developing world where, according to the media, nothing much seems to be happening (at the time of our study, Latin America) and the socialist countries of Eastern Europe. The invisibility of the latter region is mitigated in part by the apparent visibility of the Eastern European, mainly Soviet actors as highly mobile participants in international affairs, who 'move into' a news spotlight — a spotlight which is rarely directed towards their region.

It is often said (given the variety of constraints that impinge upon the production of international news) that the problem in news reporting is not so much what to include, but what to omit. Perhaps more important than the question of whether the West is over-represented in international news is the problem of the several under-representation of certain other parts of the world. There is even a marked shortage of news about other developing regions in the media of any given developing nation, so that it is still true to say that 'the peripheral nations do not write or read much about each other, especially not across bloc borders'.(3) Latin America was the most invisible region during the period of his study, but in general the news flows across the developing world are little more than a trickle, so that for example Latin American media carried little news on Africa, and the Middle Eastern media paid little attention to East Asia.

As other research has also indicated, regions of the developing world make news when undergoing some kind of disturbance that makes them, for a time, at least, a 'hot-spot' of tension and crisis. News in most media systems seems to be defined as the exceptional event, making coups and catastrophes newsworthy wherever they occur. It is not so much that the developing world is singled out for such 'negative' attention, but that the developing countries tend to be reported only in this manner. These countries are neither the source of, nor themselves apparently particularly interested in, presenting 'softer' news items. Third World media systems concentrate heavily on 'hard' news, and the tendency is that the smaller the amount of general coverage, the more it concentrates on a few topic areas and reflects the specific events of the time. News tends to stereotype all regions in some way or another.

The media of Eastern Europe tend to report on a wider and more positive life space with a greater focus on cultural and scientific items than do the Western European media with a comparable amount of 'soft' news. Although our analysis did not concentrate on 'development news' —that is, news that presents a more complete analysis of changes in the developing world than what is found in 'normal'coverage there appears to be very little evidence from any country to suggest that this kind of news plays a significant role in international news reporting. Again it is a problem of omission.

The difficulties associated with identifying and recording the sources of international news items have already been mentioned, so the research results relating to sources should be treated with more than the usual degree of caution. In addition to a very high rate *of non-attribution,* there was a marked reported use of local sources, mainly national news agencies and own correspondents. However, such information still does not allow us to say anything very definitive about the exact role of such local sources, whether as original news-gatherers (either generally, or for particular kinds of stories), or as translators and editors of items originating elsewhere.

Assuming that the second possibility is the more common, it would appear that national systems are exerting important secondary gate-keeping functions of selecting, interpreting and processing news from external sources. It could also be argued, however, that the selection is restricted, as it is taken from an already limited agenda —an agenda which is influenced, if not entirely provided, by the major news agencies. Moreover, these well-nigh universal agencies, because of their dominance and the support of other forces, have contributed to the socialization of news professionals by reinforcing certain understandings and beliefs as to what news really is, thereby (one word) helping to set the agenda in yet another way. Certainly, this research shows that the Western agencies are the second most important source of international news, coming after the home agency or own correspondent.

It is interesting to note that TASS was hardly mentioned as a news source, and the growing number of alternative sources, such as the Non-Aligned News pool, Depth News,* IPS, etc., which in the analyses would have been grouped under the general heading 'other agencies', were never prominent. Obviously there is a large gap between the practices that might generally be thought to be associated with the new information order, and what is actually happening at the present time. Moreover, this tends to be the case even in those countries which would claim to be in favour of a New World Information and Communication Order.

It is worth noting that the homogeneity in the structure of international news across all twenty-nine media systems in the quantitative analysis offers *little support* at this level for the argument that 'free flow' produces diversity. In the current situation of international news, the dominant producers determine the nature of the product, its marketing and distribution, and even its presentation. There is not a great deal of room for alternative producers, or for different conceptions and approaches to international news. The quite remarkable similarity between the patterns of attention identified in so many media systems, and what is actually produced by the major wire services as presented in the parallel analysis in Appendix 6, suggests strongly that these services not only continue to set the agenda for what counts as news, but also (despite the aforementioned 'secondary gate-keeping' function) continue to provide much of the language in news presentation.

Still, as mentioned earlier in our comments on comparative methodology, we need to be very cautious in our interpretations, and particularly in any generalizations we may be tempted to make. The greater variety of content, both between and within national systems as reflected in the thirteen qualitative reports (compared with the quantitative analysis) suggests that an adequate understanding of the essence of international news reporting requires several levels of analysis.

The main problems would appear to lie on at least two different planes. one of these has to do with the narrow determination of what constitutes international news, and the corresponding omission of certain kinds of events, actors and localities. The second has to do with the structure of bias and interpretation through which selected stories are actually presented. The relative weight and impact of each of these on those who receive the news, and the wider implications of this, remains to be assessed by other research. Which we hope might follow and benefit from this study.

Some policy recommendations

Although politically and theoretically the question of the definition of news is still problematic, the actuality of news presentation around the world, as we have seen, shows a certain homogeneity at a number of important levels.

This homogeneity is influenced, amongst other things, by production constraints, and it has been suggested that this means that radical changes are not likely to be easily achieved. It could be argued, therefore, that it would be rather naîve and unrealistic to call for a conception of news that would include process, background, context, evolution, and so on, and not merely the immediate, the negative, the conflicting and the sensational. Perhaps this more detailed and comprehensive coverage of events can be dealt with only in what is 'not-the-news', i.e. the special reports, feature articles and investigative journalism in the press, or in documentaries and current affairs programmes in the electronic media — areas which were deliberately not covered in this study.

Yet even on the basis of what we know, and within the existing frame-work of news operations, recommendations could be made for the presentation of a broader picture and, more specifically, for a deliberate and sustained attempt to improve the news flows between the different developing regions so that, *inter alia,* they may come to appreciate the nature of their common problems and the various ways of dealing with them. A supportive recommendation would be for a greater utilization of new and different news sources. This would include reliance on neighbouring newspapers as sources, as well as regional attempts at news gathering which might help to challenge the conventional, universal news agenda that currently prevails.

Third World journalists must also be trained to be more critical of professional practices and journalistic values which, hitherto, seem to have been accepted without much question, and should be helped to assess these values and practices in the light of the requirements of their own situations. More co-operation between media professionals in developing countries, particularly in providing easier access to information sources, would be another step in the right direction.

If news and information are to be seen as social resources rather than as commodities, then the universal standardization of the structure of news presentation as revealed by this study, which reflects the practices and professionalism of Western media systems and news agencies, must still present problems for the developing world. Both sides so to speak, may be colluding in maintaining this operation in a variety of ways and for different reasons, but whatever the case the emphasis still seems to be on news as a commodity rather than as a social resource.

Suggestions for future research

There is an urgent need to define positive alternatives to the dominant system of news production which would go well beyond the oft repeated negative criticisms. Such attempts in turn, must be underpinned by valid and relevant research.

---

* Depth News, which is sponsored by the Press Foundation of Asia, is a weekly news and feature service offering articles on development, economic and population themes. It began operations in 1969.

This international comparative project has provided up-to-date information which, on the whole, is in line with several other studies conducted over the past twenty years. However, now may be the time to move away from these broad mappings of international news towards deeper, more refined and more focused studies. The results of our research definitely point in this direction.

The difficulties of devising comparative international procedures for in-depth content analysis can probably best be overcome by choosing only a few selected topics for intensive analysis. The analysis should cover not only manifest but, more importantly, latent message structures, ideological orientations and imagery proper. A first step has been taken in this direction by four of the countries (Hungary, Netherlands, India and Malaysia) who participate in the main study and also agreed to take part in a further study on developmental news. Ideally, in this type of work the analysis will attempt to get behind and underneath the formal categories in the hope of tapping the essence, the real meaning of what is portrayed. Other specific issues, such as the media coverage of peace and disarmament, might also be studied in this way.

The notions of 'development journalism' and a 'Third World perspective' themselves need to be clarified and put into practice so that they may be effectively used in international communications research. Comparisons between the outputs of the big news agencies and the alternative sources such as IPS and the Non-Aligned Pool are also needed. Furthermore, whatever changes are made need to be carefully monitored and evaluated, if only to determine whether or not they represent an improvement on what went before, and if the claims that are made for them can be substantiated. Studies of Third World 'gate-keepers', along the lines suggested by Cruise-O'Brien and Golding, are also required. These studies should be evaluations of attempt to explain why alternative sources are as yet so underutilized by making critical evaluations of the patterns of prevailing news values as well as news production constraints.

It is, perhaps, also time to examine more thoroughly, and within the appropriate contexts, one of the basic assumptions of this study, namely that because of their 'regularity, ubiquity and perserverance', the news media are the major international image makers. In fact, the role played by the news media in structuring our 'pictures of the world' is increasingly being questioned. It has been suggested that the 'cultural significance in terms of transferring cultural values of international news is not as decisive as the influence that is exerted through advertising, educational publishing, children's comics, or women's magazines'.(4) This hypothesis should be further investigated.

There is no doubt that the public must be brought back into the research operation, and that we should carry out comparative studies' of images in the mind' as well as media images. Some useful ideas may be gleaned from a 'Prix Jeunesse study' of children's attitudes towards foreigners, undertaken by the Centre for Mass Communication Research at the University of Leicester. The open survey technique tried by Cantril in the 1940s, and the newer Galileo mapping techniques, may also be useful here. After all, social consciousness, its formation and its implications, are at the heart or our concerns.

We must also remember that international news plays only a modest, albeit a publicly accessible, part in the totality of international information flows. Decision-makers rely increasingly on very different kinds of transborder information flows, which include everything from credit data to remote sensing, but which are again controlled by a limited number of Western sources. It is arguable that although a comparatively informed public debate is under way about news flows, a potentially far more insidious form of information dependency, posing new threats to national sovereignty and the right to be informed, is not yet firmly on the agenda. Long-term chartings of the variety of information flows, alongside flows of trade, weapons, and personnel as the main lines of international relations in the late twentieth century, are yet another challenging task for research.

References

Chapter 1

1. Johan Galtung and Mari Holmboe Ruge, 'The Structure of Foreign News', *Journal of Peace Research,* 1965, 1, pp. 64-90.

2. From the conference document of the Fourth Conference of Heads of State or Government of Non-Aligned Countries, Algiers, September, 1973; quoted by Tran Van Dinh, 'Non-Alignment and Cultural Imperialism', in *National Sovereignty and International Communication,* ed., K. Nordenstreng and H. Schiller, New Jersey: Ablex, 1979.

3. Discussion of the four 'Ds' as cornerstones of the New Information Order can be found in Kaarle Nordenstreng, 'Defining the New International Information Order', Paper presented at the Conference, *World Communications: Decisions for the Eighties,* The Annenberg School of Communication, University of Pennsylvania, May 1980.

4. Jonathan Gunter, *The United States and the Debate on the World 'Information Order',* Washington, AED and USICA, 1979.

5. Tran Van Dinh, op. cit; see also A. W. Singham and Tran Van Dinh, eds.,*From Bandung to Colombo,* New York; Third Press Review; 1976; Cees J. Hamelink, *The New International Information Order: Development and Obstacles,* Vienna Institute for Development, Occasional Paper 80/2.

6. See, in particular, the supporting documents (Nos. 31-35 inclusive) of the International Commission for the Study of Communication Problems, plus the final report itself.

7. The resolution can be found in Unesco document 19 C/DR. 170, submitted initially by Denmark, Finland, Norway and Sweden, and supported later by Yugoslavia and India.

8. Jacques Kayser, *One Week's News,* Paris: Unesco 1953, International Press Institute, *The Flow of The News,* Zurich, International Press Institute, 1953.

9. George Gerbner and George Marvanyi, 'The Many Worlds of the World's Press', *Journal of Communication,*1977, 27, 1; Wilbur Schramm, et al., *International News Wires and Third World News in Asia,* Murrow Reports, Medford, Mass, Tufts University, 1978; see for example, *Media Asia,* 'Humanising International News',1978, 5,3; *Communications and Development Review,* 'What's News', 1978, 2, 2.

10. William Nuchanan and Hadley Cantril, *How Nations See Each Other,* Urbana, Illinois University Press, 1953.

11. This and the following quotations are taken from the IAMCR correspondence over the years 1977-1979.

12. Kaarle Nordenstreng and Markku Salomaa, 'Studying the Image of Foreign Countries as Portrayed by the Mass Media: A progress Report', presented at Eleventh Scientific Conference of the International Association for Mass Communication Research, Warsaw, September 1978.

Chapter 2

1. Guido H. Stempel III, 'Sample Size for Classifying Subject Matter in Dailies', *Journalism Quarterly,* 29, Summer 1952, pp. 333-4.

2. Peter Golding and Philip Elliott, *Making the News,* London, Longman, 1979; Denis McQuail, *Analysis of Newspaper Content,* Royal Commission on the press, Research Series 4, London, HMSO, 1977.

3. See the discussion in Philip Elliott, and Peter Golding, 'Mass Communication and Social Change: The Imagery of Development and the Development of Imagery', in E. de Kadt and C. Williams, eds., *Sociology and Development,*London, Tavistock, 1974.

4. William A. Scott, 'Reliability of Content Analysis: The Case of Nominal Scale Coding', *Public Opinion Quarterly,* 1955.

Chapter 4

1. *Keesing's Contemporary Archives,* London, Longmans, 1980; *Whitacker's Almanac,* London, 1980; *The Guardian* and the *Daily Telegraph,* April-July 1980.

2. Jacques Kayser, *One Week's News,* op. cit., p. 11.

3. Australian National Report, written by Grant and Elizabeth Noble.

4. Roland Barthes, *Mythologies,* London, Jonathan Cape, 1972.

Chapter 5

1. Supported by a grant from the United States International Communication Agency.

2. See for example, Kim Kyu Whan, *Information Imbalance - The Case of Korea,* Regional Conference on Information Imbalance in Asia, Colombo, Sri Lanka, April 1976; Annabell SrebernyMohammadi, *Seven Days in May - News Reporting in Iran,* Iran Communications and Development Institute, 1976.

3. Phil Harris, *News Dependence: The Case for A New World Information Order,* Centre for Mass Communication Research, University of Leicester, 1977; Philip Elliott and Peter Golding, 'The News Media and Foreign Affairs', in R. Boardman and A. J. R. Groom, eds., *The Management of Britain's External Relations,* Macmillan, 1973.

4. Al Hester, 'An Analysis of News Flows from Developed and Developing Nations', *Gazette,* 17, 1-2, 1971.

5. Peter Golding and Philip Elliott, *Making the News,* op. cit.

6. Johan Galtung, 'A Structural Theory of Imperialism', *Journal of Peace Research,* 8, 2, 1971.

7. Denis McQuail, *Analysis of Newspaper Content,* op. cit.

8. Harris, op. cit; Oliver Boyd-Barrett, *The International News Agencies,* London, Constable, 1980.

9. Wilbur Schramm, et al., *International News Wires and Third World News in Asia: A Preliminary Report,* Hong Kong, Centre for Communication Studies, Chinese University, 1978.

10. Oliver Boyd-Barrett, op. cit., p. 18.

Chapter 6

1. Taken from p. 11 of the National Report of the Federal Republic of Germany, written by Winfried Schuls.

2. Phil Harris, *International News Media Authority and Dependence,* Centre for Mass Communication Research, University of Leicester.

3. Johan Galtung, op. cit.

4. Cees Hamelink, 'The New International Economic Order and the New International Information Order', International Commission for the Study of Communication Problems, Unesco, Document 34, p. 4.

Appendix 1: The Participating Teams

Dr Grant Noble and Elizabeth Noble
Department of Psychology
The University of New England
Armidale, New South Wales
Australia

Professor Kaarle Nordenstreng
Department of Journalism and Mass Communication
University of Tampere
Tampere
Finland

Professor Winfried Schulz
Institut fur Publizistik
Westfälische Wilhelms-Universität
Münster
Federal Republic of Germany

Dr J. S. Yadava, Director
Indian Institute of Mass Communication
New Delhi
India

Annabelle Sreberny— Mohammadi
Iran Communications and Development Institute
Tehran
Iran

Tamas Terestyeni
Mass Communication Research Center
Hungarian Radio and Television
Budapest
Hungary

Professor Nabil Dajani
Department of Social and Behavioural Sciences
American University of Beirut
Beirut
Lebanon

Dr Brajesh Bhatia
Asia-Pacific Institute for Broadcasting Development
Kuala Lumpur
Malaysia

Dr A. Kaiser
Vakgreop cultuursociologie en massacommunicatie
Subfakuteit sociaal-culturele wetenschappen
Rijksuniversiteit
Utrecht
Netherlands

Dr Frank Ugboajah
Department of Mass Communication
University of Lagos
Lagos
Nigeria

Dr Jerzy Oledzki
Institute of Journalism
University of Warsaw
Warsaw
Poland

Dr Richard Cole
Dean, School of Journalism
University of North Carolina
Chapel Hill, North Carolina
United States

Slavko Splichal
Faculty of Sociology, Political Science and Journalism
University of Ljubljana
Ljubljana
Yugoslavia

Appendix 2; Coding: General Guide, Instructions and Schedule

CODING

Media to be covered

(a) Three or four daily papers in each country, including wherever possible the largest circulation national daily. Papers should be selected so as to be broadly representative of the national press. Since conditions vary from country to country —there may not be a national press, for instance— choice of papers is left to the local investigators bearing in mind the overall objectives of the research.

(b) The main broadcast news, whether radio or television, or both. Only news bulletins as such are to be included, not documentaries or current affairs or sports programmes. Only the main news bulletin of the day is to be analysed for any one broadcasting channel, to avoid duplication of data. Broadcast news must be tape-recorded for analysis; if video equipment is not available for television, at least the sound must be recorded - notes can be made on the visuals as necessary.

Sampling

The study design calls for one continuous week and one composite week (excluding Sundays) in 1979. Since the sample of days is so small it is important that all participants code the same days' output. In the interests of completing the study within a reasonable time the composite week has been chosen to span a limited period only rather than the whole year. Sample day dates are as follows:

Continuous week 1979.	*Composite Week 1979.*		
Monday 23 April	Monday of 1st full week of April	-	2 April
Tuesday 24 April	Tuesday a fortnight later	-	17 April
Wednesday 25 April	Wednesday ” ”	-	2 May
Thursday 26 April	Thursday ” ”	-	17 May
Friday 27 April	Fryday ” ”	-	1 June
Saturday 28 April	Saturday ” ”	-	16 June

Missing dates: Should a paper or bulletin not be available for a particular sample day —e.g. because of a strike or public holiday— it should be replaced by the nearest available issue before or after the missing day (and not already included in

the sample). This will probably result in an imbalance in days of the week in the sample (e.g. two Mondays), but it is felt that in such circumstances the principle of maintaining maximum contiguity to original sample dates is more important than that of balancing days.

Participants wishing to apply the coding schedule to the earlier years as well (1969, 1959, 1949) should choose their sample on the same basis as for the composite week of 1979, i.e. Monday of the first full week of April, Tuesday a fortnight later, and so on. (The first full week is the week containing the 7th day, where Sunday is taken to be the first day of the week.) In this way all such optional coding will remain comparable across institutions and (seasonally) across years; it will also span a manageably small number of major events. The paper chosen for this historical analysis should as far as possible be the same maximum circulation paper as the one included in the 1979 analysis.

Qualitative analysis

A qualitative analysis is to be prepared for the material covered in the coding schedule for 1979 as well as for the maximum circulation paper for the earlier years. For this historical material participants should include in their analysis the composite weeks selected as described in the previous paragraph (in the interests of comparability). They need not (and perhaps ought not to) restrict them selves to these days, however. This applies to 1979 as well. A suggested framework for this qualitative analysis is to be sent to participants shortly.

CODING INSTRUCTIONS

Unit of analysis

The unit of analysis is the news item. In newspapers this means all the material printed under a single heading (or, occasionally, under a sub-heading in larger items where material under other sub-headings deals with different subject matter). For broadcast news an item is all the material following an introductory statement on one topic. The announcement of a new (though possibly related) topic signals a new item that should be coded separately. The use of a linking phrase between items, such as 'Meanwhile in Tel-Aviv...' does not of itself mean that the two topics should be treated as one item. In practice there is little difficulty in distinguishing one item from another.

Material to be included

Include only items dealing with events or situations outside the home country, or events in the home country in which foreign nationals take part or which are presented as having substantive relevance to foreign situations, Stories at home about private individuals whose foreign nationality is incidental to the story, like 'Mr Rossini, an Italian living in Bonn, has won a lottery...' should not be included. Include such material only where the foreign nationality is an important element in the story; and here it is nationality, not ethnic membership, that matters. Similarly, passing references to foreign countries in material about home events in phrases like 'Russian-made' or 'The Minister, back from his holiday in Spain...' do not qualify an item for inclusion.

Some problems may arise where for instance there is a foreign immigrant group resident in the home country or where foreign troops form an integral part of the home country's armed forces. The local investigator will be the best judge in these circumstances, but generally speaking such groups would not automatically make an item 'foreign news' unless their presence or activity is presented as pertaining in a non-incidental way to a foreign country.

For broadcast bulletins, sports reports as such are to be ignored, for purposes of the 'core' analysis.

The coding schedule

The schedule is designed to record the data in a form suitable for direct transfer to standard eighty-column punch cards for computer analysis, using only numerical values and no more than one hole-site per column. A zero should be entered in all columns (boxes on the schedule or coding sheet) where no positive coding is made (except of course where boxes are left blank for later coding). Otherwise the appropriate number(s) are to be entered in the box(es) provided.

1. *Institution code.* Code numbers have been allocated to distinguish between different participants. As a matter of convenience in most cases participants have been coded by institution, even though they may be participating in the study in a personal capacity. Where it is necessary to combine the codings from different participants in the same country this can easily be done at the analysis stage.
Code numbers are as follows:

01 University of New England, New South Wales.

02 Karl-Marx Universität, Leipzig.

03 Westfälische Wilhelms-Universität, Münster.

04 Jorg Becker, Frankfurt.

05 University of Tampere, Finland.

06 Bangalore University, India.

07 Indian Institute of Mass Communications, New Delhi.

08 Iran Communications and Development Institute.

09 American University of Beirut.

10 Asia-Pacific Institute for Broadcasting Development, Kuala Lumpur.

11 Rijksuniversiteit, Utrecht.

12 Universiteit van Amsterdam.

13 University of Lagos, Nigeria.

14 University of Warsaw.

15 Comitetul de Stat al Radioteleviziunii Romane, Bucharest.

16 Nordicom-Sweden, Goteborg.

17 University of Illinois.

18 University of North Carolina (1).

19 University of North Carolina (2).

20 University of North Carolina (3).

21 University of Moscow.

22 Universitad Central de Venezuela, Caracas.

23 University of Ljubljana, Yugoslavia.

Always enter your institution code —or have it pre-printed on the coding sheet.

2. *Item serial number.* Each item coded is to be given a number between 0001 and 9999. These need not be consecutive but must all be different for the items processed by one institution. Institution, may wish to arrange their numbering so that the first digit distinguishes between coders. The serial number in conjunction with the institution code will give a unique number for every item in the analysis internationally.

3. *Medium.* To identify each paper or programme covered in the analysis, participating institutions will need to draw up a coding list for themselves using the following principle:

Codes to be allocated for Newspapers in the range 01 - 09

Television in the range 10 - 19

Radio in the range 20 - 29

This will facilitate grouping by medium at the analysis stage if desired.

4. *Sample day numbers*

Continuous week 1979	*Composite week 1979*
01 - Monday 23 April	11 - Monday 2 April
02 - Tuesday 24 April	12 - Tuesday 17 April
03 - Wednesday 25 April	13 - Wednesday 2 May
04 - Thursday 26 April	14 - Thursday 17 May
05 - Friday 27 April	15 - Friday 1 June
06 - Saturday 28 April	16 - Saturday 16 June

Sample days for previous years should be numbered 1 to 6 (Monday to Saturday) in the same way, but prefixed by the decade number in order to distinguish them, i.e. 61 to 66 for 1969, 51 to 56 for 1959 etc. 'Substitute' days (if any) for missing issues should be given the suffix digits 7, 8, 9, 0 while retaining the appropriate prefix digit.

5. *General/Specialized.* For the 'common core' of the study only material on general news pages is to be included. This coding is provided for anyone wishing to analyse material in specialized sections as well, so that a distinction between core and additional material can be made. Specialized sections are sports pages, business and financial sections, women's, children's, and hobbies pages, travel and leisure sections, and so on. A specialized section can normally be readily identified by a heading, such as 'Business news', by being spatially demarcated from the rest of the paper, dealing only with material of a particular type, and possibly being separately edited as an entity in itself. A by-line such as 'From our Economics Editor' by itself does not make the item specialized; it must be in a distinct and specialized *section* of the paper (specialist editors often contribute to the general news pages as well). A general news page is anything not specialized as defined above.

General news pages carry news of *varied* kinds although this is sometimes organized under headings like 'Home News' and 'Foreign News', both of which are to be included under the 'general' category.

6. *Type of item.* Presumably all broadcast news will be coded '1' News Story. 'Picture only' means picture-plus-caption or short two-or-three-sentence explanation.

Participants coding material additional to the common core may extend these codes —e.g. '6' Advertising— for additional material only. All 'core' material (general news pages) must be coded under the five categories provided.

7. *Source of item.* A separate column is given for each in order to take account of multiple sources. 'Unidentifiable' is an exclusive category; if it is coded 'Yes' all others must be coded 'No'. 'Own correspondent' should be coded 'Yes' only if this is stated or quite obvious —don't guess.

8. *Length.* The length of a broadcast item is timed in seconds. The length of a newspaper item is the total column length occupied by the item (including the space taken by headline and picture, if any) measured in centimetres, based on the standard column width for that paper. Thus a two-column wide block of print ten centimetres high measures twenty column centimetres (entered as 0020). Adjustments for comparability between papers with different column widths can be made later at the data processing stage.

9. *Length of picture.* Applies to the press only, is measured for overall length, and includes the caption.

10. *Story event or issue.* Write in a brief phrase like 'Middle East peace negotiations' or 'Rhodesian elections' to describe the event or issue that the story concerns. It should then be possible to separate out any major or persistent issues for analysis.

11. *Story type.* 'Abroad' means in a country other than the home country. Colonies of the home country are to be treated as foreign, and so is the metropolitan country if the home country is (or was) a colony.

'Home news abroad': news event located in a foreign country whose main actors are of the home country, or whose importance is explicitly shown to be because of domestic events.

'Foreign news at home': news events located in home country involving foreign actors or with main reference to events or situations abroad. This includes domestic debate on foreign affairs in general.

'Foreign news': all events located outside home country other than 'home news abroad'.

12. *Location.* This concerns the first and main events in the story. The location is that of the immediate news event. Thus Geneva peace talks on Rhodesia take place in Switzerland. The only exceptions are meetings of the United Nations; these take place at 'the United Nations'. For events at sea, in international air space, write in 'At sea' etc.

The numerical coding will be done after data collection when the actual countries that need codes will be known and any 'difficult cases' (e.g. East Pakistan/Bangladesh historically) can be decided upon.

13. *Relations between states.* This concerns relations between states considered as political entities, not just between individuals and groups of different nationalities. Thus an Egyptian marrying an Israeli, or an international sporting contest, should be coded 'No', unless these events are presented as having implications for or resulting from political relations between the states concerned.

14. *Topics.* These concern the kind of event or situation that the item is mainly about. It will be possible to analyse this data at two levels: (a) the level of broad categories of the main headings —Political, Military, Economic, and so on; and (b) in more detail at the level of the subtopics within each broad category, e.g. military topics are subdivided into armed conflict, peace moves, and other. The prime classification is the Main Topic— what the item is mainly about. Each item is to be allocated to one —and only one— main topic category. There will then be as many main topics as there are items. There will inevitably be some ambiguous cases and difficult decisions. This problem can be partly overcome by the classification of subsidiary topics. Thus if there is some doubt as to whether a story is mainly about political or military matters, and it is decided to classify it as 'Military' as the main topic, the political aspect can still be retained in the data by coding 'political' as a subsidiary topic. There is provision for coding up to three subsidiary topics. Three are not obligatory; many stories will deal with only one topic, the Main Topic. The criterion for recording a subsidiary topic is whether it forms a substantive part of the item, that is, if it were absent, would the sense of the item be substantially changed? Thus a passing reference to a recent drought in an economic story would not make 'Natural desister' a subsidiary topic. If the story were about the economic consequences of the drought then 'disaster' probably would be a subsidiary topic.

15 & 16 *Actors.* Actors are the subjects of the story; individuals groups or other entities doing things or affected by events, in a way that is essential to the story or commentary. Where a person or group could be omitted from the story without altering its substance, they should not be recorded as actors. 'President Carter arrived in Paris today for discussions with the french prime minister' - here the President and the Prime Minister are both actors. President Carter, accompanied by his wife, arrived in Paris for discussions...' here 'his wife' may not need to be recorded as an actor, particularly if she is not mentioned again. If in doubt in such cases include them as actors. The object is not to fill the data with marginal 'actors' that are only mentioned in passing.

Actors may be individual, plural or institutional. Thus each of the following could be an actor: 'the president', 'the crowd', 'troops', 'the committee', 'the party', 'Britain'. The main actor is the main subject of the story, usually the first mentioned. 'Other' actors are others essential to the story. There may be no human actor, e.g. 'A hurricane has caused extensive damage. . .', or no main human actor. e.g. 'A hurricane has caused extensive damage, and killed five people.' Here the five people would probably only be 'other' actors unless the story is mainly about their deaths, rather than about the hurricane. Unless they are further differentiated they would be entered only once as a group under 'other actors'.

(a) Nationality —write this in the space provided.
(b) Position/sphere —record here (by entering the appropriate code number in the boxes), the position of the actor, the capacity in which he appears, or his sphere of activity as presented in the story. Sports people will normally be coded *18* 'Sports'. A sportsman who is also a politician will be recorded as such if that is the main capacity in which he appears in the story. The ruling party in a country would be recorded as such; an individual representative of the party (e.g. a leader or official) acting in that capacity would similarly be recorded as 'ruling party'.

'Legitimate political opposition' means opposition political parties or their representatives operating within the normal constitutional arrangements of the country in question, as officially understood in that country. 'Non-legitimate political opposition' means political parties, or groups contending for power, that are outlawed or denied constitutional means of political activity in their country —e.g. certain black parties and movements in South Africa. (N.B.: There is no evaluation implied here. 'Legitimate/Illegitimate' is as officially regarded within the country concerned). A similar distinction applies between regular and irregular military forces. Sometimes guerrillas and non-legitimate political opposition groups may be the same people; they should be classified as political or military according to whether they are presented in the news item mainly in their political or in their military roles. A pressure group is a group pursuing some limited objective or interest short of winning political power itself —e.g. pressing for changes in the law or the recognition of the rights of minorities by means other than gaining office.

Ther is a certain inadequacy in the 'Position/sphere' classification in that two principles of classification are involved —that of position or role as such, and that of sphere of activity— and that these overlap in some cases and not in others. Thus an 'actor' classified as 'Chief executive, president, etc.' is always unambiguously an individual in a political role. In other cases, 'actors' classified as 'Ruling Party', 'Industry', or 'Sport', for instance, may be individuals, collectivities, or even near-abstractions, e.g. 'The chairman of General Motors has said. . .', 'General Motors has announced a new range of products. . .', 'The industrial sector has performed well. . .' would all be coded 'Industry'. It seems that this part of the coding works well enough in practice.

(c) Quoted? Where any actor is quoted directly or indirectly, code 1 'Yes'. 'The President said that . . .' is a quote just as much as if his words were given in quotation marks or actually broadcast.

After completing the sections Nationality, Position/sphere, and Quoted? for the main actor, do the same for 'other actors' using the same coding scheme, for up to three other actors. Enter zeros throughout in boxes where there is not an 'other actor' to be recorded.

17. *Themes and references.* Each of these is simply coded as present or absent. The idea is to pick up news angles, conceptual frameworks and the like that are present in the content but which may not emerge clearly from the classification of Topics and other coding. The 'themes' and 'references' suggested vary somewhat in their levels of generality, and in some cases overlap with some of the Topics. Mostly, however, they are conceived as aspects of news coverage that cut across the topic classification. The overall rule is that the theme or reference in question should be quite clearly present in the news item in a way that would be recognized by almost anyone. In the case of the asterisked items, only the actual words in the list (or forms of them) are to be taken as indicating the presence of the theme. Otherwise, the practical rule is that if the theme is clearly in evidence (in the text, and not just in the mind of the analyst) code it as present, even if it is only a marginal aspect of the coverage; if in doubt, do not code it as present.

Foreign news coding schedule

Card 1
Col

1. *Institution code*

1 ☐
2 ☐

2. *Item serial number*

3 ☐
4 ☐
5 ☐
6 ☐

3. *Medium*

7 ☐
8 ☐

4. *Sample day number*

9 ☐
10 ☐

5. *General/specialized* (Press only)
1 On general news page
2 In specialized section

11 ☐

6. *Type of item*
1 News story
2 Editorial
3 Feature
4 Reader's letter
5 Picture only (press only)

12 ☐

7. *Source of item*
(Check 1 Yes, 0 No for each)
Home country agency

Reuters   13 ☐
UPI   14 ☐
AP   15 ☐
AFP   16 ☐
Tass   17 ☐
Other agency   18 ☐
Own correspondent
or staff reporter   19 ☐
                       20 ☐
Other medium - home
Other medium - foreign 21 ☐
Other   22 ☐
Unidentifiable   23 ☐
                       24 ☐

8. *Length* (in column cm. or seconds)

25 ☐
26 ☐
27 ☐
28 ☐

9. (a) *Is there a picture ?* (press only)
   1 Yes
   2 No   29 ☐

   If yes:
   (b) *Length of picture* (col. cm.)

   30 ☐
   31 ☐
   32 ☐

10. *Story event or issue* (write in)

    33 ☐
    34 ☐

11. *Story type*
    1 Home news abroad
    2 Foreign news at home   35 ☐
    3 Foreign news abroad
    4 Other or uncertain

12. *Location* (write in name of country
    in which main event occurs)

    36 ☐
    37 ☐

13. Does the story concern *Relations between states*
    (or groups of states) ?
    1 Yes
    2 No   38 ☐

14. *Topics* (identify one - and only one - main topic
    by entering '1' against that category. Code '2'
    for no more than three subsidiary topics. Enter
    '0' against all other categories).

    Diplomatic/political activity between states

    39 ☐

    Politics within states:
    Internal conflict or crisis
    Elections, campaigns, appointments,   40 ☐
    government changes

    Other political, including legislation   41 ☐

                                                   42 ☐

    Military and defence:
    Armed conflict or threat of

    43 ☐

    Peace moves, negotiations, settlements

    44 ☐

    Other, including arms deals, weapons,
    bases, exercises

    45 ☐

Economic matters:
   Agreements on trade, tariffs, etc.

                                              46 ☐
   Other international trade, imports, exports,
   trade balance   47 ☐
   Capital investment, stock issues, state
   investments (not aid)   48 ☐
   Stock exchange, share prices, dividends,
   profits (not new stock issues)   49 ☐
   Other economic performance, output, growth
   sales, etc. (for economy as whole or   50 ☐
   particular enterprise)
   Prices, cost of living, inflation, etc.

                                              51 ☐
   Industrial projects, factories, dams, ports,
   roads, etc.   52 ☐
   Agricultural matters, projects, crops. harvests,
   etc.   53 ☐
   Industrial/labour relations, disputes, negotia-
   tions, wages   54 ☐
   Monetary questions, exchange rates, money
   supply   55 ☐
   Other economic

                                              56 ☐

International aid:
   Disaster or famine relief

                                              57 ☐
   Aid for economic purposes, e.g. industrial
   development   58 ☐
   Military aid, weapons, advisers, training

                                              59 ☐
   Other aid, e.g. for education, family planning,
   etc   60 ☐

Social services:
   Social problems generally, health, housing,
   illiteracy, etc.   61 ☐
   Educational provision

                                              62 ☐
   Health provision (not family planning)

                                              63 ☐
   Family planning

                                              64 ☐
   Other social services and social welfare matters

                                              65 ☐

Crime, police, judicial, legal and penal:
   Non-political crime, police, judicial and penal
   activity   66 ☐
   Political crime, as above

                                              67 ☐
   Non-criminal legal and court proceedings,
   e.g. claims for damages   68 ☐
   Other crime/legal

                                              69 ☐

Culture, arts, archaeology

                                              70 ☐

Religion

                                              71 ☐

Scientific, technical, medical

                                              72 ☐

63

Sports:
International

73 ☐

Non-international

74 ☐

Entertainment, show business (except personalities)

75 ☐

Personalities (not politicians):
Sports

76 ☐

Entertainers

77 ☐

Others

78 ☐

Human interest, odd happenings, animals, sex, etc.

79 ☐

80 ☐

Institution and Item No.

1 ☐
2 ☐
3 ☐
4 ☐
5 ☐
6 ☐

Student matters

7 ☐

Ecology
Energy conservation

8 ☐

Pollution

9 ☐

Other

10 ☐

Natural disasters - floods, earthquakes, drought, etc.

11 ☐

Other

12 ☐

15. *Main actor*
(a) Nationality (write in)

13 ☐
14 ☐

(b) Position/sphere:
01 Symbolic/nominal head of state

15 ☐
16 ☐

02 Chief executive, prime minister, president

03 Other executive, government minister, cabinet, the government as a whole

04 Legislature, parliament, congress, etc. or committee thereof

05 Ruling party

06 Legitimate political opposition

07 Non-legitimate political opposition

08 Other politician (national)

09 Local government official or politician

10 Ambassador or diplomat

11 Military - regular forces of state

12 Military - irregular, guerrillas, terrorists, etc.

13 Industry

14 Trade unions, workers or equivalent, as distinct from management

15 Pressure group

16 Religious

17 Sports

18 Media - 'this paper', etc., the one being coded

19 Other medium, or media in general

20 Academic/education/scientific

21 Police

22 Judiciary/lawyers

23 Criminals/prisoners

24 Celebrities/show business

25 Aristocracy, royalty (in non-political capacity)

26 Nation(s)

27 United Nations

28 Other inter-governmental bodies, OAU, NATO, OPEC, EEC, etc.

29 Other international bodies, e.g. Red Cross

30 Ordinary people, citizens

31 Other

00 No human actor

(c) Quoted?
1 Yes
2 No

17 ☐

16. *Others actors* (up to three), as above
(a) Nationality
(write in)

	1.		2.		3.	
	18 ☐		23 ☐		28 ☐	
	19 ☐		24 ☐		29 ☐	
(b) Position/sphere	20 ☐		25 ☐		30 ☐	
	21 ☐		26 ☐		31 ☐	
(c) Quoted?	22 ☐		27 ☐		32 ☐	

17. *Themes and references* (Code '1' Present, '0' Absent, for each)
Nuclear arms proliferation/limitation

33 ☐

Espionage

Racialism, racial discrimination, apartheid   34 ☐

Religious or ethnic antagonism   35 ☐

Political independence (of any nation)   36 ☐

Economic self-sufficiency (of any nation)   37 ☐

Home country as benefactor to foreign country   38 ☐

Home country as beneficiary of foreign country   39 ☐

Aid to developing country(ies)   40 ☐

Development of Third World countries   41 ☐

Population explosion/control   42 ☐

Energy shortage/oil supply   43 ☐

Ecology, environment, pollution (not energy)   44 ☐

Human rights   45 ☐

Religious freedom   46 ☐

Freedom of speech, opinion   47 ☐

Individual freedom (other than speech or religion)   48 ☐

Torture   49 ☐

50 ☐

Subversion

Terrorism   51 ☐

East-West detente, coexistence   52 ☐

East-West division (political), Iron Curtain, etc.   53 ☐

USSR-China division   54 ☐

Rich-poor, developed-developing, North-South division   55 ☐

Social equality/inequality   56 ☐

Corruption in public life   57 ☐

* Imperialism/colonialism/neo-colonialism (on the part of any power)   58 ☐

* Socialism   59 ☐

* Communism   60 ☐

* Fascism   61 ☐

* Democracy   62 ☐

* Capitalism   63 ☐

* Totalitarianism   64 ☐

65 ☐

80 ☐

* These words only (or forms thereof)

65

Appendix 3: Sample Coding Sheet

Card 1
Col

Institution code	1 ☐	Picture Length	30 ☐	
	2 ☐		31 ☐	
			32 ☐	
Item No	3 ☐	Event/Issue	33 ☐	
	4 ☐		34 ☐	
	5 ☐			
	6 ☐	Story type	35 ☐	
Medium	7 ☐	Location	36 ☐	
	8 ☐		37 ☐	
Day No	9 ☐	Relations	38 ☐	
	10 ☐			
General/Specialized	11 ☐	Topics	39 ☐	
			40 ☐	
Type	12 ☐		41 ☐	
			42 ☐	
Source	13 ☐		43 ☐	
	14 ☐		44 ☐	
	15 ☐		45 ☐	
	16 ☐			
	17 ☐	Topics (cont'd)	46 ☐	
	18 ☐		47 ☐	
	19 ☐		48 ☐	
	20 ☐		49 ☐	
	21 ☐		50 ☐	
	22 ☐		51 ☐	
	23 ☐		52 ☐	
	24 ☐		53 ☐	
			54 ☐	
Length	25 ☐		55 ☐	
	26 ☐		56 ☐	
	27 ☐		57 ☐	
	28 ☐		58 ☐	
			59 ☐	
			60 ☐	
Picture ?	29 ☐		61 ☐	

Card 1
Col.2

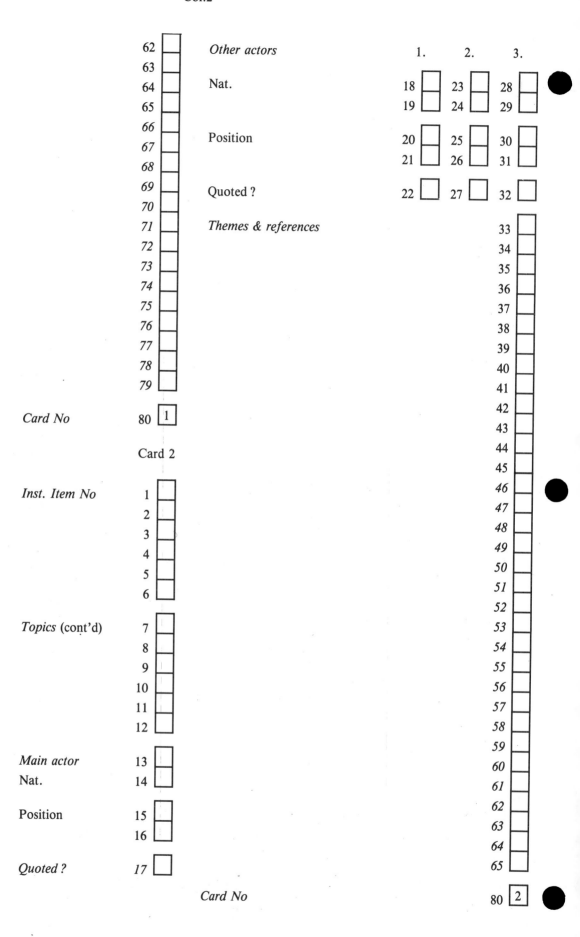

62	☐	*Other actors*		1.	2.	3.
63	☐					
64	☐	Nat.		18 ☐	23 ☐	28 ☐
65	☐			19 ☐	24 ☐	29 ☐
66	☐					
67	☐	Position		20 ☐	25 ☐	30 ☐
68	☐			21 ☐	26 ☐	31 ☐
69	☐	Quoted ?		22 ☐	27 ☐	32 ☐
70	☐					
71	☐	*Themes & references*				33 ☐
72	☐					34 ☐
73	☐					35 ☐

Other actors

Nat.

Position

Quoted ?

Themes & references

Card No 80 ☐1

Card 2

Inst. Item No 1
2
3
4
5
6

Topics (cont'd) 7
8
9
10
11
12

Main actor 13
Nat. 14

Position 15
16

Quoted ? 17

Card No 80 ☐2

33
34
35
36
37
38
39
40
41
42
43
44
45
46
47
48
49
50
51
52
53
54
55
56
57
58
59
60
61
62
63
64
65

Information is provided herein on the structure of the media and the actual channels chosen for analysis in the sixteen additional countries covered by the United States team.

LATIN AMERICA

Argentina

Argentina is considered to have one of the most literate populations in the developing world. There are almost 200 daily newspapers and a highly developed broadcasting system. Most radio and television stations are privately owned, although there are a certain number of government and universities stations. Since 1976, all of the media have been closely supervised. Two of the papers included in this study, *Clarín* and *Crónica* are popular tabloids with circulations of 450,000 and 250,000, respectively. *La Opinión,* although published in tabloid format, is a more serious élite-oriented paper with a circulation of 87,000. Newscasts from Radio Rivadavia, TV Eleven and Tele-Noche were also included.

Brazil

The daily papers in Brazil operated in the early 1970 s under government control. The two newspapers included here were subjected to less pressure thanks to their prestige, strong financial base and large circulation. *O Estado de Sao Paulo* is an independent paper with a circulation of 200,000. *Jornal do Brazil,* published in Rio de Janeiro, is Catholic-conservative, with a circulation of 170,000. News broadcasts were not included.

Mexico

Of the 200 daily papers, some twenty-six are published in Mexico City, including the two examined in this study. *Excelsior* is an independent morning paper with a circulation of 154,000. *El Universal* is a centre-left morning paper with a circulation of 174,000. Broadcasting is a mixture of private commercial and government cultural networks. The *TV Horas* news bulletin was also included.

AFRICA

Algeria

Until independence, all daily papers in Algeria were owned by Europeans and printed in French. In the 1970s, all private publishing was banned, leaving four daily papers, *El Moudjahid* was first published by the Front de Libération Nationale (FLN) in the 1950s and smuggled into Algeria from Tunis; it remains the only daily published in French. *Al Chaab* (The People) was founded in the 1960s and is printed in Arabic. Radiodiffusion-Télévision Algérienne, the only domestic broadcasting organization, is a state-owned but financially self-sufficient co-operative. An *Algiers TV* newscast of twenty-eight minutes was included in this study.

Ivory Coast

Of the two daily papers published in the Ivory Coast *Fraternité Matin* was selected for analysis. The official daily organ of the single party, the Democratic Party, it is published in French in the capital, Abidjan, and has a circulation of 30,000. Broadcasting is government-owned and controlled by the Ministry of Information. A *Télévision Ivoirienne* newscast of twenty-seven minutes was analysed for this study.

Kenya

Of the country's three daily papers, the two English-language papers were selected for analysis. The *Standard,* which once represented white settler interests, has a circulation of 30,000. The *Daily Nation,* a prestigious English-language paper in Africa, has a circulation of 90,000. Both devote about 30 per cent of their space to advertising. *Voice of Kenya* is the government-owned and —operated radio-television network, broadcasting mainly in English, Swahili and eighteen vernacular tongues. One radio newscast was included in our study.

Tunisia

Tunisian newspaper circulation is divided between the French and Arabic press, with four daily papers. *La Presse de Tunisie,* with a circulation of 40,000, and *L'Action* and *Al'Amal*, the French and Arabic organs of the Destour Socialist Party with 50,000 circulation each, were all included. A television newscast by *Radiodiffusion Télévision Tunisienne* was also selected.

Zaire

The six daily papers in Zaire are all printed in French, the language in which most publications appear. The two included in this study, *Elima* and *Salongo,* are both published in the capital, Kinshasa. *Voix de Zaire,* a half-hour radio newscast by the national broadcasting service, was also analysed.

Zambia

Zambia's two dailies are both published in English, the nation's official language. The *Times of Zambia* has a circulation of 65,000 and is published in Lusaka and Ndola, the copperbelt town. The *Zambia Daily Mail* is government-controlled and published in Lusaka. The Zambia Broadcasting Service operates all broadcasting under the Ministry of Information. A fifteen-minute broadcast by *Radio Zambia* and two channels of *Television-Zambia* were covered for this study.

MIDDLE EAST

Egypt

Egypt has seventeen daily papers with a total circulation of 700,000. However, the actual readership, as in other parts of the developing world, may be much higher, for papers are read aloud in coffee-houses and other public places. Radio also reaches a broad public under the state-owned broadcasting organization. *Al-Ahram,* the semi-official voice of the government, *Al Akhbar* and *Al-Gomhuria* were all included in this work as was a newscast by *Radio Egypt.*

ASIA

Indonesia

There are 120 dailies in Indonesia, mainly published in Bahasa Indonesian, but also in English and Chinese. The following dailies were included in this study: *Kompas,* with a circulation of 265,000; *Sinar Harapan,* with a circulation of 180,000; and *Merdeka* with a circulation of 130,000. One radio and one television newscast from the government-controlled broadcasting service were also analysed.

Thailand

Of thirty-five dailies, three Thai-language papers were selected. *Siam-Rath* has a circulation of 120,000, *Thai-Rath,* 600,000 and *Dao Siam,* 140,000. Broadcasting operates under both public and private ownership. One newscast from *Radio Thailand* and from *TV Channel Three* were covered.

EASTERN EUROPE

USSR

The USSR has 640 daily papers, published in fifty-eight national languages and dialects and nine foreign languages. *Pravda* (Truth), founded by Lenin in 1912, is the most important paper. It is based in Moscow, but simultaneously printed in a number of cities across the country. As the official publication of the Communist Party, it has a circulation of over 11 million copies daily. *Izvestia* (News), the official organ of the Praesidium of the Supreme Soviet, has a daily circulation of 9 million, while *Komsomolskaya Pravda* (Communist Youth Pravda) has a circulation of 10 million. *Vremya* (Time), the main newscast on Moscow television, was also included.

WESTERN EUROPE

Greece

Of 104 daily papers, twelve are published in Athens. One of those with the largest circulation, *Ta Nea,* a liberal evening paper, was selected for analysis. Broadcasting was not covered.

Iceland

Iceland is reputed to have one of the highest readerships of newspapers throughout the world. Of the six daily papers, most are the organs of political parties. *Morgunbladid,* a conservative paper, has a circulation of 40,000; *Thjodviljinn,* the labour movement paper, has a circulation of 12,000; *Dagbladid,* which is independent, has a circulation of 25,000. Icelandic State Broadcasting competes with the American Armed Forces station for audiences. Radio and television newscasts by the main network were included in our study.

Turkey

Of the 400 daily papers, *Milliyet,* a high circulation (330,000) morning paper, was selected for analysis. Broadcasting was not covered.

Appendix 5: Other Research and the World of the News

Robert L. Stevenson

School of Journalism University of North Carolina, United States

Introduction

One of the problems of any descriptive analysis of news content is external validity: to what degree are the results a function of methodological considerations, that are unique to the study, whether they be theoretical, pragmatically necessary or merely arbitrary.

While most of the analysis of this study has covered national media systems, we, of course, would like to extend the findings in two directions. The more important generalization is from the twelve day sample period to a vaguely defined universe of news at the turn of the decade. We are interested in international news in general at the time of the study. We are also interested, although probably to a lesser degree, in filling in geographic gaps in our study so that we will come closer to the title of this project, 'The News of the World', rather than the more prosaic but accurate, news of the media of twenty-nine countries.

Both of these purposes can be served by considering other studies which have also examined the nature of foreign news. To the extent that other research has focused on countries not included in our study, we can fill in some of the national gaps; and to the extent that other methodologies have produced compatible results, we can be more confident of the external validity of our project. Another benefit of a review of pertinent research is that we may find studies which addressed questions our study did not examine but which are important in the debate on international communications.

In this appendix, we present a very selective review of recent, published research dealing with international news. We have not taken into consideration any study published before 1970, on the assumption that foreign news has changed steadily and therefore some of the important research carried out in the 1950s and 1 960s probably is no longer valid. We also have examined only studies that are essentially comparable to ours, that is, quantitative studies that focus on foreign news in national media in terms of geographic origin, topic, source and the like. We also emphasize studies of countries that are not included in our research. Exclusion of a particular study ought not to be taken as an indication that we do not consider it important or competent but only that it did not meet the criteria defined above or, as surely must have happened, that it did not come to our attention.

Threats to external validity

Content analysis, the least satisfactory of social science methodologies, necessarily involves decisions that may or may not limit the drawing of general conclusions from the results. The most important of these are the sample of time, the sample of media and the unit of analysis.

Time. The problem of choosing a specific sample of time is twofold. On the one hand, the universe of 'news' is undefinable, so that any sample will be arbitrary rather than random. The news of the 1960s differs from that of the 1970s, and surely the news of the 1980s will differ from both. Some elements of the news, such as geographic origin, shift rapidly. But others, such as the newsworthiness of natural disasters and wars, are relatively stable. And still other elements, like the importance of politics as a news value, may well be permanent.

On the other hand, studies that attempt to extend a sample over too long a time period in hopes of avoiding the zigzags of daily headlines simply become unwieldy. Occasionally, one finds studies based on true random samples drawn over a year or even a decade, but in most cases such a sampling technique is impractical and based on an artificially defined universe. Unless one has some important reason for examining the 'News of 1971' or the 'news of the 1970s', such a cumbersome sample design serves no purpose.

Media. In our study, participants were asked to include the largest-circulation newspaper in the country, but beyond that, no specifications were established for what media were to be covered. The number of papers varied from one to six; in some countries, electronic media were excluded. In all countries, only daily media were examined, omitting weekly magazines, magazine-format broadcasts and even the Sunday editions of newspapers.

Nor did we specify a random sample of newspapers in countries where enough papers exist to make a reasonable random sample possible. But is a randon sample appropriate where circulation varies from paper to paper and where influence is not necessarily even related to circulation? One could argue, for example, that the *New York Times* and the *Times* of London, whose circulations are well below those of popular competitors, have national and even international influence far beyond what the numbers would suggest. And to equate a small daily in the American heartland or even the New York *Daily News* with twice the circulation, to the *New York Times*, Washington *Post* or Los Angeles *Times* is to ignore the most obvious differences among American newspapers.

Unit. If one chooses, as we have done, to count individual news stories rather than total space, then a one-column-centimetre filler at the bottom of an inside page gets as much weight in the analysis as the lead story on the front page. If one ignores position, as we have done, a front page banner headline with pictures counts as much as an item in a roundup of foreign news on the back page.

An immediate reaction to these considerations is that any methodological decision is arbitrary and, as a result any finding must be a prisoner of method. If this is the case, we have no power to generalize findings beyond the specifics of the time, media and units of analysis of each project. However, such pessimism is unwarranted. We can compare our results with those of similar studies to determine whether or not and in what way the arbitrary decisions influenced the outcome. In some cases, we can analyse our own data in different ways to address the same questions.

First of all, we will summarize other recent studies that meet the criteria outlined above. We will then report some test analysis of our own data in order to examine how results might differ if we had chosen other techniques of sampling and analysis. Finally, we will analyse how the gaps in our study could be filled in with other research, what limitations methodological decisions impose on 'our results and what added strengths and insights can be derived from similar studies.

Other studies

As noted above, this review is not intended to be exhaustive, either in the listing of studies or in the consideration of results. Instead, we will focus on research that is recent, compatible with our own in terms of methodology and purpose and complementary to our geographic coverage and findings.

Douglas A. Boyd and Donald R. MacKay, 'An Analysis of Ten International Radio News Broadcasts in English to Africa,' Medford MA, Tufts University (Murrow Reports), 1978.

This report is based on a monitoring of English language broadcast to sub-Saharan Africa on 12 December, 1977. Eight broadcasters were included: British Broadcasting Corporation (BBC), Radio Station Peace and Progress (USSR), Radio Moscow, Voice of America (VOA), Voice of Nigeria, Radio Canada International, Broadcasting Service of the Kingdom of Saudi Arabia, Israeli Broadcasting Authority, Radio Nederland and Radio South Africa Authority.

Twenty separate news stories were identified, none of which was carried by all ten services. Two stories, United States Secretary of State Vance's visit to Jordan and Syrian reaction to peace initiatives, were carried by seven services; the average story was reported on three of the ten services. The percentage of African-related stories ranged from 100 per cent on station Peace and Progress to 0 per cent on the Israeli broadcast. The medium proportion was 42-45 per cent. The two major Western broadcasters, BOA and BBC, devoted 68 per cent and 45 per cent respectively, to African-related news.

Jack B. Haskins, 'What We Know About Bad News,' in Joseph P. McKerns, ed., Proceedings of the Third Annual Communications Research Symposium, Knoxville, University of Tennessee, 1980.

This is an extensive literature review of 'bad news' —what it is, who selects it, who pays attention to it, and so forth. Haskins' conclusions are as follows:

Since 1950, the proportion of bad news in a variety of media, places and times seems remarkably stable, varying between 25 per cent and 50 per cent of the total news content (of American media). On the average, about one-third of all editorial content is bad news and about the same proportion can be described as good news.

Bad news is more likely than other news to get preferential display techniques, in both newspapers and television: the stories are longer, more likely to be portrayed in photographs, more likely to appear on the front page or early in the newscast.

The meagre amount of evidence available indicates that news magazines, newspapers and TV prime time shows do not reflect the world of real events very faithfully. More specifically, the most serious crimes are probably overrepresented in Houston and British newspapers. Bad news is also more likely to contain factual errors than other news.

Bad news appears to be overselected from the real world for inclusion in the news media and to be given more prominent display after selection. When given a choice between a pair of items on the same topic, London editors will overwhelmingly choose the one with more conflict. This is contrary to a general tendency among the public to be more reluctant to transmit bad news than good news in person-to-person transactions. The journalists' affinity for bad news probably derives from the conventional wisdom of the trade, being among the high-priority values transmitted implicitly if not explicitly from one generation of newsmen to the next.

Both the general psychological evidence and specific evidence on news strongly indicate that the public probably over-perceives the amount of bad news contained in the mass media.

The reading public can be aptly described as 'bad news bears.' Reader interest in bad news averages about one-fourth to one-third higher than for all other kinds of news combined. Bad news appears to stimulate interest in pictures even more than in article reading. War news appears to be the most interesting type of bad news, while minor crimes and other local bad news trivia are below average in interest.

While men may be more generally interested in bad news than women, the opposite may be the case in the under-35 age group, at least for certain specific types of bad news. Not much else is known at the moment, without further analysis of existing data. However it is suspected that bad news interest may be associated with low intelligence and with certain personality types.

Items with happy endings, optimistic titles, and problem solutions are almost invariably more interesting to the public than the same items without positive appoaches. The acceptability of such approaches to newsmen is unknown.

Ronald G. Hicks and Avishag Gordon, 'Foreign News Content in Israeli and U. S. Newspapers,' Journalism Quarterly 51:641-644 (1974).

This study examines eleven issues of 'rest day' papers, Friday in three Israeli papers and Sunday in the New Orleans *Times-Picayune,* from February to April, 1973. Results are analytical rather than descriptive and test several hypotheses about the nature of foreign news and foreign news flow. Results:

This modest study offers some support for the arguments that international news tends to be more factual and straightforward than analytical, that it is more concerned with coverage of élites than with common people, that it tends to be concerned with Big Power nations, and that the news flow tends to be one-way from these large nations to the smaller ones.

The study does not support the argument that foreign news tends to be negativistic in nature, nor that it is entirely all hard news. Insofar as rest day papers are concerned, the evidence indicated that positive news outweighs negative news and that a substantial amount of soft news is published,

While it may be argued that excessive emphasis on elites in foreign news coverage creates unreal stereotypes of other nations, the publication of substantial amounts of soft news (news of sports, amusements, cultural events, etc.) at least offers some prospect of giving readers a more balanced perception of what is going on in other countries.

John A. Lent and Shanti Rao, 'A Content Analysis of National Media Coverage of Asian News and Information,' Gazette 25 (1): 17-22 (1979).

The Survey is based on an analysis of six issues of the *New York Times* and *Washington Post* (excluding Sunday), six evening news programmes from ABC and one issue of *Newsweek* in September-October 1977. The major question was how much and what kind of news from Asia was available to average United States viewer or reader. Results:

If one depended on these four media for a week's coverage of Asia, he would probably receive about four full pages in both the *New York Times* and *Washington Post*, 2 1/2 pages in *Newsweek* and approximately ten minutes from ABC News.'

The range of topics 'probably does not give the reader viewer a very broad perspective on Asia. . . All four media used large percentages (ranging from 37.1 per cent to 82.5 per cent) of news that had implications for United States domestic and foreign policy. . .

The study also noted that during the sample week, the Associated Press 'A' wire (major domestic news wire) moved eighty-five different stories, measuring about 1,000 column inches, about Asia.

Denis McQuail, Analysis of Newspaper Content, Research Series 4, Royal Commission on the Press, London, HMSO, 1977.

This detailed analysis of nine national papers published in London and two in Scotland in November, 1975, is very similar to our study and reflects the similar intellectual heritage. Major conclusions are:

Even according to the relatively narrow definition of foreign content adopted for this study, the amount is generally very high. In none of the national dailies was the proportion of news space given to foreign news less than 9 per cent and in one case it was as high as 27 per cent . . .A majority of items (58 per cent) were about an action or event rather than about a statement or background information. An assessment of the level of 'predictability' of news shows 29 per cent of the items to be classifiable as about 'predictable' events and 36 per cent about 'unexpected' events. On the other hand, only 20 per cent of the items could be classified as having a ''dramatic'' character and 73 per cent were judged 'undramatic'. Fourthly, a general assessment of whether items involved 'good news' (e.g. constructive positive) or 'bad news' (negative, violent, etc.) showed the largest proportion (48 per cent) to be assignable to the latter category and only 26 per cent to be judged as positive. . .

The majority of stories (60 per cent) were about events occurring in a single foreign country, rather than having an 'international' character. Europe (including USSR) and the USA predominate as the regions most involved in all foreign news, accounting for 40 per cent and 18 per cent respectively, of the allocations of all items to regions. The EEC countries and the USA on

their own account for 32 per cent. . . News coverage is evidently much more closely related to 'nearness to home' and level of economic development than to the population or size of regions. One could interpret the evidence as indicating that the routine coverage of normal activities in much of the world is thin: outside Europe and the USA, it takes a major event to make news. . .

Most news or features concern either international diplomatic events, foreign domestic political matters or economic and trade matters (each about 20 per cent of all items). The next larges categories are crime and human interest, at 15 per cent and 4 per cent respectively. Different regions show different 'topic profiles.' For instance, Third World regions are lacking in 'human interest' and generally have more news of political violence. The USA has an above average proportion of news of crime, show business and human interest and least 'crisis' news. The Middle East leads in the latter respect.

C. B. Pratt, 'The Reporting and Images of Africa in Six U. S. News and Opinion Magazines: A comparative Study', Gazette 26(1): 31-45 (1980).

This heavily qualitative study analysed coverage of Africa for a sixteen-week period in 1976 in the three major American news magazines; *Time, Newsweek* and *U. S. News and World Report,* and three opinion journals; the *Nation, New Republic* and *National Review.*

Results showed that *Time* and *Newsweek* averaged about one story per week from Africa (fifteen and nineteen, respectively during the period studied). *U. S. News* carried thirty-four African stories in the sixteen weeks. The two liberal Journals, the *Nation* and *New Republic,* carried only one story per month while *National Review* carried twenty-three stories in the sixteen-week period.

The author concludes:

All the magazines project Africa as struggling against a cornucopia of divisive, malignantly centrifugal forces that are somewhat paralleled in immutability by the fate that had befallen the legendary Sisyphus in his bid to push a boulder uphill. As a baby continent, its livelihood is umbilically tied to the dictates of the economically developed nations.

The miniscule coverage of the continent, both in terms of geographic areas and typology, and the emphasis of the latter on violence, portray the continent negatively. However, it is true that some African nations are plagued by a destabilizing wave of crises. Also true is their dirt-poor characteristic. But it is indeed distressing to observe media staffers' rationalization of a Pavlovian response to turbulent, one-type news on the basis that it provides gratifications for reader needs.

Gehan Rachty. Foreign News in Nine Arab Countries, Medford MA: Tufts University (Murrow Reports), 1978.

One newspaper in each of nine Arab countries, Egypt, Jordan, Lebanon, Qatar, United Arab Emirates, Yemen Democratic Republic, Algeria, Iraq and the Syrian Arab Republic, was analysed for five days in December 1977. Only 'international news items', presumably events outside the country, were included.

Major results:

News from Arab states accounted for 44 per cent of foreign news; 36 per cent were from Western countries (including Japan and Israël), 15 per cent from other Third World areas; 5 per cent were from Eastern Europe and China.

'Congruence of political and economic interests is not an important determinant of the flow of information:' that is, the pro-socialist (or at least anti-Western) states did not differ from the others in their news orientation.

Western news agencies provided 46 per cent of the items; 26 per cent of the items were credited to Arab news agencies; 26 per cent were not credited.

'Hard news' (foreign, military, political, economic and human rights news) accounted for 87 per cent of the items; 'soft news' for 13 per cent.

'Positive news' accounted for 58 per cent of the items, while 43 per cent were categorized as 'negative'.

Wilbur Schramm, et al., 'International News Wires and Third World News in Asia,' Medford MA, Tufts University (Murrow Reports), 1978.

This is one of the most comprehensive and important studies of international news flow. Schramm and his colleagues examined the files of the four Western news agencies for five days in 1977 and issues of sixteen Asian newspapers for seven days overlapping the same period. Most of the analysis focused of Third World news, but for one day of the sample period, all news content was coded.

Even the preliminary, largely quantitative analysis addresses many of the questions about international communications our study examined. A book on the project expanding a qualitative and quantitative analysis promises to be a major contribution to the current debate. Some of the conclusion Schramm drew from a preliminary analysis are as follows:

. . . it is clear that the international wire services are delivering rather more Third World news to their clients in Asia than had been the general opinion. It is apparent also that the Asian daily newspapers, at least in so far as our sample represents them, are printing rather less Third World news from outside their own countries than had been the expectation.

The figures are striking. The four international news agency wires we have studied are carrying a total of 105,000 words, over 400 stories, of Third World news per day. The 'average' wire (which does not exist, of course, because there are great differences between wires) carries about 26,000 words, a little over 100 Third World stories, each day. The 'average' daily in our sample of fifteen Asian newspapers (an average daily is just as mythical as an average wire, for the newspapers differ even more than do the news services) carries twenty-three stories, a little less than 13,000 words each day, of Third World news from other countries.

Quite simply, these (qualitative)studies are showing that the apparent similarity of wire to wire, and wire to newspapers, in news selection, begins to fall away when we probe beyond aggregate data to individual stories. The wires are quite different, not only in total length and size of stories, but also in the particular stories they choose to cover, the kind of coverage they give to events within a country, and the 'angle' from which they approach some of the same events. All of them cover the Tripoli meeting and President Sadat's initiative, of course. All of them cover the Malaysian airplane crash. But there is considerable variation in what else they cover and how they do it.'

As part of the qualitative analysis, Schramm and his colleagues examined how the four wires covered India during the five-day period and how it was reported in the sample of Asian papers. 'The four wires carried 135 stories, about 35,000 words on India, an average or 8,700 words each. Thirteen Third World newspapers outside India carried 70 stories, totalling 24,000 words, with an average of 1,850 words each. The range, however, was very wide. One Asian paper carried no news at all from India in those five days. Two newspapers, the *New Straits Times* and the *South China Morning Post,* on the other hand, actually carried more news on India than did one of the wires. . . These papers, of course, had all four news wire services as well as other sources available to them'.

The study found that only one paper out of the thirteen carried a story, covered by all four wire services, about Prime Minister Desai's plans to visit Nepal for an official visit at the end of the week. In contrast, the most frequently used story (six newspapers out of thirteen) concerned recovery from an explosion at a nuclear heavy water plant which had put the plant out of operation and raised questions of sabotage. Five papers reported the work of a committee investigating President Gandhi's 'national emergency' and a violent protest at a textile mill.

'Seven Days in May: Major News Stories in the Press and on TV', Newspaper Advertising Bureau, Inc. (New York), 1978.

This report is part of a national study in the United States of 'How the Public Gets Its News', which included a personal interview survey of a national sample of more than 3,000 adults. Part of the project involved a content analysis of commercial network television news, morning and early evening programmes, for the period 14-22 March 1977, and a similar analysis of 300 daily newspapers for the single day prior to the interview during the same period. This analysis included only stories of more than five column inches and content categories generally consistent with national television news (i. e., excluding fashion, sports, state and local government). A second analysis focused on fourteen major metropolitan papers, two per day for the same seven weekday period.

Two parts of this report are pertinent to this study: the amount of foreign news and the diversity of coverage across and within media.

The coders counted 362 stories on the three networks, of which 46 per cent were categorized as foreign news; 12 per cent dealt with 'war, rebellions, arms control' and 33 per cent were classified as 'diplomatic, foreign events.' Thirteen events were covered with ten or more stories, nine of which were international news: Zaire invaded by rebel forces; delegation sent to Vietnam to investigate the cases of soldiers 'missing in action'; Indira Gandhi confronts controversy; President Carter approves ban on Rhodesian chrome; Italian man hijacks Spanish airliner; Left scores major victory in French elections; Soviets warn Carter on human rights stand; Lebanese leader Jumblatt assassinated; Japanese Prime Minister Fukuda visits Carter.

The newspapers devoted a far lower percentage to international news: 16 per cent of what was similar to our definition of 'main news section', less national and local news. Of this 4 per cent of the items were 'wars, rebellions, arms control', and 12 per cent were 'diplomatic, foreign events'.

The study found a high degree of overlap of coverage among the three networks: 71 per cent of fifty-two major stories were covered by all three, and 27 per cent were covered by two out of three. In the newspapers, however, far more diversity was apparent. The study quotes an extended comparison of the front pages of the three most influential newspapers —the *New York Times,* Washington *Post* and los Angeles *Times*— which concluded that '60 per cent of the time, the front pages of these three papers had only one or two of their eight or ten stories in common'. And only '20 per cent of the time, 33 days (out of 155), there was not a single story that appeared on the front page of all three papers, and on only 32 days did the three front pages have more than two stories in common'.

W. A. E. Skurnik, 'Foreign News Coverage in the Ivory Coast: A Statistical Profile of Fraternite-Matin.' Gazette 24 (4): 271-282 (1978).

This study is based on an analysis of the Ivory Coast newspaper for January and April 1975, and March 1976. Results:

About 15 per cent to 20 per cent of the overall news output of the paper was devoted to international news. 'This amounts to a daily average of 15.1 articles about 4.7 countries and subjects, and to a length of 213 column/centimeters'. The geographic origins (based on number of articles) are: Africa, 40 per cent; Europe, 24 per cent; Middle East/North Africa, 13 per cent; Asia, 6 per cent; the Americas, 7 per cent; world, 10 per cent. When calculated by total space, the proportion for Europe drops to 14 per cent while that of the middle East/North Africa increases to 16 per cent.

From 35 per cent to 40 per cent of the stories were attributed. The sources varied considerably over the three months,but on the average, 25 per cent were attributed to news agencies (including, apparently, the national news agency), 61 per cent to the paper's own staff, and 12 per cent to miscellaneous sources.

The author concludes that 'Fraternité-Matin seems to follow a pan-African news policy inasmuch as the largest percentage of its foreign news is devoted to events in sub-Saharan Africa. . . Articles about Africa seem oriented mainly toward two areas of news coverage: 1. the post-independence inter-African structure to which the Ivory Coast belongs and, to a lesser extent, the Francophone states of Africa, Zaire included; and 2. current events, in the case of the period under review, chiefly the problems of Southern Africa.'

'Finally, it is apparent that, at least from a quantitative perspective, dependence on predominantly European written news sources need not prevent a strong African accent in the editorial policy of an African newspaper's coverage of international news.'

Results

The easiest way to array the results of these and other studies in order to compare them with the findings of our research is to examine the geographic origins of foreign news. Most of the studies have divided the world along similar geographic and political lines. There are differences, notably as to whether the 'Middle East' includes the Moslem countries of Northern Africa and Asia, and deciding how to deal with stories that have no single geographic focus. But on the whole, the classifications we adopted for our study mirror those in other research, and allow us to compare our results with those of similar studies using different methodologies and to fill in some of the gaps of our project.

Table 1 shows the results of other studies, representing analyses of forty-two national media and news agency files, from ten separate studies. Some of the studies were described above; others, for various reasons, have been excepted only for data. The studies cover samples of media from one newspaper to a 'composite paper' made up of 15 individual papers, and time periods from one day to the equivalent of a full month. The samples begin as early as 1970 with some as recent as 1977.

Two kinds of comparisons are appropriate here. The first is to compare the results of our study of individual countries with studies of the same countries from Table 1; the analysis of Indian or Nigerian media, for example, with the comparable analysis by Pinch* who looked at one paper for five days in 1977. The second analysis is to compare the results of our project to the findings of other studies which looked at the media of other countries in the same geographic region. Here, for example, we would compare the results of our analysis of the Egyptian or Lebanese media with the findings reported by Dajani and Donohue from studies of twenty-one days in 1971 of a single paper each in Kuwait, Saudi Arabia and Syria.

If analyses of the media of one country at two points in time with different methodologies and different media samples produce essentially the same results, we can be confident that our results are widely generalizable to the national news media as they existed in the 1970s. If studies of national media systems not included in our study produce findings compatible with ours, we can be reasonably certain that our results are broadly representative of the various press systems of the world, not only the twenty-nine countries in the study.

Precise comparisons with other studies based on other criteria become more difficult. In fact, after several attempts, we have abandoned efforts to array the results of some of these studies into comparable categories of topic, theme or direction. The categories chosen by different researchers vary too much to permit us to recast them into a single table. However, we can examine the conclusions of the different studies to determine to what extent they agree and whether disagreements can be attributed to methodological differences.

In our own study, we can also make some important comparisons. In Table 2, we present some sample comparisons between analyses based on number of items and total amount of space. Although differences do appear when the data are divided into small subcategories, at the level of analysis by country, which is the one used in most of our report, the similarities are remarkable. It simply makes very little difference whether you count stories or measure total space; the results for each country are nearly identical.

What is the effect of including only the main news sections of two six-day weeks? In the sample of United States papers, we included two Sunday editions, thus making fourteen news sections in all, and coded all foreign news (although for the analysis in this report,we excluded this additional material) so that we could get a better picture of all foreign news available in the daily United States Press. In table 3, we compare frequency distributions from the United States sample as they appear in the report with those based on the total content of all fourteen issues. The results, on one hand, are predictable, but on the other hand, they also carry a warning for the interpretation of the results of our project.

Sports and other material usually found in special sections are under-represented in our study as is material not written to meet a daily deadline. By focusing on the main news sections of daily papers, we overrepresent the fast-breaking, event-oriented news, politics, foreign affairs and war. We underrepresent economics, sports, culture and 'soft news' in general. We also underrepresent, to a substantial degree, the amount of foreign news available in the United States press, and perhaps therefore in other systems also. The limited sample of the main news pages

---

* See Table 1, sources (pages 77).

Table 1 : Geographic origin. of foreign news (See list of sources at end of table)

Country	Source	Sample	No. of Stories	North America	Latin America	Africa	Middle East	Asia	Western Europe	Eastern Europe	General
North America											
United States UPI 'A' Wire	Rimmer	6 days, 1977	214	25 %	14	9	10	12	22	6	2
United States Wash. Post	Pinch	5 days, 1977	186	NA	7	11	17	25	29	11	NA
United States Network TV	Hester	1 newscast per month, 1972-76	610	NA	3	7	19	32	29	5	5
Latin America											
Peru	Pinch	1 paper, 5 days, 1977	195	12 %	33	4	9	6	31	5	NA
Venezuela	Pinch	1 paper, 5 days, 1977	134	17 %	30	0	10	6	36	1	NA
Africa											
Madagascar	Pinch	1 paper, 5 days, 1977	78	14 %	1	26	24	5	14	15	NA
Mali	Pinch	1 paper, 5 days, 1977	56	4 %	2	54	16	2	21	2	NA
Tanzania	Skurnik	1 paper, 1976	159	5 %	3	43	14	5	20	4	6
Guinea	Skurnik	1 paper, 1976	171	5 %	1	58	9	2	14	3	6
Ivory Coast	Skurnik	1 paper, 1976	247	1 %	4	49	19	2	14	0	0
Kenya	Skurnik	1 paper, 1976	264	7 %	5	41	18	6	17	3	2
Kenya	Pinch	1 paper, 5 days, 1977	212	13 %	5	32	18	14	26	3	NA
Nigeria	Pinch	1 paper, 5 days, 1977	58	7 %	2	53	10	5	22	0	NA
Nigerian TV	Golding-Elliott	28 programmes 1971-72	?	8 %	3	30	0	17	14	6	14
Tanzania	Pinch	1 paper, 5 days, 1977	129	3 %	2	73	12	4	6	1	NA
Senegal	Skurnik	1 paper, 1976	160	7 %	5	51	13	2	16	1	5
Senegal	Pinch	1 paper, 5 days, 1977	156	2 %	3	67	7	5	13	3	NA
Ghana	Pinch	1 paper, 5 days, 1977	79	4 %	1	58	14	10	8	5	NA
Reuters to West Africa	Harris	11 days, 1973	1792	12 %	4	32	6	14	26	2	4
Algeria	Dajani*	1 paper, 3 weeks, 1971	See next page	11 %	8	9	22	3	7	7	34
Tunisia	Pinch	1 paper, 5 days, 1977	91	8 %	0	8	46	4	32	2	NA
Middle East											
Kuwait	Pinch	1 paper, 5 days, 1977	211	8 %	0	4	54	7	21	6	NA
Syria	Dajani	1 paper, 3 weeks, 1971	See right	12 %	3	3	35	3	7	16	20
Egypt	Pinch	1 paper, 5 days, 1977	201	14 %	2	7	38	3	29	6	NA
Egypt	Dajani	1 paper, 3 weeks, 1971		14 %	2	5	35	4	6	12	23
Kuwait	Dajani	1 paper, 3 weeks, 1971	Standardised units, based on column inches	9 %	1	2	55	3	8	5	17
Lebanon	Dajani	1 paper, 3 weeks, 1971		10 %	1	1	54	6	7	9	12
Saudi Arabia	Dajani	1 paper, 3 weeks, 1971		15 %	1	2	36	1	7	4	35
Asia											
Composite wire	Schramm	4 wires, 5 days, 1977	2464	9 %	4	8	19	49	9	2	NA
Composite paper	Schramm	5 papers, 1 day, 1977	1977	19 %	1	5	6	48	19	2	NA
Indonesia	Pinch	1 paper, 5 days, 1977	125	8 %	2	1	10	59	16	5	NA
India	Pinch	1 paper, 5 days, 1977	79	6 %	0	5	15	59	9	5	NA
Singapore	Pinch	1 paper, 5 days, 1977	267	9 %	1	4	13	51	19	3	NA
Malaysia	Pinch	1 paper, 5 days, 1977	220	16 %	2	5	9	42	23	3	NA
Western Europe											
Eurovision	Golding-Elliott	28 days, 1971-72	345	9 %	2	4	4	21	41	14	5
Visnews	Golding-Elliott	28 days, 1971-72	371	9 %	4	16	11	23	27	3	7
AFP to W. Europe	Harris	5 days, 1975	1394	11 %	5	13	8	17	39	4	3

Table 1 : Geographic origin. of foreign news (See list of sources at end of table)

Country	Source	Sample	No. of Stories	North America	Latin America	Africa	Middle East	Asia	Western Europe	Eastern Europe	General
Western Europe											
Reuters to W. Europe	Harris	5 days, 1975		14 %	5	9	8	14	41	4	5
United Kingdom	McQuail	11 papers, 12 days, 1975	2483	19 %	3	12	10	13	35	6	2
Irish TV	Golding-Elliott	28 programmes, 1971-72	?	3 %	1	3	2	8	75	3	5
Swedish TV	Golding-Elliott	28 programmes, 1971-72	?	7 %	3	5	5	20	40	8	12
Eastern Europe											
Hungary, Czechoslovakia	Gerbner	10 papers, 1 week, 1970	?	8 %	14	2	5	10	25	34	NA

* In this study, Western Europe includes only Britain and France ; only China is included in Asia ; Turkey, Pakistan and Cyprus are coded under General.

Sources

Dajani, Nabil, and John Donohue, 'A Content Analysis of Six Arab Dailies', *Gazette* 19, 155-170 (1973).

Gerbner, George, and George Marvanyi, 'The Many Worlds of the World's Press', *Journal of Communication* 27, 52-66 (1977).

Golding, Peter, and Philip Elliott, *Making the News,* London and New York, Longman, 1979.

Hester, Al., 'Five Years of Foreign News on U.S. Television Evening Newscasts', *Gazette* 24, 86-95 (1978).

Harris, Phil, *Final Report of a Study of the International News Media,* Leicester : University of Leicester, 1977 (mimeo).

McQuail, Denis, *Analysis of Newspaper Content,* Research Series 4, Royal Commission on the Press, London, HMSO, 1977.

Pinch Edward T., *A Brief Study of News Patterns in Sixteen Third World Countries,* Medford MA, Tufts University (Murrow Reports), 1978.

Rimmer, Tony, 'Foreign News in UPI's "A" Wire in the USA : a Descriptive Analysis of Content for February 13-18, 1977', presented to the International Communication Association, meeting in Acapulco, 1980.

Schramm, Wilbur, et al., *International News Wires and Third World News in Asia,* Medford MA, Tufts University (Murrow Reports), 1978.

Skurnik, W.A.E., 'Foreign News Coverage Compared : Six African Newspapers', presented to the African Studies Association, Los Angeles, 1979.

Table 2 : Comparison of results of analysis by total length and number of stories in Mexican sample

	Column centimeters n = 136,070	Number of stories n = 2,436		Column centimeters n = 136,070	Number of stories n = 2,436
Geographic origin of news			*Main Topic*		
North America	20%	23%	International politics	10%	11%
Latin America	28	32	Domestic politics	12	12
Africa	3	3	Military, defence	3	3
Middle East	6	6	Economics	17	21
Asia	4	5	International aid	2	1
Western Europe	20	21	Social problems	1	1
Eastern Europe	9	3	Crime, justice	4	5
General	10	8	Education, science, culture	22	14
	r = .97		Sports	17	18
			Human Interest	10	12
			Accidents, disasters	2	2
			Other	1	1
				r = .92	

r = correlation coefficient between columns 1 and 2.

of a six-day week eliminated 45 per cent of the total foreign news available in the U. S. newspapers over the course of a week. The same may well be true for other, particularly Western, press systems.

But, of course, none of these studies tried to estimate how much news is available in the United States in general. For that, we would have to include the weekly news magazines, weekly and monthly opinion journals and a representative sample of the 10,000 or so general circulation magazines. And we would have to expand the sample of broadcast news to include the all-news radio stations, listener-supported talk stations and the new non-stop TV Cable News Networks.

The problem of trying to define the population of news available from which a representative sample could be drawn might not be so difficult in countries less saturated with mass media. And yet all of the studies examined in this appendix as well as our own faced similar problems and dealt with them in similar ways, by focusing on the news available on a daily basis in the fast media which emphasize events as they happen.

What do these various studies tell us about the three threats to external validity noted earlier?

Time. The studies earlier in the decade emphasized Asia, while those closer to our own typically found more media attention on the Middle East. This is not surprising given the nature of events over the decade. Those which used a limited sample of time, one day to one week, produced results strikingly similar to those which used a larger sample of time spread over a longer period. As long as the analysis is general, the conclusions noted in the main report about the adequacy of a relatively small sample are supported. We conclude that our findings are broadly representative of news at the end of the decade.

Media. None of the studies we examined attempted to define the population of news available to the public or even to draw a probability sample of newspapers. In all cases, the samples were purposive, generally emphasizing the influential, élite media. The number of papers, on the whole, is relatively unimportant; studies based on one newspaper were compatible with those based on four, five or six papers; surveys of élite papers generally produced findings similar to those based on a broad range of papers.

Some differences are apparent among media —broadcast media generally present a narrower range of geographic origins and topics— but as long as we keep in mind the warning that our study deals with the main news available in leading fast media, we conclude that our criteria for sampling media did not influence the results.

Unit. We opted to count numbers of stories rather than total space or some index of prominence for simplicity in computer analysis. Pragmatism, in this case, was a good guide because other studies based on space and our own methodological comparisons demonstrate that various approaches produce approximately the same results. As with earlier considerations, we emphasize the caveat that differences do become important when the sample is divided into small subsamples or when fine distinctions in content are made.

For each of these considerations, the same cautions apply to our study as to most of the others we have examined: the study represents the news available at the end of the decade in the main parts of fast media. The decisions whose influence appears, as it were, below the surface of the results, do not seem to influence the results. To argue that our study and other similar studies carried out in the past decade, are not representative of the total universe of news is to attack a straw man. The emphasis in the main body of the report has been on comparisons across national media rather than on projections to an undefined, and undefinable, universe of international news. From comparisons within our own data and comparisons with other studies, it is clear that these kinds of analyses have the strongest claims to external validity.

Other findings

Thus far, the examination of other studies has focused on the effects of arbitrary decisions that do not deal directly with results, media samples, time frame and unit of analysis. What may be said about other methodological decisions, some equally arbitrary, which are more closely tied to the results? Such decisions would include the selection of geographic origin of the news, identification of a single main topic and other evaluations of the nature of the content.

Geographic emphasis. Because most of the studies categorized the foreign news on the basis of its geographic origin, this is the one area where we were successful in arraying the results of other studies in a format that was directly comparable to our own. In some of the studies, criteria did produce differences, notably as to whether 'foreign news' could take place in one's own country and the way in which the 'Middle East' was defined. But on the whole, we can test our results with those of other studies and can fill in a number of important geographic gaps in our data.

The results are quite overwhelming in their consistency. Almost without exception, the data shown in Table 1, from forty-two countries, derived from ten separate studies, are in perfect harmony with the results of our study. The pattern is so strong and so consistent in all of the studies that one wonders how impressions to the contrary could have gained acceptance. And the pattern is simple: regional news is emphasized in the media of countries in all parts of the world with all kinds of political and media systems; in second place, behind the dominance of 'own region', is news from Western Europe and North America; the 'invisible' parts of the world are the socialist countries of Eastern Europe and parts of the Third World outside the immediate area.

This pattern allows us to predict, to a certain degree, the pattern of foreign news in media of countries not in our study. What would we expect from the media of France, for example? An emphasis on Western Europe with fair attention to North America and little coverage of Latin America and Eastern Europe. The press of Guatemala? Heavy coverage of Latin America with moderate attention to North America and Western Europe but little space for events in Asia and Eastern Europe. And so on.

Topic. Almost all studies of news describe where it is from and what it is about. The second element, what it is about, is harder to deal with than the first. Because so many different definitions of content, topic, or emphasis were used in these various studies, it is not possible to array them in a single table or to compare them directly with the list of main topics in our study. Nevertheless, some comparisons can be made.

All of the studies which deal with the category of main topic found, as we did, that news in the fast media emphasizes a narrow range of topics. Generally speaking, news is politics or, as Clausewitz might have put it, politics by other means, such as war and economics. Almost all of the news involves the affairs of governments and, where distinctions can be made, the affairs of the executive branch of governments.

Whether the news is full of 'bad' events or 'good' events or merely reports events themselves is largely a matter of one's perspective. Some of the studies found an emphasis on

Table 3 : Comparison of main section, six-day analysis and total paper, seven-day analysis in United States media sample

	Full sample n = 2,675	Limited sample n = 1,487		Full sample n = 2,675	Limited sample n = 1,487
Geographic origin of news			*Main Topic*		
North America	35%	26%	International politics	13%	18%
Latin America	6	7	Domestic politics	15	21
Africa	7	10	Military, defence	11	16
Middle East	11	16	Economics	14	9
Asia	13	14	International aid	1	2
Western Europe	17	16	Social services	2	2
Eastern Europe	7	6	Crime, justice, legal	9	12
General	5	5	Culture	7	2
	r = .94		Religion	2	2
			Science	1	2
			Sports	10	2
			Entertainment	1	1
			Personalities	4	1
			Human Interest	3	2
			Student affairs	0	0
			Ecology	2	3
			Accidents, natural disasters	3	4
			Other	2	2
				r = .84	

r = correlation coefficient between columns 1 and 2.

Table 4 : Evaluations of nations in foreign news

	Positive	Negative	Neutral, mixed
Egypt n = 2035	21%	13%	66%
Indonesia n = 1079	3	3	94
Thailand n = 800	4	6	90
Iceland n = 801	9	13	78
Turkey n = 298	9	3	88
Soviet Union n = 938	8	8	84
AP to Latin America n = 2250	5	2	93
Reuters to Latin America n = 521	9	2	90
AFP to Latin America n = 1326	2	3	95
United States n = 2675	10	7	84
Mexico n = 2220	8	8	81
Argentina n = 1707	20	10	70
UPI to Latin America n = 802	6	3	91
Brazil n = 1096	29	11	60
Tunisia n = 1628	7	5	88
Algeria n = 1137	7	10	83
Zaire n = 499	2	1	97
Ivory Coast n = 407	0	1	99
Kenya n = 821	7	8	85
Zambia n = 586	1	3	96
Reuters to Middle East n =	1	3	96

disruptive events —wars, violence, other kinds of hostility— but even this truism is not universally supported. What could be construed as positive developments in the affairs of nations —the election in then-Rhodesia, the Camp David accords, the summit between Presidents Brezhnev and Carter, the election in the United Kingdom also got heavy coverage in the media of most of the countries in our study. And most, although not all, of the other studies we examined found more good news than bad or at least bad events reported neutrally.

What we can conclude from our survey of other research is broadly supportive of our own findings: a strong emphasis in foreign news on the affairs of governments as they relate to politics and economics, an emphasis on disruptive events but by no means coverage of only that part of the human drama. And, of course, we must remember our caution that our study and most of the others excluded exactly those parts of the media and even certain media themselves where a broader, more thoughtful, and perhaps more positive, approach to foreign news is emphasized.

Evaluations. As the qualitative analysis in our study makes clear, the same event can appear very different when filtered through the national news agencies and editors of different countries. Even the most cursory reading of the press of different countries shows how different the world appears from varying perspectives. Is the news essentially negative, as is often charged, or is bias, like beauty, more in the eye of the beholder?

Our study did not address this question directly. In the United States contribution to the project, we added a code which characterized the presentation of each nation in the news as positive, negative or mixed; that is, the interpretation would depend on the perspective or passions of the reader. A few of the other studies also looked at this aspect of news.

It is not easy to decide whether the news is really good or bad. If we are to avoid the problem of reflecting our own personal prejudices, a point we have made in urging a reconsideration of bias in the news*, we need to formulate explicit rules that are widely agreed on and to follow them carefully. With our coders who were working in almost a dozen languages, we developed a set of rules but also offered the following rule of thumb: would an enemy of the country you are evaluating agree with the categorization within that country as 'positive' or 'negative'? If you cannot be sure, then you must assume that different people would see the story differently and categorize it as 'mixed' or 'neutral'. This is an artificial perspective, of course, but reliability of measurement is essential for any research.

When we remove our own perspectives from an evaluation of the news, as we have done in Table 4, the results show that news is for the most part neither good nor bad; mostly it is

---

* Robert L. Stevenson and Mark T. Greene, 'A Reconsideration of Bias in the News,' *Journalism Quarterly* 57: 115-121 (1980).

neutral, and where direction is involved, it is sometimes even more positive than negative. This finding is consistent with several of the other studies we looked at that also demonstrated the reliability of their observations.

Why, then, does just about everyone feel that the media are biased against his or her candidate, his or her country? The reason seems to be that, as our study of bias argued, news which is not compatible with our expectations is seen as biased and negative. The phenomenon is not new, of course. Walter Lippmann, in his classic study, *Public Opinion,* written a half century ago, argued that we usually define in our heads, then see, rather than the other way around. His observation has been supported in most research since then, including the United States study here which shows that most coverage of foreign news in the media of most countries is essentially neutral.

Conclusions

In this appendix, we have considered more than a dozen studies of foreign news. All were relatively recent, competently executed and addressed to the same broad considerations that inspired our study. The purpose of looking at other research was twofold: to test our study against others that approached methodological and substantive questions somewhat differently, and to see what gaps in our study could be filled in by colleagues who have also been concerned with some of the same problems in international communication.

Across a wide range of methodological and substantive considerations, we found support for our study. The specifics of our research design, time and media samples, unit of analysis, definitions of coding categories, do not appear to have influenced the outcome beyond the limitations we have noted. Where direct comparisons can be made with other studies, these other studies consistently supported our conclusions. From this wide-ranging survey of studies, we offer the following generalizations:

1. Geographic proximity is the overwhelming factor in foreign news. Regional news dominates news from all other parts of the world. The 'invisible' parts of the globe as locations for international news events are generally the socialist world, and alternating areas of the Third World.

2. Foreign news is mostly political news and associated topics of economics, military and diplomatic activity. Disruptive events do get heavy coverage but by no means the only coverage. Positive developments figure prominently in foreign news even though 'bad news' does attract readers and is generally considered newsworthy by journalists.

3. 'Bias' is largely in the eye of the reader. Most news does not single out any country or group of countries for negative coverage. Most news is essentially neutral, and when evaluation is presented, coverage is generally balanced between favorable and negative.

Appendix 6: The News of the World in Four Major Wire Services

A Study of Selected Services of the Associated Press, United Press International, Reuters, and Agence France-Presse

by

David H. Weaver, G. Cleveland Wilhoit, Robert L. Stevenson, Donald Lewis Shaw and Richard R. Cole

School of Journalism Indiana University United States

School of Journalism University of North Carolina United States

About two-thirds of foreign news in the Third World press, and a great proportion in more developed countries, originates in the major wire services.(1) It is small wonder, then, that the big four Western services —The Associated Press, United Press International, Reuters, and Agence France-Press— are singled out for criticism in the debate about world news flow. The big four agencies are accused of monopolizing the international flow of news, of failing to serve the needs of the Third World, and of misrepresenting two-thirds of humanity to itself and to the rest of the world.

This report briefly examines the structure and functions of the major wire services and takes a close look at their foreign coverage in selected samples from wire news in 1979. Using methodology similar to that of the larger study reported in this volume, the report suggests greater balance of wire service coverage between North and South nations than claimed by the critics, but calls for re-evaluation of the definitions of news that seem to dominate much wire service coverage.

News definition and the emergence of wire news

Definitive histories of the major wire services have yet to be written. One Historian, however, correlates the rise of Western-style 'objectivity' with the development of wire news in the latter part of the nineteenth century in the United States.

Donald Shaw argues that marketing news to partisan newspapers of widely differing political views led to an emphasis on speed, presentation of facts without elaborate interpretation, and roughly equal attention to different points of view.(2)

Michael Schudson rejects Shaw's interpretation of the role of the American wire services in fostering objectivity in American journalism. Schudson argues that the notion of objectivity did not become central to journalism until the 1930s, suggesting that the general emergence of logical positivism and of the scientific method was the broad social force that produced Western journalistic 'objectivity'.(3)

In any case, it is clear that news written in the Western wire service style has been widely used around the world. For example, a recent study found that in Yugoslavia —a nation which has been a cradle of many of the ideas supporting a New World Information and Communication Order— press coverage of the United States comes largely from Western news agencies. Lee Becker and Paul Underwood found, further, that the Yugoslav papers did very little editing of the original wire copy. In tone and topic, the view of United States in Yugoslav newspapers was largely that of the Western wires.(4)

Alternative sources to the Western news agencies are widely available, however. Third World editors and national news agency staffs (staple users of the wire agencies) have access to the Soviet news agency TASS, the Non-aligned News Agencies pool, and a rapidly increasing number of regional and specialty news services. TASS is used in Eastern Europe and a small number of Third World countries, but the Yugoslav study cited above and recent work by Wilbur Schramm suggest the Western wires are still used substantially, even in Eastern Europe.(5)

International news distribution: The national news agencies

Ninety national news agencies, fifty of which are controlled by the government, are listed in the 1975 Unesco directory of world communications.(6) All Asian nations from the eastern Mediterranean to the Pacific had news agencies, except Cyprus, Kuwait, Saudi Arabia, Singapore, and Thailand. Of forty African countries, thirteen had no agency. Only five Latin American countries had national news agencies.

Since the publication of the Unesco directory, dozens of other national and regional agencies have emerged, many with Unesco encouragement. A recent survey found 104 government news agencies, a figure which represents 68 per cent of the world's nation-states.(7)

Many of the national news organizations also supply news to other news agencies. For example, the national news agencies of Zaire (AZAP), Congo (ACI), Chad (ATP), and the Federal Republic of Germany (DPA) supply news to Cameroon's national news organization (ACAP). The agencies of the German Democratic Republic (ADN), the Federal Republic of Germany (DPA), Romania (AGERPRES), Czechoslovakia (CTK), and Yugoslavia (TANJUG) supply news to the Egyptian agency (MENA), an important regional wire. The Tunisian news agency (PAP) exchanges dispatches with twelve news agencies, and Syria's SANA has agreements with fifteen news agencies.(8)

The news agency of the German Democratic Republic in 1975 had contracts with sixty-five foreign news services.

Romania's AGERPRES received news from thirty-six agencies. CTK of Czechoslovakia had fifty agreements.

Hungary's MTI had exclusive distribution contracts with seventeen foreign agencies. Poland's PAP had thirty-two external wire sources (9) and 5,200 subscribers, including 2,000 in foreign countries.

In a study in 1977, Phil Harris noted that the Ghana News Agency used twelve external wires, six of them on a regular basis. Five of the services were from the West, five from socialist countries, and two were services of Northern Africa.(10)

A major study of Asian prestige newspaper use of wire news found heavy reliance upon the Western wires for their foreign news, including news about the Third World. Wilbur Schramm's research, published in the 1980 *Mass Communication Review Yearbook,* suggested, however, that the Asian newspapers were regional and local in orientation, using an average of only twenty-three foreign Third World stories on a typical day. Non-Third World news use was significantly less.

The roughly 100 national news agencies, then, appear to be an important element in world news flow about which little is known. Edward Pinch found that about three-quarters of Third World nation-states (with Latin America being a major exception) channel wire service news through their national news agencies. The mass media in those countries, then, are not direct subscribers to external news services, making the national news agency a focal gatekeeper for external wire news.(11)

While little definitive published work is available about the structure and function of the major wire services in international information flow, several conclusions appear plausible: (1)the four major western wire services supply the great bulk of foreign news used by most of the world's mass media; (2) the Western wires supply a great deal more foreign news than domestic mass media use; and (3) the more than 100 national news agencies, primarily in the Third World, are in a position to play major gatekeeping and news-supply roles, although very little is known about the extent to which those roles are exercised in the present global communication picture.

Wire Service Coverage of the Third World for Western Consumption

A few published studies have looked closely at Western wire service coverage of foreign lands, particularly of their coverage of the Third World. A quarter century ago, Scott Cutlip analised the content and flow of the AP wires in the United States, finding that only about 5 to 10 per cent of state wire copy dealt with foreign news. Two decades later, Al Hester found that foreign datelines constituted about 20 per cent of the Interbureau wire. Hester also found evidence that foreign wire news was heavily oriented to European countries and that news about developing societies tended to emphasize violence, famine, and social disintegration.(13)

Others have argued that wire news is more balanced in foreign coverage than critics say, and that the problem lies in the news selection patterns of mass media editors.(14) Thus, the background studies suggest a need for much more extensive baseline data on wire service foreign coverage performance than now exists.

In addition to these studies concerning United States wire service coverage of foreign countries, many other studies suggest that general American media coverage of the rest of the world —especially the Third World countries— tends to be crisis-oriented and drawn to sensational and atypical happenings. Tattarian argues that there is an acknowledged tendency among Western media, including the wire services, to devote greater attention to the Third World in times of disaster, crises and confrontation.(15) Aggarwala concludes that most of the Third World news is negative and deals with such subjects as famines, natural disasters, and political and military intrigues.(16) Lent and Woollacott, in separate papers, support the crisis orientation of news from the less developed countries of the world.(17) Golding and Elliott argue that much of the coverage of developing nations is centred on nations subject to repetitive crisis or military conflict.(18)

Other scholars suggest that news about the less-developed countries of the world is likely to constitute a rather small proportion of all Western foreign news. Hester found that news concerning Western Europe predominated in the foreign news coverage of United States wire services and that Television 'news from Asia, Africa and Latin America was generally little evidenced, unless United States interests were directly involved.'(19) Gerbner and Marvanyi, studying foreign news coverage in nine countries, found that foreign news content constituted about 16 per cent of total news space for the *New York Times* in 1970, as Kayser found in 1951, and that only 3 per cent of American press coverage was devoted to central and southern Africa.(20)

In short, these previous studies and recent complaints of Thid World countries regarding Western news coverage led us to expect that the less developed countries of the world as a group would receive less of the foreign news coverage in the wire services we studied than would the more developed, and that the wire service coverage of the less developed countries would be more crisis-and conflict-oriented than would the coverage of the more developed countries.

Content analysis method: wire service coverage of other lands

A standartized content analysis scheme, developed primarily by Paul Hartmann at the University of Leicester and used by all of the national research teams working on the project described in the earlier report, was used in the wire service study. The Associated Press, Agence France-Presse, the Non-Aligned News Agencies Pool, Reuters, TASS, and United Press International were asked to provide files of their major international (regional) services for two types of sample periods during the first half of 1979. The four Western agencies responded, but TASS and the Non-Aligned News Agencies Pool did not, so the study does not include them.

The content analysis deals with these services:

1. The Associated Press (AP) Interbureau (IB) wire to smaller media in the United States;
2. The United Press International (UPI) state (regional) wire to smaller media in the United States;
3. The AP wire to Latin America;
4. The UPI wire to Latin America;
5. The Agence France-Presse (AFP) wire to Latin America;
6. Reuters wire to Latin America;
7. Reuters wire to the Middle East (Beirut);
8. The AFP wire to Francophone Africa.

The content sample for AP and UPI corresponds to the approach described in the larger report, while only the continuous six-day week 23-28 April 1979, was sampled for the other wire services. Coding procedures followed the common-core schedule described in the report. The full instructions and schedule can be found in Appendix 2.

Findings

The structure of western wire service international news.
Tables 1 to 8 reveal the amount, location and kind of international news being carried by selected services of the Associated Press, United Press International, Reuters, and Agence France-Presse during sampled days in the spring of 1979. As in the main report on newspaper, radio and television news, these figures must be interpreted with caution because of the problems inherent in any classification scheme that involves fairly abstract categories. In spite of such problems, however, these figures do provide a general map of the amounts and kinds of international news flowing through selected services of the 'big four' Western news agencies in the spring of 1979.

Average news day. Table 1 provides some idea of the amount of international news reporting available to subscribers of the AP and UPI regional wires in the United States, all four wire services to Latin America, and the services of Reuters to the Middle East (Beirut) and AFP to Francophone Africa. It appears at first glance that AP and UPI provide ten times more international news to Latin America than to small-and medium-sized news organizations in the United States. This is true, however, in large part because the domestic news originating in the United States is coded as foreign, or international, news on the Latin American wires. About one-fourth of the news on the AP wire to Latin America originates in the United States and nearly one-third of such news on the UPI wire to Latin America is located in the United States. But nearly 40 per cent of the news on both these wires is located in Latin American countries, the figures in Table 1 suggest that a large amount of international news is available each day for use by subscribers en Latin America and Francophone Africa, a moderate amount to subscribers in the Middle East, and a modest amount to smaller media in the United States.

Judging from these figures, and the other studies referred to earlier in this report, there is little problem with the sheer amount of international news available to various national news agencies and media. In fact, there is evidence from earlier studies that the Western wires supply a great deal more foreign news than domestic media in most countries can, or do, use.(21)

In the main report, the press systems with a large amount of international news reporting include those of countries in Latin America and Africa, areas that receive large amounts of wire service international news. The press systems of at least two countries in the Middle East (Egypt and Iran) contain relatively small amounts of international news, matched by small amounts of foreign news in the wires serving those nations. Thus, there does appear to be at least a rough correlation between the amount of Western wire service international news flowing into a region of the world and the amount of international news in the press of that region.

Type of story. Table 2 shows that in the United States Regional wires of AP and UPI, the bulk of international news reporting concerned foreign news abroad, as was true in the press systems of most of the countries included in the main report. Because the stories of the other wire services were not coded into these categories, it was not possible to tell if this is a common pattern, but the international news content of the press systems analysed in the main report leads us to suspect that it is. Roughly half of the AP and UPI international news stories concerned relations between states, and the percentage of such news in the U.S. press analysed in the main report (42 per cent) closely reflects that proportion, suggesting again that there is a correlation between the amount of wire service international news and the amount of such news in the press of a given country or region.

Table 1 : Amount of international wire news on a average day

	Number of stories	Length column centimeters
AP regional wire to United States	17	250
UPI regional wire to United States	12	236
AP to Latin America	125	2,962
UPI to Latin America	134	2,626
AFP to Latin America	222	3,844
Reuters to Latin America	87	2,010
Reuters to Middle East	59	457
AFP to Francophone Africa	160	2,864

Table 2 : Type of Wire Service Story

	Home news abroad	Foreign news at home	Foreign news abroad	Other or uncertain	Percentage concerning relations between states
AP Regional wire to United States (n = 199)	18	1	81	0	41
UPI Regional wire to United States (n = 138)	21	0	79	0	49
AP to Latin America (n = 2,250)	—*	—	—	—	—
UPI to Latin America (n = 802)	—	—	—	—	—
AFP to Latin America (n = 1,326)	—	—	—	—	—
Reuters to Latin America (n = 521)	—	—	—	—	—
Reuters to Middle East (n = 346)	—	—	—	—	—
AFP to Africa (n = 944)	—	—	—	—	—

* These story categories were not used for analysing wire service news to countries other than the United States.

Location of international news. Table 3 presents the frequencies for location of international wire service news by region of the world. As is true of the press systems analysed in the main report, the single most important finding is that the Western wire-services going into various other regions (Latin America, the Middle East, and Africa) concentrate on foreign news about the countries of those regions. All four wire services to Latin America contain more news originating in Latin America than in any other region (from 40 per cent to 48 per cent, as reported in Table 3). Reuters to the Middle East contains far more news originating in the Middle East (55 per cent) than in any other region. Likewise, AFP to Francophone Africa countains more news originating in Africa (35 per cent) than in any other region. The AP and UPI regional wires in the United States do, of course, contain more overall news originating in North America than in any other region, but only foreign datelined stories were coded, so the percentages reported in Table 3 are negligible for North America. It is noteworthy, however, that the American regional wires carried nearly the same proportions of news originating in Asia and the Middle East as in Western Europe.

Taken together, these findings suggest that the big four Western news agencies are not ignoring Third World countries in favour of the more developed First World countries. As Table 4 shows, news from Latin America was ranked first by all four wire services going into Latin America, news from Africa was ranked first in the AFP wire to Africa, news from the Middle East was ranked first in the Reuters wire to Beirut and second in the UPI regional wire in the United States, and news from Asia was ranked second in the AP regional wire to the United States. These rankings, averaged across all eight wire services, suggest that Western Europe was the most heavily covered region of the world, with the Middle East a close second, followed by Latin America, North America, Africa, and Asia. Eastern Europe and the general world (news not occurring in one of the seven regions, or news of international organizations not clearly tied to a single region) were the two consistently least-covered regions.

Of course, the selection of the wire services for study must be kept in mind when discussing the relative ranking of different areas of the world. But there is evidence here to support Schramm's finding that the Western news agencies deliver much more Third World news than the Asian newspapers he studied chose to use.(22) There is also support for the claim, however, that Latin America is largely ignored in the Western wire services flowing into the United States the Middle East, and Africa. Even though geographical proximity appears to be the prime criterion for determining newsworthiness in the big four Western news agencies, just as it was for the press systems studied in the main report, political and economic ties and critical events undoubtedly play an important role in determining news coverage priorities. Thus, the Middle East and Western Europe are ranked high by all eight wires, regardless of their geographical destinations.

Topics in international wires news. Table 5 shows the proportions of news from each wire service devoted to each of eighteen major topics. As in the main report, only the main topic of each story is represented in this table; the subtopics are not reported here. The general finding, as in the main report, is that international wire news reporting equals politics. There is some deviation from this pattern in the four wires to Latin America, where economic matters and sports are emphasized more heavily than in the other wires, but it is clear that political and military matters comprise the bulk, of Western wire service reporting, leaving little space for cultural, religious, scientific and medical news. It is also equally clear, however, that the wires do not devote as much coverage to natural disasters and crime as has been claimed by some critics.

It appears that Reuters and AFP emphasize international politics (diplomatic and political activity between states) more than does AP or UPI, and the two regional wire services in the United States, emphasize domestic politics and military matters more than do the wires to the other regions, except for Reuters to the Middle East, which had the highest proportion of stories about military and defence matters.

The main report found that the press of the more developed industrialized nations concentrated less on political, military and economic matters than did the press of the less developed countries, but no such difference emerged in our study of the Western wire services. About the same proportion of news was devoted to the first four 'hard news' categories by the wire services flowing into the United States, as by those flowing into the other areas of the world (roughly 50 per cent to 70 per cent). Reuters to the Middle East and Agence France-Presse to Africa carried the most such news, while UPI and AFP to Latin America carried the least.

Thus, the topics of international reporting by the big four Western wires are quite similar, regardless of their destination. The only noticeable exceptions are more emphasis on economics and sports in the wires going to Latin America, and more emphasis on crime, religion and human interest matters in the regional wires going to media in the United States.

Topics in international wire news by region. A cross-tabulation was made of the topics of news by the region for each of the eight wire services included in this report. For reasons of space, however, the table is not reproduced here but is available from the Centre for Mass Communication Research, University of Leicester.

In the regional wires to the United States, there are only five foreign-datelined news stories originating in North America, and these five stories deal mainly with what can be called 'hard news' —politics, economics and crime. In the four wire services to Latin America, the news from North America is mainly about politics, economics and sports, with little mention of military matters and some coverage of crime and science. This pattern also holds to a large extent for Reuters to the Middle East and AFP to Africa, but with much less coverage of sports by both wires and much more coverage of domestic politics and crime by Reuters to the Middle East.

News coverage of Latin America by AP and UPI regional wires in the United States focuses heavily on domestic politics, with some coverage of international politics, crime, science and natural disasters. In the four wires going to Latin America, however, there is much less emphasis on domestic politics in Latin America and much more coverage of Latin American economics and sports. Latin America is nearly invisible in the Reuters wire to the Middle East, and in AFP's African wire the coverage of Latin American countries focuses on politics, economics, crime and natural disasters.

Turning to news coverage of Africa, it is apparent that coverage in the United States regional wires deals mainly with military matters and domestic politics. Whereas military and defence were nearly ignored in Latin American coverage, these topics constitute nearly one-half of the coverage about Africa in the AP and UPI wires going to smaller media in the United States. But for some unknown reason, the AP and UPI wires to Latin America concentrate much less on military matters in their coverage of Africa, and the same is true for Reuters and AFP to Latin America. There is considerable emphasis on African domestic politics in all the wires to Latin America and generally more coverage of international politics and sports from Africa than in the American regional wires. Reuters's middle East wire covered Africa almost entirely in terms of politics and military matters, and AFP's African wire

Table 3 : The location of international news

Source	Number of stories	North America %	Latin America %	Africa %	Middle East %	Asia %	Western Europe %	Eastern Europe %	General world %
AP regional wire to United States	199	1	5	13	18	23	28	11	1
UPI regional wire to United States	138	1	7	15	23	20	25	8	0
AP to Latin America	2,250	23	40	4	7	3	16	3	3
UPI to Latin America	802	30	40	3	7	3	14	3	1
AFP to Latin America	1,326	14	47	3	9	4	19	2	1
Reuters to Latin America	521	10	48	4	11	6	13	4	4
Reuters to Middle East	346	3	1	13	55	8	18	3	0
AFP to Africa	944	6	3	35	18	4	26	4	4

Table 4 : Rank ordering of regions in international news*

Source	North America	Latin America	Africa	Middle East	Asia	Western Europe	Eastern Europe	General
AP regional wire to United States	7	6	4	3	2	1	5	7
UPI regional wire to United States	7	6	4	2	3	1	5	8
AP to Latin America	2	1	5	4	7	3	7	7
UPI to Latin America	2	1	6	4	6	3	6	8
AFP to Latin America	3	1	6	4	5	2	7	8
Reuters to Latin America	4	1	7	3	5	2	7	7
Reuters to Middle East	5	7	3	1	4	2	5	8
AFP to Africa	4	8	1	3	6	2	6	6

* A « 1 » indicates that the largest proportion of news from each wire service was located in a certain region, whereas a « 7 » indicates that the smallest proportion of stories originated in that region. These rankings are based on the percentages in Table 3.

Table 5 : Topics in international news

Source	Number of stories	International politics %	Domestic politics %	Military, defence %	Economic matters %	International aid %	Social services %	Crime, legal %	Culture %	Religion %	Scientific, medical %	Sports %	Entertainment %	Personalities %	Human interest %	Student matters %	Ecology %	Natural disasters %	Other %
AP regional wire to United States	199	13	21	18	8	1	2	11	3	6	1	0	1	2	6	1	1	4	2
UPI regional wire to United States	138	25	28	14	4	1	0	13	2	4	1	0	0	1	4	0	0	2	1
AP to Latin America	2,250	21	12	3	18	1	1	8	1	1	1	19	1	1	1	1	1	6	4
UPI to Latin America	802	11	14	3	18	1	0	9	1	2	3	23	1	2	1	0	1	6	4
AFP to Latin America	1,326	12	18	6	16	1	1	9	1	1	2	23	1	1	1	0	1	4	3
Reuters to Latin America	521	30	14	4	14	1	1	6	0	0	0	19	0	2	1	1	1	4	2
Reuters to Middle East	346	35	18	25	7	1	0	7	1	1	0	0	1	0	0	0	0	5	0
AFP to Africa	944	32	16	11	15	2	1	8	1	0	1	5	0	0	1	1	0	2	3

concentrated more on economics and noticeably less on domestic politics in its coverage of Africa than did the other Western news agency wires. This pattern of focusing less on domestic politics and more on economics in covering the region to which the wire service is directed is also evident in Latin America. Perhaps there is so much coverage of domestic politics in the media indigenous to a given region or in the national wire services that the Western wires do not wish to compete with, or duplicate, such coverage. Or perhaps such coverage is politically more sensitive when directed toward the region to which it refers. It must be remembered, too, that in terms of absolute numbers of stories, there is not actually less coverage of domestic politics in those regions to which the wires are directed. Because of the larger number of total stories devoted to the 'home' regions by each wire service, it is only the proportions of news about domestic politics that are smaller, not the number of stories.

Coverage of the Middle East by the American regional wires concentrates on politics, military matters, and crime. This pattern is generally repeated in the other Western wire services studied here. With the exception of AFP to Africa, it is clear that international politics is more heavily emphasized in coverage of the Middle East than in coverage of North America, Latin America, or Africa. And in all eight wires, international politics is the most heavily covered topic in the Middle East, a finding that is not surprising in view of the Middle East peace negotiations between Israël and Egypt and the Iranian revolution. This finding is also consistent with the coverage of the Middle East in the press systems of other regions, as revealed in the main report, and suggests that the emphases in Western wire services are reflected to some extent in the press systems of other countries.

American regional wire service coverage of Asia concentrated on political, military, and prime matters, as was true for Middle Eastern coverage, but more attention was paid to human interest material in Asia than in the Middle East. The same general pattern was followed by the four wires to Latin America, with more coverage of sports by AFP and Reuters than by AP or UPI. The picture of Asia presented to the Middle East by Reuters featured international politics, military, and economic news, with a sprinkling of crime. AFP covered Asia mainly in terms of international politics, domestic politics and sports for its African customers.

Western Europe was covered mainly in terms of politics and crime by the American regional wires of AP and UPI, and there was noticeably more reporting of religious news than in the five regions discussed thus far. In the four wires to Latin America, coverage of Western Europe focused on politics, economics, and sports, as it did in the AFP wire to Africa. Only in the Reuters wire to the Middle East was military and defence news from Western Europe emphasized much. These findings are at odds with the conclusion in the main report that the Western European media systems show a far greater spread of interest in 'softer' news items than is apparent in either the socialist or developing worlds. And this discrepancy suggests that the big four Western news agencies are not very effective agenda-setters of news for the Western European media systems, perhaps because there are so many other sources of international information available to these diverse media systems.

News coverage of Eastern Europe concentrates heavily on international politics and religion in the American domestic wires, and on international politics, crime and sports in the four wires to Latin America. Economic news from Eastern Europe is stressed more by Reuters to the Middle East than by the other wires, military matters are stressed more by AFP to Africa. The emphasis on international politics by the Western wire services parallels the emphasis on international politics by the domestic media of the Eastern European region, and is in line with Becker's finding that the Yugoslav press relied strongly on Western news agencies for its coverage of the United States.(23)

Aside from news of these seven regions, there is really no coverage of other parts of the world in the AP and UPI regional wires to the United States, and in Reuters's wires to Latin America and to the Middle East. The AFP wires to Francophone Africa and to Latin America carry the most coverage of other areas of the world, and this coverage deals mainly with economic matters and to a lesser extent with sports events. This pattern is partly reflected in the AP and UPI wires to Latin America, but UPI offers no coverage of sports and replaces that gap with news about military and cultural matters.

Thus, the major finding from all these cross-tabulations is that the Western news agencies consider politics to be the most newsworthy topic in news from all areas except Africa (where military matters prevail) and the 'general world' category (where economics dominate). Close behind politics are military, economic and crime news, regardless of the destination of the wire services. Once again, the evidence suggests that the topics of international news reporting by the Western news agencies are quite similar.

For some reason, however, there is generally more coverage of sports from most regions in the wires directed to Latin America than in the wires directed to other areas. And there is a trend towards more coverage of economics and less coverage of domestic politics of countries in the region to which a wire service is directed, perhaps because the press of a given region already contains much coverage of domestic politics or because such material is more politically sensitive than other kinds of news.

Finally, there is evidence that the big four Western news agencies are agenda-setters for the various national press systems, except in Western Europe where there appears to be much more 'soft' news (dealing with cultural, scientific and human interest subjects) than is carried by the Western wires.

Actors in international wire news. Just as the topic of politics dominates Western international news reporting, so politicians are the most frequently mentioned actors in the news, as Table 6 illustrates. Government figures are especially prominent in Reuters' wire to the Middle East and in Agence France-Presse's wire to Africa. Thus, the conclusion from the main report that international news in the press systems of twenty-nine countries is comprised of political news with political actors is supported by this analysis of eight Western wires.

The only other actor categories to receive double-digit percentages were those of military figures (especially irregular military or terrorists in the American wires) sports personalities (in the wires to Latin America), and ordinary people (in the American wires). Ordinary people were also featured in the reporting by the press of Australia, the Soviet Union, the Federal Republic of Germany, Greece, Iceland, the Netherlands, the United States and Thailand, as pointed out in the main report. Such ordinary people and citizens included Vietnamese refugees, the Harrisburg, Pennsylvania, inhabitants, and Iranian demonstrators.

These parallel findings once again suggest that what is emphasized in the Western news agencies is also, to some extent, what is emphasized in the press systems of many countries. Whether this is because the press systems take the lead from the wire services, or because the wires pick up stories from the press systems, is not clear from our data, which have been collected for a single period in time. But it seems likely from past studies and from our knowledge of how wire service

Table 6 : Actors in international wire service news

	Head of state/government	Other leading govt	Non-legitimate opposition	Other legitimate govt	Local govt. official	Diplomat/ambassador	Regular military	Irregular military terrorists	Industry	Workers, unions	Pressure groups	Religious	Sports	Media	Academic, scientific	Police	Judiciary/lawyers	Criminals/prisoners	Celebrities/show biz	Aristocracy/royalty	Nation(s)	United Nations	Other inter-govt bodies	Other international bodies	Ordinary people, citizens	Other	No human actor
	%	%	%	%	%	%	%	%	%	%	%	%	%	%	%	%	%	%	%	%	%	%	%	%	%	%	%
AP regional wire to United States (n = 199)	17	10	1	2	1	1	5	12	2	1	1	3	0	4	3	0	1	3	1	1	1	1	3	0	19	2	4
UPI regional wire to United States (n = 138)	28	15	0	7	0	1	6	11	0	1	1	1	0	1	1	1	1	1	1	1	3	0	1	0	15	1	3
AP to Latin America (n = 2,250)	7	17	1	3	1	2	4	2	8	3	3	1	21	3	2	1	1	2	1	1	3	1	1	0	6	2	4
UPI to Latin America (n = 802)	6	13	1	3	1	2	4	2	6	5	1	1	24	3	3	2	1	2	1	1	2	1	1	1	6	3	4
AFP to Latin America (n = 1,326)	6	18	1	3	1	4	4	2	5	3	1	2	20	2	3	1	1	1	3	1	4	0	1	1	5	6	2
Reuters to Latin America (n = 521)	8	20	0	4	1	5	8	2	6	3	1	1	18	3	2	1	1	3	1	0	3	1	1	1	5	1	1
Reuters to Middle East (n = 346)	15	42	0	2	0	1	11	5	4	1	1	2	0	2	1	1	1	2	0	1	1	1	1	1	1	1	2
AFP to Africa (n = 944)	14	29	1	4	1	3	6	2	4	1	1	1	5	3	2	1	1	1	1	0	2	0	3	2	1	2	8

news is used that the wires have more influence on the press systems than vice versa. Table 8 in the main report suggests that only four of the twenty-nine nations analysed obtain more than 50 per cent of their international news from the big four Western news agencies (Mexico, Iran, Egypt and Indonesia), and most of the rest receive 20 per cent to 50 per cent from them. But it is not clear what the next major source of international news for most systems (home news agencies or national media) is. There may be a kind of "two-step" flow —from the big four Western agencies, to home news agencies to various media— which masks the true influence of the Western wires.

Themes in international wire news. In addition to being coded in terms of length, type of story, location of news, topic of news and actor, each news story was also coded for the presence or absence of thirty-three 'themes and references' which tended to be a bit more detailed and illustrative of the orientations of the news than did the topics. Table 7 shows the three most frequently mentioned themes in the international news of each wire service. When these themes are ranked in terms of number of mentions in the top three lists of all eight wire services, the results are:

T e r r o r i s m	6 mentions
Political independence	4 ,,
Individual freedoms	4 ,,
Religious/ethnic antagonism	3 ,,
Energy	3 ,,
Third World development	2 ,,
Subversion	2 ,,

It is particularly striking that the first four themes in this list are the first four most frequently mentioned themes in the twenty-nine national media systems included in the main report (in the same rank ordering). This finding lends even more support to the argument that the Western news agencies are either agenda-setters for the national press systems of the countries included in the larger Foreign Images study, or that these news agencies are very sensitive, indeed, to what themes are being emphasized in the national press systems. As mentioned earlier, we think that agenda-setting by the news agencies is more probable than agenda-setting by the national press systems, but it is possible that both processes occur in a kind of reciprocal fashion over time.

Additonal evidence of the close correspondence between the topics and themes emphasied by the big four Western news agencies and by national press systems was found in a separate analysis for Latin América. Pearson correlations between the main topics emphasised by the four wires and the media in Mexico, Argentina, and Brazil ranged from .70 to .90 indicating that the ranking of topics by the news agencies and the ranking by the press are very similar. The correlations for the themes are weaker (from .31 to .68, with an average of .55), but still indicate a general similarity between rankings of the themes by the news agencies and the media of the three countries. (25)

A comparison of less-developed and more-developed wire news. In addition to the results reported above, we also carried out a more detailed comparison of the coverage of the more developed and less developed countries, using only the AP and UPI regional wire service sample to media in the United States.

Table 7 : The three most frequently-mentioned themes

AP Regional wire to United States	UPI Regional wire to United States	AP to Latin America	UPI to Latin America
Terrorism	Religions or ethnic antagonism	Other individual freedoms	Other individual freedoms
Religions or ethnic antagonism	Political independence (of any nation)	Terrorism	Third world development
Subversion	Subversion	Energy	Energy/Terrorism

AFP to Latin America	Reuters to Latin America	Reuters to Middle East	AFP to Africa
Other individual freedoms	Third World development	Terrorism	Political independence (of any nation)
Terrorism	Political independence	Religions or ethnic antagonism	Terrorism
Political independence/ Energy/pollution/Human Rights/North-South division/Socialism/Communism/Democracy	Aid to developing countries	East-West detente	Other individual freedoms

The data for this comparison were obtained in the same manner as the other data analysed in this report, and a 'pretest' sample from 5-9, February 1979, and 20, 22, 26, February and 7 and 16 March 1979, was also included. This 'pretest' sample represented one consecutive five-day week chosen randomly from the first two months of 1979, and one constructed week sample chosen from the first three months of the year.

In order to compare the amount and kind of regional wire service coverage of more developed and less developed countries of the world, it was necessary to divide the ninety-one countries included in our study into these two groups. This is, of course, a somewhat problematic and difficult task, given the absence of any 'official' list to serve as a baseline. Our classification was based primarily upon a North-South geographical dimension, with the more developed countries tending to fall into the northern hemisphere and the less developed countries tending to fall into the southern hemisphere. This classification follows the logic behind the first North-South dialogue conference on International Economic Co-operation held in Paris in December 1975.

We decided to put the countries of Europe and the USSR, North America, Japan, Australia and South Africa in the more developed (Northern) category because of their economic development status. We also included Greece in the more developed group because of its ties with the Western world. (See Table 8).

In the less developed (southern) category, we included Africa (minus South Africa), Asia (minus the eastern USSR), South America and Oceania (minus Australia). Yugoslavia was also included in this group, although it is a European country by any geographical standard, and because of its leading role in New World Information and Communication Order debate and in the Non-Aligned Nations movement.

Other debatable cases - especially Turkey, Israel, Hong Kong and Portugal - were classified according to their concern with the Unesco sponsored debate on a New World Information and Comunication Order. Of these four, only Portugal was classified as a more developed country. Israel was classified as a less developed country because of its comparative newness, its concern with developmental problems, and its sensitivity to the issue of cultural imperialism, especially in the form of imported television programming. (See Table 8).

The most frequently covered less developed countries in the 'official' wire service sample were Iran, Uganda, Israel, Egypt, China and Nicaragua. And the same was generally true for the pretest sample as well, with Iran dominating the list and Vietnam replacing Nicaragua and Uganda. (See Table 8). The frequencies of stories about the less developed countries of the world in Table 8 also suggest that most of these Sixty-six countries received some coverage during the four weeks we studied, even if this coverage was rather sparse.

Among the twenty-five more developed countries included in our study, Austria, France, the Federal Republic of Germany, the United Kingdom, Italy, Japan, and the Soviet

Table 8 : Frequency of United States regional wire service foreign coverage, Spring 1979

Less-developed countries (n = 66)

Location of Story	Prestest sample (n = 194 stories)	'Official' sample (n = 336 stories)
Afghanistan	0.5	0.6
Algeria	—	1.8
Argentina	—	—
Brazil	1.0	0.3
Burma	—	0.3
Cambodia	1.5	0.3
Chad	0.5	0.3
China (People's Republic)	3.1	3.6
Colombia	—	0.6
Cuba	—	—
Cyprus	0.5	0.6
Dominican Republic	—	—
Ecuador	0.5	—
Egypt	2.6	4.2
El Salvador	1.0	—
Ethiopia	—	—
Fiji Islands	—	—
Ghana	—	0.9
Guyana	1.5	—
Hong Kong	1.5	1.2
India	0.5	0.9
Indonesia	1.0	0.3
Iran	19.1	8.3
Iraq	—	—
Israël	3.1	5.0
Jordan	0.5	—
Kenya	—	—
Korea (Democratic People's Republic)	—	0.3
Korea	—	0.6
Kuwait	0.5	0.9
Laos	—	1.2
Lebanon	2.1	0.6
Liberia	—	0.6
Lybia	—	—
Malaysia	0.5	1.2
Republic of Maldive	0.5	—
Mauritania	—	—
Mexico	1.0	1.5
Mongolia	—	—
Nepal	—	0.3
Nicaragua	—	3.0
Nigeria	—	—
Pakistan	0.5	2.7
Palestine	—	—
Panama	—	0.6
Peru	—	—
Philippines	2.1	0.6
Portugal	—	—
Puerto Rico	0.5	—
Saudi Arabia	—	—
St. Lucia	0.5	—
St. Vincent	—	0.3
Sudan	0.5	—
Syrian Arab Republic	—	0.3
Taiwan	0.5	—
Tanzania	—	—
Thailand	1.0	2.1
Tunisia	—	—
Turkey	1.0	—
Uganda	1.5	7.4
United Arab Emirates	—	0.3
Vietman	5.7	2.1
Yemen (Arab Republic)	0.5	0.3
Yemen (Democratic)	—	—
Yugoslavia	1.5	0.6
Zimbabwe-Rhodesia	1.5	2.1

More-developed countries (n = 25)

Location of Story	Prestest sample (n = 194 stories)	'Official' sample (n = 336 stories)
Australia	0.5	0.9
Austria	0.5	4.0
Belgium	—	0.6
Canada	0.5	0.9
Czechoslovakia	—	0.6
Denmark	—	—
France	1.5	4.2
Germany (Democratic Republic)	—	—
Germany (Federal Republic)	—	1.2
Greece	—	0.3
Hungary	—	—
Ireland	0.5	0.9
Italy	8.8	5.0
Japan	3.6	3.0
Norway	1.0	0.3
Poland	—	1.5
Portugal	0.5	—
South Africa	—	0.9
Spain	—	0.9
Sweden	—	—
Switzerland	1.0	0.3
United Kingdom	10.8	6.2
United States	0.5	0.6
USSR	2.6	7.1
Vatican City	2.6	1.8

Table 9 : Comparison of United States regional wire service foreign coverage - Number of stories

Number of stories from:	Less-developed	More developed	TOTAL
AP	107 (54 %)	91 (46 %)	198 (100%)
UPI	90 (65 %)	48 (35 %)	138 (100%)
TOTAL ...	197 (59 %)	139 (41 %)	336 (100%)

Corrected chi-square = 3.74, 1 df, p = .05

Table 10 : Comparison of United States regional wire service foreign coverage - Average length of stories in column centimeters

Average length of stories of:	Less-developed	More developed	F-Test significance
AP (n = 198)	17.1	12.1	p = .002
UPI (n = 138) ...	20.1	18.9	p = .56
AP and UPI combined (n = 336) ...	18.5	14.4	p = .001

Union received the most frequent coverage. As with the less developed countries, most of the more developed countries received some coverage in either the pretest or official samples. In fact, we were surprised at the number of countries receiving some coverage in the AP and UPI regional wire services during the four weeks we studied. There were considerably more countries represented (sixty-nine) than we expected to find in such a relatively short time period.

Number of stories. The AP and UPI carried significantly more foreign news stories from the less developed countries than from the more developed countries in the official two-week sample period, with UPI carrying almost twice as many stories from less developed countries as from more developed countries. (See Table 9). The same was also true for the pretest sample, where 117 stories were located in less developed countries and 74 were located in more developed countries. (The other three stories wer located in 'non-countries', such as the United Nations and the Caribbean).

However, it should be remembered that the less developed countries in our study outnumbered the more developed countries nearly three to one, so one would expect nearly three times as much coverage of the less developed countries as of the more developed countries, if an equal number of stories were carried about each country. But this seems to us to be an unreasonable demand to place inform the wire services, when many of the less developed countries of the world are far less populated than are the more developed countries.

In short, the sheer numbers of foreign datelined stories carried by the regional wire services do not support the claim that the United States wire services are ignoring the less developed countries of the world in favour of the more developed countries in their foreign news coverage.

Length of stories. Both AP and UPI carried foreign news stories that were, on the average, longer when located in the less developed countries of the world than when located in the more developed countries. (See Table 10). This was especially true for AP, where the average length in column centimeters of the foreign news stories about the less developed countries was one and one-half times as great (17.1) as the average length for more developed countries (12.1). (We could not compare the pretest sample with the official sample because length was not measured for the pretest stories).

In short, the average lengths of the foreign news stories in our sample do not support the claim that United States wire services are devoting more foreign news coverage to the more developed countries of the world than to the less developed countries.

Subjects of Stories. Each story was coded in terms of one main topic and no more than three subsidiary topics. The comparison of the subject matter of stories from more developed and less developed countries which follows is based on main and subsidiary topics combined. All differences noted between more developed and less developed countries are significant to the .05 level or beyond, as measured by the chi-square test.

The bulk of the regional wire service coverage for both more developed and less developed countries was about diplomatic and political activity between states, internal conflict or crisis,

Table 11 : Comparison of subject matter of United States regional wire service foreign coverage, Spring 1979

Topics of wire Service stories	Percentage of stories from more-developed countries * (n = 139)	Percentage of stories from less-developed countries (n = 197)	Percentage of all stories in official sample (n = 336)	Chi-square significance between more and less-developed countries
Politics				
1. Diplomatic/political activity between states	34.5	48.3	42.6	.004
2. Internal conflict or crisis	13.7	46.7	33.0	.0001
3. Elections, campaigns, appointments, government changes	15.1	10.1	12.2	.27
4. Other political, including legislation	1.4	3.0	2.4	.45
Military and defence				
5. Armed conflict or threat of	10.8	41.6	28.9	.0001
6. Peace moves, negotiations, settlements	10.8	17.3	14.6	.11
7. Other, including arms deals, weapons, bases exercices	4.3	2.5	3.3	.59
Economics matters				
8. Agreements on trade, tariffs, etc.	3.6	3.5	3.6	.25
9. Other international trade, imports, exports	4.3	2.5	3.3	.21
10. Capital investment, stock issues (not aid)	0.7	0.0	0.3	.86
11. Stock exchange, share prices, dividends	0.0	0.0	0.0	N/A
12. Other economic performance, output, growth, etc	2.2	0.5	1.2	.39
13. Prices, cost of living, inflation, etc.	0.7	1.0	0.9	.68
14. Industrial projects, factories, dams, ports	4.4	1.5	2.7	.11
15. Agricultural matters, projects, crops, harvests, etc.	0.0	0.5	0.3	.86
16. Industrial/labour relations disputes, negociations, wages	3.6	1.0	2.1	.11
17. Monetary questions, exchange	3.6	0.0	1.5	.03
18. Other economic matters	0.0	2.0	1.2	.24
International/aid				
19. Disaster or famine relief	0.0	2.5	1.5	.17
20. Aid for economic purposes (e.g. industrial development)	1.4	1.0	1.2	.87
21. Military aid, weapons, advisors, training	0.7	7.1	4.5	.01
22. Other aid (e.g. education, family planning)	0.7	0.5	0.6	.64
Social services				
23. Social problems in general (health, housing, illiteracy, etc.)	3.6	1.5	2.4	.36

Topics of wire Service stories	Percentage of stories from more-developed countries * (n = 139)	Percentage of stories from less-developed countries (n = 197)	Percentage of all stories in official sample (n = 336)	Chi-square significance between more and less-developed countries
24. Educational provision	0.0	0.5	0.3	.86
26. Family planning	0.0	0.0	0.0	N/A
27. Other social services and social welfare	0.0	0.5	0.3	.86
Crime, Police, Judicial, Legal, Penal matters				
28. Non-political crime, police, judicial, and penal activity	14.4	3.6	8.1	.001
29. Political crime	9.4	17.8	14.2	.02
30. Non-criminal legal and court proceedings (e.g. claims for damages)	0.0	0.5	0.3	.86
31. Other crime/legal	2.9	0.0	1.2	.06
32. Culture, arts, archeology	5.7	3.0	3.2	.29
33. Religion**	10.8	1.0	5.1	.0001
34. Scientific, technical, medical	7.9	3.0	5.1	.12
35. International	0.0	0.0	0.0	N/A
36. Non-international	0.0	0.0	0.0	N/A
37. Entertainment, show business (except personalities)	0.7	1.0	0.9	.68
Personalities (not politicians)				
38. Sports	1.4	1.0	1.2	.47
39. Entertainers	0.0	1.0	0.6	.49
40. Others	0.7	2.0	1.5	.47
41. Human/interest, odd happenings, animals, sex, etc.	22.3	4.5	11.9	.0001
42. Student matters	0.7	2.0	1.5	.56
Ecology				
43. Energy conservation	1.4	0.5	0.9	.48
44. Pollution	0.0	0.0	0.0	N/A
45. Other	0.7	0.0	0.3	.86
46. Natural disaster (floods, etc.)	2.2	3.6	3.0	.68
47. Other	4.3	2.0	3.0	.42

* These percentages for stories about more-developed countries (and the percentages for stories about less-developed countries and for all stories combined) total more than 100 % because each story was coded into one main topic and up to three subsidiary topics. The percentages in this table are based on the combined main and subsidiary topic tables.

** These percentages for the 'religion' topic are based only on the main topic totals. Including the subsidiary topic totals would obscure the difference between the wire service coverage of the more-developed and less-developed countries.

armed conflict or the threat of it, peace moves and negotiations, elections and campaigns, crime and human interest and odd happenings. (See Table 11) In short, the wire services concentrated mostly on 'official' news — that which flows mainly from government and military sources.

There was very little news dealing with social problems, culture, education, health, family planning and other social services. And there was very little wire service news dealing with international aid and economic matters, especially agricultural projects.

Overall, it may stared that **the subject** matter of the regional wire service stories in general supports the claim that the Western news agencies do not report much about social and economic development as compared to political and military events. But is this tendency more pronounced in news from the less developed countries of the world as compared to the more developed countries ?

A comparison of the 139 stories from the more developed countries with 197 stories from the less developed countries indicates that stories from the *less developed* countries are significantly more likely than are stories from more developed countries to be about diplomatic/political activity between states, internal conflict or crisis, armed conflict or the threat of it, military aid, and political crime. (See Table 11 for exact percentages).

Wire service stories from the more developed countries of the world, on the other hand, are significantly more likely than stories about the less developed countries to be about non-political crime, religion, and human interest or odd happenings. (See Table 11 for exact percentages).

These trends are generally supported by the pretest data. Significantly more stories from the *less developed* countries focus on elections, political violence, internal conflict or crisis, and armed conflict than do stories from the more developed countries. And significantly more stories from the more developed countries concentrate on prices, labor relations and culture than do stories from the less developed countries. In addition, there are very few stories about social problems, education, health, the family and other social services from either the less-developed or the more developed countries of the world.

In short, our data on the subject matter of United States regional wire service foreign news coverage in the spring of 1979 supports those who claim that Western coverage of the less developed Third World countries tends to concentrate on conflicts and crises. The largest differences we found between wire service coverage of the more developed and less-developed countries were on the topics of internal conflict, or crisis, and armed conflict.

As mentioned earlier, previous studies and more recent charges by Third World countries led us to expect that the less developed countries would receive less of the foreign coverage by the regional wires we studied than would the more developed countries. But our data on number and length of wire service stories did not support this expectation. In fact, there were more foreign news stories from the less developed countries than from the more developed countries in both the AP and UPI regional wires, and these stories were, on the average, longer than those from the more developed countries. Of the sixty-nine countries reported on in the four weeks we studied, forty-eight of them were 'less-developed'.

Some will argue that this finding is not typical because of the time period we studied. The Iranian revolution, the conflict between Israel and some of her Arab neighbours, and the fighting in Uganda and Vietnam and Nicaragua did increase the number (and probably the length) of many wire service stories from less developed countries of the world. But we would argue that it is difficult to find a time period when such

events are not occuring somewhere in the world. Because of this tendency for armed conflict to be happening in some region of the world at any given time, our findings are probably more typical than they might appear at first.

Although our data do not support the claim that the less developed countries of the world are neglected in favour in the more developed countries in the foreign coverage of the two United States regional wire services, our findings do point out that Western news agencies focus on conflicts and crises when covering the less developed or Third World countries. This may be true, however, because there simply is more open armed conflict and crisis in these countries than in the more developed countries.

But even in the more developed countries, the bulk of the wire service stories we analysed concentrated on political and military activity and crime. Economic matters, international aid efforts (except for military aid), social services, culture, scientific and medical achievements, and ecological issues such as energy and pollution were all but neglected in the coverage of both less developed and more developed countries of the world in favour of the more 'official' news from governmental and military authorities.

These findings suggest that basic questions of news values among Western editors and reporters may be more fundamental and, in the long run, more important than are the amount and kind of coverage of less developed and more developed countries of the world. Radically different definitions of news from those that exist today might help greatly in promoting not only international but also intranational understanding and co-operation.

Qualitative Summary of United States Wire News. To give the reader a better sense of the flavour of the news flowing on the AP and UPI regional wires in the United States, the following description is provided:

Invasions and peace treaties, the comings and goings of world leaders, and revolutions and terrorist violence dominated Associated Press and United Press International regional wire service reports to America's small—and medium-sized daily newspapers during the study period.

The fighting between China and Vietnam, the meeting between Presidents Carter and Brezhnev in Vienna to sign the Salt II treaty, and the peace treaty between Egypt and Israel received the most extensive wire service coverage. The Middle East also figured prominently in the wire reports as the new Islamic government in Iran struggled to establish itself against domestic opposition. The overthrow of Idi Amin in Uganda by Tanzanian forces and Ugandan guerrillas dominated the news from Africa.

The affairs of a number of other nations also received extensive, if less continuous, wire coverage during the study period. Some of the most important wire stories in this category were as follows: the attack on the Somoza government in Nicaragua by Sandinista guerrillas; the visit of Pope John Paul II to Poland, elections in Spain, the United Kingdom, and the Soviet Union; and terrorist attacks in Northern Ireland and Italy.

The wire services devoted extensive news and feature coverage to the summit between Presidents Brezhnev and Carter on strategic arms in Vienna. An AP story analysed the arms limitation treaty from the perspective of the balance of power between Soviet and North Atlantic Treaty Organisation (NATO) forces in West Europe, concluding that the treaty would not affect the military standoff in the region. A UPI story focused on questions about the Soviet president's health, quoting at length Soviet statements stressing Brezhnev's continued vigour. UPI also reported on how the city of Vienna copes with high-level summit meetings. Both wire services reported extensively the statements of Presidents Carter and

Brezhnev on the need for peace and improved United States — USSR relations.

AP and UPI covered as best they could the military conflict in Vietnam and Cambodia. The wire services reported from Thailand on military moves and diplomatic efforts to end the fighting. A UPI story noted that negotiations were likely to be drawn out. Another UPI story focused on the deterioration of Soviet-Chinese relations as a result of the conflict.

Peace rather than war was the theme of a number of wire service reports on the successful negotiations of an Israeli-Egyptian peace treaty and subsequent relations between the former enemies. AP provided extensive coverage on President Carter's shuttle diplomacy between Cairo and Jerusalem in his efforts to remove the final obstacles to an agreement. UPI reports stressed the substantial agreement that already had been reached. Both wire services also noted the hostile reaction to the completed treaty by the other Arab powers in the Middle East and subsequent moves by these powers to break off diplomatic relations with Egypt.

Summary of Main Findings. Our analysis of eight selected services of the big four Western news agencies (Associated Press, United Press International, Agence France-Presse, and Reuters) suggests the following conclusions:

1. Much more international news is available each day from the big four Western news agencies, especially in Latin America and Africa, than most domestic media can, or, do, use.

2. There is at least a rough correlation between the amount of Western wire service international news that flows into a region and the amount of international news in the press of that region.

3. Most of the international news carried by the Western wire services is about the region into which these services are flowing. Thus all four wires going to Latin America contain more international news originating in Latin America than in any other region. In short, geographical proximity appears to be the prime criterion for determining newsworthiness.

4. Western news agency international reporting concentrates most heavily on political actors, almost regardless of the region being reported.

5. The topics of international reporting are quite similar for all four news agencies studied here, regardless of their destination. Politics, military and defence matters, and economics dominate Western news agency international reporting, followed by crime and sports.

6. There appears to be proportionally greater coverage of economics and less coverage of domestic politics of the region to which a wire service is directed as compared to other regions in that wire.

7. The topics and themes emphasized by the Western news agencies tend to be the topics and themes emphasized by the press in many countries. In other words, the big four Western wires seem to be rather powerful agenda-setters for the presses of many nations.

8. The themes most heavily emphasized in international news reporting by the big four Western wires include terrorism, political independence, individual freedoms (human rights), religious and ethnic antagonism, energy, Third World development, and subversion.

9. A separate analysis of the news from 'more developed' and 'less developed' countries in the AP and UPI regional (state) wires in the United States shows that the less developed countries as a group receive more international coverage (more and longer stories) than do the more developed countries.

10. United States wire service stories about less developed countries were significantly more likely to deal with internal conflict or crisis, armed conflict, and military matters than were such stories from the more developed countries, supporting those who claim that Third World coverage is more conflict — and crisis — oriented than is First World coverage. This may be true, however, because there simply is more open armed conflict and crisis in Third World countries than in others.

11. In both more developed and less developed countries, the bulk of Western wire service coverage tends to concentrate on political and military matters, with very little reporting of cultural, scientific and medical achievements.

Conclusions

The findings from this study of eight wire services of the big four Western news agencies lead us to many of the same conclusions as those of the main Foreign Images report, which is based on the analysis of the press in twenty-nine countries of the world by scholars from thirteen different countries. There is a rather standard pattern of reporting, in terms of topics and themes, in the wires of the Associated Press, United Press International, Agence France-Presse, and Reuters, even though there are some relatively minor differences. And the heavy attention given to political topics and actors appears to be reflected in the press systems of the twenty-nine countries in the main report. Our analysis suggests that international news in the wire services reflects patterns of news definition similar to those which emerge in domestic news media coverage. There appears to be a reliance on 'officialdom' for news, clearly reflected in the concentration on politics and political actors. Equally strong, though, is a reliance on the exceptional event, as indicated by the frequent reporting of terrorism and military actions.

We agree that the problem in news reporting is not so much what to include, as what to omit, given the time, space, economic and governmental restraints on international news reporting. But even with such restraints, we agree with the main report that there is a need for seeing the world more broadly and for expanding the definition of news to include such subjects as international aid efforts, social services, culture, and scientific and medical achievements.

It is likely that one of the main reasons for the widespread use and influence of the big four Western news agencies is their ability to provide timely reports of important events around the world for a reasonable price. But use of these news agencies should not preclude use of other sources of news, such as regional news agencies and other national media, for coverage of topics and themes not on the agendas of the big four Western agencies. Our findings suggest that basic questions of news values among Western editors and reporters are fundamental to the pictures of the world presented in the press of many nations. As long as the big four Western news agencies continue to play such an influential role in setting the world agenda of news, such news values should be constantly questioned not only by those within the news agencies themselves, but also by others outside these organizations, especially other journalists and mass communication scholars such as those in IAMCR.

As is true in the larger report dealing with the press systems of twenty-nine nations, we have not studied the content of Western wire service news in detail. Instead, we have focused in the main on the structure, or the basic patterns, of international reporting by these agencies.
Differences in cultural perspectives and values are not reflected in our findings. Nevertheless, what is being reported may be more important than how it is reported. We have dealt here only with the what of Western wire service international reporting; the how of such reporting remains to be studied.

1. Wilbur Schramm, 'Circulation of News in the Third World: A Study of Asia', in G. Cleveland Wilhoit and Harold de Bock (eds.), *Mass Communication Review Yearbook,* (Beverly Hills, Sage Publications, Inc., 1980, p. 618.

2. Donald L. Shaw, 'News Bias and the Telegraph: A Study of Historical Change', *Journalism Quarterly,* Spring 1967, 44: 3-12. For a good history of the American news agencies, see Richard A. Schwarzlose, *The American Wire Services: A Study of their Development as a Social Institution,* New York, Arno Press, 1979.

3. Michael Schudson, *Discovering the News: A Social History of American Newspapers,* New York, Basic Books, Inc., Publishers, 1978 pp. 3-11.

4. Lee B. Becker, Paul Underwood and Dafna Lemish, 'Coverage of the U.S.: A study of the Yugoslav Press'. Paper presented at the 12th General Assembly and Scientific Conference of the International Association for Mass Communication Research, Caracas, Venezuela, August, 1980.

5. Wilbur Schramm, op. cit., p. 600.

6. Unesco, *World Communications,* New York, Unipub, 1975, pp. 3-9.

7. Leonard Sussman, 'Press Control: Is There a Middle Ground' Paper presented at the World Communications Conference II, Ohio University, Athens, Ohio, (Summer 1980).

8. Unesco, *World Communications,* op. cit., pp. 44, 54, 122.

9. Unesco, *World Communications,* op. cit., pp. 390, 438, 405 and 431.

10. Phil Harris, 'News Dependence: The Case for a New World Information Order', A mimeographed paper, Leicester, The University of Leicester, 1977, p. 237.

11. Edward T. Pinch, 'A Brief Study of News Patterns in sixteen Third World Countries'. Unpublished paper, 'Medford, Maine. Fletcher School of Law and Diplomacy, Tufts University, 1978.

12. Scott, M. Cutlip, 'Content and Flow of A news —From Trunk to TTS to Reader', *Journalism Quarterly,* Winter 1954, 31: 434-446.

13. Al Hester, 'An Analysis of News Flow from Developed and Developing Nations', *Gazette,* 1971, 17: 29-43.

14. John Maxwell Hamilton, 'Ho-hum, Latin America', *Columbia Journalism Review, June* (May/june, 1977), 16: 9-10.

15. Roger Tattarian, 'News Flow in the Third World: Some Problems and Proposals'. Paper presented at a conference on the Third World and Press Freedom at the Edward R. Murrow Center for Public Diplomacy, Fletcher School of Law and Diplomacy, New York, 12-13 May 1977.

16. Narinder Aggarwala, 'Third World News Agency'. Paper presented at a conference on the Third World and Press Freedom at the Edward R. Murrow Centre for Public Diplomacy, New York, 12-13 May 1977.

17. John Lent, 'Foreign News in American Media', *Journal of Communication,* 27 Winter 1977. Martin Woolacott, 'In Search of Bad News', *New Straits Times,* Kuala Lumpur, September 1975.

18. Peter Golding and Philip Elliott, 'Mass Communication and Social Change: The Imagery of Development and Development of Imagery', in E. de Kadt and G. Williams, (eds). *Sociology and Development,* London; Tavistock, 1974.

19. Al Hester, 'Foreign News on U.S. Television: Though a Glass Darkly or Not at All'. Paper presented at the biennial conference of the International Association for Mass Communication Research, Leicester, England, 1976.

20. George Gerbner and George Marvanyi, 'The Many Worlds of the World's Press', *Journal of Communication,* 27; Winter 1977.

21. See, for example, Schramm, op. cit.; and Harris,op. cit..

22. Schramm, op. cit..

23. Becker et al., op. cit...

24. This suggests that Schramm's finding that two-thirds of the foreign news originates in the major wire services may be unusually high, but it is difficult to know the origins of many news stories in the press of both the more developed and less developed countries.

25. For the complete set of correlations, see Robert L. Stevenson, Richard R. Cole and Donald Lewis Shaw, 'Patterns of World News Coverage: A Look ath the Unesco Debate on the 'New World Information Order'. An invited paper presented to the Association for Education in Journalism's annual convention in Boston, Massachusetts, August 1980.

ALBANIA: N. Sh. Botimeve Naim Frasheri, TIRANA.
ALGERIA: Institut Pédagogique National (IPN), 11, rue Ali-Haddad, ALGER; Office des Publications Universitaires (OPU), Place Centrale Ben Aknoun, ALGER; ENAL, 3 Bd Zirout Youcef, ALGER. *Periodicals only:* ENAMEP, 20, rue de la Liberté, ALGER.
ANGOLA: Distribuidora Livros e Publicações, Caixa Postal 2848, LUANDA.
ARGENTINA: Librería El Correo de la Unesco, EDILYR, S.R.L., Tucumán 1685, 1050 BUENOS AIRES.
AUSTRALIA: *Publications:* Educational Supplies Pty. Ltd., P.O. Box 33, BROOKVALE 2100, N.S.W. *Periodicals:* Dominie Pty., Subscriptions Dept, P.O. Box 33, BROOKVALE 2100, N.S.W. *Sub-agents:* United Nations Association of Australia, P.O. Box 175, 5th Floor, Ana House, 28 Elizabeth Street, MELBOURNE 3000; Hunter Publications, 58A Gipps Street, COLLINGWOOD, Victoria 3066.
AUSTRIA: Buchhandlung Gerold & Co., Graben 31, A-1011 WIEN.
BAHAMAS: Nassau Stationers Ltd, P.O.Box N-3138, NASSAU.
BANGLADESH: Bangladesh Books International Ltd., Ittefaq Building, 1 R.K. Mission Road, Hatkhola, DACCA 3.
BARBADOS: University of the West Indies Bookshop, Cave Hill Campus, P.O. Box 64, BRIDGETOWN.
BELGIUM: Jean De Lannoy, 202, Avenue du Roi, 1060 BRUXELLES. CCP 000-0070823-13.
BENIN: Librairie nationale, B.P. 294, PORTO NOVO; Ets. Koudjo G. Joseph, B.P. 1530, COTONOU; Librairie Notre-Dame, B.P. 307, COTONOU.
BOLIVIA: Los Amigos del Libro, casilla postal 4415, LA PAZ; Avenida de las Heroínas 3712, casilla postal 450, COCHABAMBA.
BOTSWANA: Botswana Book Centre, P.O. Box 91, GABORONE.
BRAZIL: Fundaçao Getúlio Vargas, Serviço de Publicaçoes, caixa postal 9.052-ZC-02, Praia de Botafogo 188, RIO DE JANEIRO (GB).
BULGARIA: Hemus, Kantora Literatura, boulevard Rousky 6, SOFIJA.
BURMA: Trade Corporation no. (9), 550-552 Merchant Street, RANGOON.
CANADA: Renouf Publishing Company Ltd., 2182 St. Catherine Street West, MONTREAL, Que., H3H 1M7.
CHAD: Librairie Abssounout, 24 av. Charles de Gaulle, B.P. 388, N'DJAMENA.
CHILE: Bibliocentro Ltda., Constitución n° 7, Casilla 13731, SANTIAGO (21).
CHINA: China National Publications Import and Export Corporation, P.O. Box 88, BEIJING.
COLOMBIA: Instituto Colombiano de Cultura, Carrera 3A n.° 18-24, BOGOTÁ.
COMOROS: Librairie Masiva, 4 rue Ahmed Djoumi, B.P. 124, MORONI.
CONGO: Commission Nationale Congolaise pour l'Unesco, B.P. 493, BRAZZAVILLE; Librairie Populaire, B.P. 577, BRAZZAVILLE (branches in Pointe Noire, Loubomo, Nkayi, Makabana, Owendo, Ouesso and Impfondo).
COSTA RICA: Librería Cooperativa Universitaria, Cuidad Universitaria 'Roderigo Facio', SAN JOSÉ.
CUBA: Ediciones Cubanas, O'Reilly No. 407, LA HABANA. *For "The Courier":* Empresa Coprefil, Dragones No. 456 e/Lealtad y Campanario, HABANA 2.
CYPRUS: MAM, Archbishop Makarios 3rd Avenue, P.O. Box 1722, NICOSIA.
CZECHOSLOVAKIA: SNTL, Spalena 51, PRAHA 1. (Permanent display): Zahranicni literatura, 11 Soukenicka, PRAHA 1. *For Slovakia only:* Alfa Verlag Publishers, Hurbanova nam. 6, 893 31 BRATISLAVA. *For the 'Courier' only:* PNS-UED, Jindrisska 14, PRAHA 1.
DENMARK: Munksgaard Export and Subscription Service, 35 Nørre Søgade, DK-1370 KØBENHAVN K.
DOMINICAN REPUBLIC: Librería Blasco, Avenida Bolívar, No. 402, esq. Hermanos Deligne, SANTO DOMINGO.
ECUADOR: *Periodicals only:* Dinacur Cia. Ltda, Santa Prisca n.° 296 y Pasaje Sans Luis, Oficina 101-102, Casilla 112-B, QUITO. *All publications:* Casa de la Cultura Ecuatoriana, Núcleo del Guayas, Pedro Moncayo y 9 de Octubre, casilla de correos, 3542, GUAYAQUIL; Casa de la Cultura Ecuatoriana, avenida 6 de Diciembre n.° 794, casilla 74, QUITO; Nueva Imagen, 12 de Octubre 959 y Roca, Edificio Mariano de Jesús, QUITO.
EGYPT: Centre for Unesco Publications, 1 Talaat Harb Street, CAIRO.
EL SALVADOR: Librería Cultural Salvadoreña, S.A., Calle Delgado No. 117, apartado postal 2296, SAN SALVADOR.
ETHIOPIA: Ethiopian National Agency for Unesco, P.O. Box 2996, ADDIS ABABA.
FINLAND: Akateeminen Kirjakauppa, Keskuskatu 1, SF-00100 HELSINKI 10; Suomalainen Kirjakauppa Oy, Koivuvaarankuja 2, 01640 VANTAA 64.
FRANCE: Librairie de l'Unesco, place de Fonenoy, 75700 PARIS. CCP 12598-48.
GABON: Librairie Sogalivre (Libreville, Port Gentil and Franceville); Librairie Hachette, B.P. 3923, LIBREVILLE.
GERMAN DEMOCRATIC REPUBLIC: Buchhaus Leipzig, Postfach 140, 701 LEIPZIG or international bookshops in the German Democratic Republic.
GERMANY, FEDERAL REPUBLIC OF: S. Karger GmbH, Karger Buchhandlung, Angerhofstrasse 9, Postfach 2, D-8034 GERMERING/MÜNCHEN. *For scientific maps only:* Geo Center, Postfach 800830, 7000 STUTTGART 80. *For* 'The Courier' (German, English, Spanish and French edition): M. H. Baum, Deutscher Unesco-Kurier-Vertrieb, Besaltstrasse 57, 5300 BONN. 3.
GHANA: Presbyterian Bookshop Depot Ltd., P.O. Box 195, ACCRA; Ghana Book Suppliers Ltd., P.O. Box 7869, ACCRA; The University Bookshop of Ghana, ACCRA; The University Bookshop of Cape Coast; The University Bookshop of Legon, P.O. Box 1, LEGON.
GREECE: International bookshops (Eleftheroudakis, Kauffmann, etc.); John Mihalopoulos & Son S.A., International Booksellers, 75 Hermou Street, P.O.B. 73, THESSALONIKI; Commission Nationale Hellénique pour l'Unesco, 3 rue Akadimias, ATHENS.
GUADELOUPE: Librairie Carnot, 59, rue Barbès, 97100 POINTE-À-PITRE.
GUATEMALA: Comisión Guatemalteca de Cooperación con la Unesco, 3a Avenida 13-30, Zona 1, apartado postal 244, GUATEMALA.
HAITI: Librairie 'À la Caravelle', 26, rue Roux, B.P. 111-B, PORT-AU-PRINCE.
HONDURAS: Librería Navarro, 2a Avenida N° 201, Comayaguela, TEGUCIGALPA.
HONG KONG: Swindon Book Co., 13-15 Lock Road, KOWLOON; Federal Publications (HK) Ltd, 2D Freder Centre, 68 Sung Wong Toi Road, Tokwawan, KOWLOON; Hong Kong Government Information Services, Publication Section, Baskerville House, 22 Ice House Street, HONG KONG.
HUNGARY: Akadémiai Könyvesbolt, Váci u. 22, BUDAPEST V; A.K.V. Könyvtárosok Boltja, Népköztársaság utja 16, BUDAPEST VI.
ICELAND: Snaebjörn Jonsson & Co., H.F., Hafnarstraeti 9, REYKJAVIK.
INDIA: Orient Longman Ltd., Kamani Marg, Ballard Estate, BOMBAY 400 038; 17 Chittaranjan Avenue, CALCUTTA 13; 36a Anna Salai, Mount Road, MADRAS 2; 80/1 Mahatma Gandhi Road, BANGALORE 560001; 5-9-41/1 Bashir Bagh, HYDERABAD 500001 (AP); 3-5-820 Hyderguda, HYDERABAD 500001. *Sub-depots:* Oxford Book & Stationery Co., 17 Park Street, CALCUTTA 700016; Scindia House, NEW DELHI 110001; Publications Section, Ministry of Education and Social Welfare, 511, C-Wing, Shastri Bhavan, NEW DELHI 110001.
IRAN: Iranian National Commission for Unesco, Seyed Jamal Eddin Assad Abadi Av., 64th St., Bonyad Bdg., P.O. Box 1533, TEHRAN.
IRELAND: The Educational Company of Ireland Ltd., Ballymount Road, Walkinstown, DUBLIN 12; Tycooly International Publ. Ltd., 6 Crofton Terrace, DÚN LAOGHAIRE, Co. Dublin.
ISRAEL: A.B.C. Bookstore Ltd., P.O. Box 1283, 71 Allenby Road, TEL AVIV 61000.
ITALY: Licosa (Libreria Commissionaria Sansoni S.p.A.), Via Lamarmora 45, casella postale 552, 50121 FIRENZE; FAO Bookshop, Via delle Terme di Caracalla, 00100 ROME.
IVORY COAST: Librairie des Presses de l'Unesco, Commission nationale ivoirienne pour l'Unesco, B.P. 2871, ABIDJAN.
JAMAICA: Sangster's Book Stores Ltd., P.O. Box 366, 101 Water Lane, KINGSTON; University of the West Indies Bookshop, Mona, KINGSTON.
JAPAN: Eastern Book Service Inc., 37-3 Hongo 3-chome, Bunkyo-ku, TOKYO 113.
JORDAN: Jordan Distribution Agency, P.O.B. 375, AMMAN.
KENYA: East African Publishing House, P.O. Box 30571, NAIROBI.
REPUBLIC OF KOREA: Korean National Commission for Unesco, P.O. Box Central 64, SEOUL.
KUWAIT: The Kuwait Bookshop Co. Ltd., P.O. Box 2942, KUWAIT.
LEBANON: Librairies Antoine, A. Naufal et Frères, B.P. 656, BEIRUT.
LESOTHO: Mazenod Book Centre, P.O. MAZENOD.
LIBERIA: Cole & Yancy Bookshops Ltd., P.O. Box 286, MONROVIA.
LIBYAN ARAB JAMAHIRIYA: Agency for Development of Publication and Distribution, P.O. Box 34-35, TRIPOLI.
LIECHTENSTEIN: Eurocan Trust Reg., P.O.B. 5, FL-9494, SCHAAN.
LUXEMBOURG: Librairie Paul Bruck, 22, Grande-Rue, LUXEMBOURG.
MADAGASCAR: Commission nationale de la République Démocratique de Madagascar pour l'Unesco, Boîte postale 331, ANTANANARIVO.
MALAWI: Malawi Book Service, Head Office, P.O. Box 30044, Chichiri, BLANTYRE 3.
MALAYSIA: Federal Publications Sdn. Bhd., Lot 8238 Jalan 222, Petaling Jaya, SELANGOR; University of Malaya. Cooperative Bookshop, KUALA LUMPUR 22-11.
MALI: Librairie populaire du Mali, B.P. 28, BAMAKO.
MALTA: Sapienzas, 26 Republic Street, VALLETTA.
MAURITANIA: GRA.LI.CO.MA, 1, rue du Souk X, Avenue Kennedy, NOUAKCHOTT.
MAURITIUS: Nalanda Co. Ltd., 30 Bourbon Street, PORT-LOUIS.
MEXICO: SABSA, Insurgentes Sur n° 1032-401, MÉXICO 12, DF; Librería El Correo de la Unesco, Actipán 66, Colonia del Valle, MÉXICO 12, DF.
MONACO: British Library, 30, boulevard des Moulins, MONTE CARLO.
MOROCCO: Librairie 'Aux belles images', 282, avenue Mohammed-V, RABAT, C.C.P. 68-74. *For 'The Courier' (for teachers):* Commission nationale marocaine pour l'Education, la Science et la Culture, 19, rue Oqba, B.P. 420, AGDAL-RABAT (C.C.P. 324-45); Librairie des écoles, 12, avenue Hassan II, CASABLANCA; Société Chérifienne de Distribution et de Presse, SOCHEPRESS, angle rues de Dinant et St Saëns, B.P. 683, CASABLANCA 05.
MOZAMBIQUE: Instituto Nacional do Livro e do Disco (INLD), Avenida 24 de Julho, 1921-r/c e 1° andar, MAPUTO.
NEPAL: Sajha Prakashan, Polchowk, KATHMANDU.
NETHERLANDS: *Publications:* Keesing Boeken B.V., Joan Muyskenweg 22, Postbus 118, 1000 BC AMSTERDAM. *Periodicals:* D & N-Faxon B.V., Postbus 197, 1000 AD AMSTERDAM.
NETHERLANDS ANTILLES: Van Dorp-Eddine N.V., P.O. Box 200, Willemstad, CURAÇAO, N.A.
NEW CALEDONIA: Reprex SARL, B.P. 1572, NOUMÉA.
NEW ZEALAND: Government Printing Office Bookshops: Retail Bookshop – 25 Rutland Street; Mail orders – 85 Beach Road, Private Bag, C.P.O., AUCKLAND. Retail – Ward Street; Mail orders – P.O. Box 857, HAMILTON. Retail – Cubacade World Trade Center, Mulgrave Street, (Head Office); Mail orders – Private Bag, WELLINGTON. Retail – 159 Hereford Street; Mail orders – Private Bag, CHRISTCHURCH. Retail – Princes Street; Mail orders – P.O. Box 1104, DUNEDIN.
NICARAGUA: Librería Cultural Nicaragüense, calle 15 de Septiembre y avenida Bolívar, apartado n.° 807, MANAGUA; Librería de la Universidad Centroamericana, Apartado 69, MANAGUA.
NIGER: Librairie Mauclert, B.P. 868, NIAMEY.
NIGERIA: The University Bookshop of Ife; The University Bookshop of Ibadan, P.O. Box 286; The University Bookshop of Nsukka; The University Bookshop of Lagos; The Ahmadu Bello University Bookshop of Zaria.
NORWAY: *Publications:* Johan Grundt Tanum, Karl Johans Gate 41/43, OSLO 1; Universitets Bokhandelen, Universitetssentret, P.O.B. 307, Blindern, OSLO 3. *For 'The Courier':* A/S Narvesens Litteraturtjeneste, Box 6125, OSLO 6.
PAKISTAN: Mirza Book Agency, 65 Shahrah Quaid-i-Azam, P.O. Box 729, LAHORE 3.
PANAMA: Distribuidora Cultura Internacional, Apartado 7571, Zona 5, PANAMÁ.
PARAGUAY: Agencia de Diarios y Revistas, Sra. Nelly de García Astillero, Pte. Franco 580, ASUNCIÓN.
PERU: Librería Studium, Plaza Francia 1164, Apartado 2139, LIMA.
PHILIPPINES: National Book Store Inc., 701 Rizal Avenue, MANILA.
POLAND: ORPAN-Import, Palac Kultury, 00-901 WARSZAWA; Ars Polona-Ruch, Krakowskie Przedmiescie N° 7, 00-068 WARSZAWA.
PORTUGAL: Dias & Andrade Ltda, Livraria Portugal, rua do Carmo 70, LISBOA.
PUERTO RICO: Librería Alma Mater, Cabrera 867, Río Piedras, PUERTO RICO 00925.
ROMANIA: ARTEXIM Export/Import, Piata Scienteii n° 1, P.O. Box 33-16, 70005 BUCUREŞTI.
SAUDI ARABIA: Dar Al-Watan for Publishing and Information, Olaya Main Street, Ibrahim Bin Sulaym Building, P.O. Box 3310, RIYADH.
SENEGAL: Librairie Clairafrique, B.P. 2005, DAKAR; Librairie des 4 vents, 91, rue Blanchot, B.P. 1820, DAKAR.
SEYCHELLES: New Service Ltd., Kingsgate House, P.O. Box 131, MAHÉ; National Bookshop, P.O. Box 48, MAHÉ.
SIERRA LEONE: Fourah Bay College, Njala University and Sierra Leone Diocesan Bookshops, FREETOWN.
SINGAPORE: Federal Publications (S) Pte. Ltd., Times Jurong, 2 Jurong Port Road, SINGAPORE 2261.
SOMALIA: Modern Book Shop and General, P.O. Box 951, MOGADISCIO.
SPAIN: Mundi-Prensa Libros S.A., Castelló 37, MADRID 1; Ediciones Liber, apartado 17, Magdalena 8, ONDÁRROA (Vizcaya); Donaire, Ronda de Outeiro, 20, apartado de correos 341, LA CORUÑA; Librería Al-Andalus, Roldana, 1 y 3, SEVILLA 4; Librería Castells, Ronda Universidad 13, BARCELONA 7.
SRI LANKA: Lake House Bookshop, Sir Chittampalam Gardiner Mawata, P.O. Box 244, COLOMBO 2.
SUDAN: Al Bashir Bookshop, P.O. Box 1118, KHARTOUM.
SURINAME: Suriname National Commission for Unesco, P.O. Box 2943, PARAMARIBO.
SWEDEN: *Publications:* A/B C.E. Fritzes Kung. Hovbokhandel. Regeringsgatan 12, Box 16356, S-103 27 STOCKHOLM. *For 'The Courier':* Svenska FN-Förbundet, Skolgränd 2, Box 150 50, S-104 65 STOCKHOLM. (Postgiro 18 46 92). *Subscriptions:* Wennergren-Williams AB, Box 30004, S-104 25 STOCKHOLM.
SWITZERLAND: Europa Verlag, Rämistrasse 5, 8024 ZÜRICH; Librairies Payot (Geneva, Lausanne, Basel, Berne, Vevey, Montreux, Neuchâtel, Zurich).
SYRIAN ARAB REPUBLIC: Librairie Sayegh, Immeuble Diab, rue du Parlement, B.P. 704, DAMAS.
THAILAND: Suksapan Panit, Mansion 9, Rajdamnern Avenue, BANGKOK; Nibondh & Co. Ltd., 40-42 Charoen Krung Road, Siyaeg Phaya Sri, P.O. Box 402, BANGKOK; Suksit Siam Company, 1715 Rama IV Road, BANGKOK.
TOGO: Librairie Evangélique, B.P. 378, LOMÉ; Librairie du Bon Pasteur, B.P. 1164, LOMÉ; Librairie universitaire, B.P. 3481, LOMÉ.
TRINIDAD AND TOBAGO: Trinidad and Tobago National Commission for Unesco, 18 Alexandra Street, St. Clair, PORT OF SPAIN.
TUNISIA: Société tunisienne de diffusion, 5, avenue de Carthage, TUNIS.
TURKEY: Haset Kitapevi A.S., Istiklâl Caddesi, N° 469, Posta Kutusu 219, Beyoglu, ISTANBUL.
UGANDA: Uganda Bookshop, P.O. Box 7145, KAMPALA.
USSR: Mezhdunamdnaja Kniga, MOSKVA G-200.
UNITED KINGDOM: HMSO Publications Centre, P.O. Box 276, LONDON SW8 5DT; Government Bookshops: London, Belfast, Birmingham, Bristol, Edinburgh, Manchester; Third World Publications, 151 Stratford Road, BIRMINGHAM B11 1RD. For scientific maps only: McCarta Ltd, 122 King's Cross Road, LONDON WC1X 9DS.
UNITED REPUBLIC OF CAMEROON: Le Secrétaire Général de la Commission nationale de la République Unie du Cameroun pour l'Unesco, B.P. 1600, YAOUNDÉ; Librairie des éditions Clé, B.P. 1501, YAOUNDÉ; Librairie St Paul, B.P. 763, YAOUNDÉ; Librairie aux Messageries, Avenue de la Liberté, B.P. 5921, DOUALA; Librairie aux frères réunis, B.P. 5346, DOUALA; Centre de Diffusion du Livre Camerounais, B.P. 338, DOUALA.
UNITED REPUBLIC OF TANZANIA: Dar es Salaam Bookshop, P.O. Box 9030, DAR ES SALAAM.
UNITED STATES: UNIPUB, 205 East 42nd Street, NEW YORK, N.Y. 10017. *Order for books and periodicals:* UNIPUB, Box 1222, ANN ARBOR, MI 48106.
URUGUAY: Edilyr Uruguaya, S.A., Maldonado 1092, MONTEVIDEO.
VENEZUELA: Librería del Este, Av. Francisco de Miranda, 52, Edificio Galipán, Apartado 60337, CARACAS; DILAE C.A. (Distribuidora Latinoamericana de Ediciones C.A.), Calle San Antonio entre Av. Lincoln y Av. Casanova, Edificio Hotel Royal – Local 2, Apartado 50.304, Sabana Grande, CARACAS.
YUGOSLAVIA: Jugoslovenska Knijiga, Trg Republike 5/8, P.O. Box 36, 11-001, BEOGRAD; Drzavna Zalozba Slovenije, Titova C, 25, P.O.B. 50-1, 61-000 LJUBLJANA.
ZAIRE: Librairie du CIDEP, B.P. 2307, Kinshasa; Commission nationale zaïroise pour l'Unesco, Commissariat d'Etat chargé de l'Education nationale, B.P. 32, KINSHASA.
ZAMBIA: National Educational Distribution Co. of Zambia Ltd, P.O. Box 2664, LUSAKA.
ZIMBABWE: Textbook Sales (PVT) Ltd., 67 Union Avenue, HARARE.

UNESCO BOOK COUPONS
Unesco Book Coupons can be used to purchase all books and periodicals of an educational, scientific or cultural character. For full information please write to: Unesco Coupon Office, 7, place de Fontenoy, 75700 Paris (France). [51]

(B) CC/85/XVII/93 A

ISBN 92-3-202265-6